HELP ME...
I HAVE A TEENAGER!!

The Nitty Gritty Guide
to Parental Sanity

Annie Drake, MA, RN, CS, LMFT

Duckworks Publishing

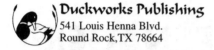

Duckworks Publishing
541 Louis Henna Blvd.
Round Rock, TX 78664

First Printing December 1998

Printed in the United States of America

10 9 8 7 6 5 4 3

Edited by Hillel Black

Design by Dan Miller, Dan Miller Graphics

Library of Congress Catalog Card Number: 98-96899

ISBN 0-9667490-9-X

To my dear parents,
Tom and Marilyn,
whose love, patience and discipline
gave me the gift of faith.

Pick your battles

Contents

PART 1   WHAT IS HAPPENING TO MY CHILD?

What does it take to Raise a Teenager?, What is it Like to be a Parent of a Teenager?, "This is Hard!", "A Crisis of Carrots", "I'm not Confused, You Are", "There are Lots of Surprises", This is a Test... Only a Test, Too Much to Worry About, Sometimes Bad Things Happen to Good People, No One Listens to Me, No One Says "Thank You", As a Parent, Will You have any Fun?, What is it like to be a Teenager?, "Confused? Who, Me?", Teenage Thrills, Just Leave Me Alone!, Are We Having Fun Yet?, Am I OK?, Traumatic Situations, You are Not Listening to Me!, Rewards, You're in it Together, A Shift in Parenting Strategy, Your Choice: Parent or Friend?, It is Only a Stage, Childhood: Absorbing Information, The New Experimenter, Characteristics, Adolescence is a Process, Their Rooms Are Their Homes, WHO AM I?, Adolescent Developmental Stage, The Last Person on Earth, When in Doubt, Say the Opposite, The Spotlight, I am the Center, The Mood, The Costume, The Rule Breaking Challenge, How Does Your Teenager Think?, Who Makes A Real Difference To Your Teenager?, You are the Balance, What Motivates Your Teenager?, The Circle of Influence, Who Influences Young People?, Peer Values, Social Values, Classic Values, Family Values, What Does Parental Guidance Mean?, TV Impact, The Parent Source ... Saying "No", Pass the Baton of Responsibility

When Their Ears Close Up, Selective Memory Loss, Responding to

Issues, Goals for Your Teenager, 6 Steps to Having a Civilized Conversation, Step One: Emotional Climate, Your Anger and Your Teenager's, Step Two: Location, Step Three: Setting the Mood, Step Four: Time and Timing, The Time Delay, Timing with an Irritable Teenager, Time Together, Listening VS Hearing, Step Five: 3 Communication Rules, The Power of Influence, Step Six: The Talk Timer Method: Solutions to Interruptions, The Value of Behavior, Faking an Opinion, The Eye Hug, The Foot Massage, Neutral Touching, Hugs for Comfort, Social Distance, How Do You Talk to Your Teenager?, No Lecture Method; Ruining a Perfectly Good Conversation, Let it Be, How to Say No, Negotiate, Negotiate, Negotiate, Words Can Hurt, Words from Parents, Angry Words at Home, Words can Encourage or Discourage, Words Focused on Actions, Behaviors, Events, Personality and Character Attacks, Behavior and the Person, "You" Statements, Questions?, "Why did you do that?", Lying "Did you..?", Focused on Others, One Minute Lecture, Situations Before They Happen, Do's and Don'ts, Ideas

Chapter 3   Who is in Charge of the Rules? 143

Am I Just the Biggest Person in the House?, Create a Vision, No Matter Where You Draw the Line, Too Much Freedom, Forgiveness, Discipline vs. Punishment, Why Discipline?, Discipline with Love, Truth or Consequences, Rules : Assumed/Unspoken, Spoken and Written, What Works Instead?, On the Road of Adolescence, Privileges and Responsibility, Jingle the Car Key, Changing the Rules, Check Up, Rebellion Means Supervision, Grounding Does Not Work, Creating Consequences, Logical Consequences, The Swiss Cheese Essay, Chore Cards and the Spotless Home, The Big Meany, the Little Pest, Make Me!!, It Takes Two to Tandem, The Swearing Tree, No Homework?, Feeding Spotty, Taxi Fare, Verbal and Written Apologies, When in Doubt Take Away TV for a Week, Sarcastic Statements, The Ball, the Window & the Estimate, Curfew: Beat the Clock, Jingle the Car Keys, Get a Phone , Get a Permit, "If You're Going To Yell...", Mousse and the Hairdryer, The Bedroom Door, Garbage In, Garbage Out, The Car Fender, Borrowers Beware, No Nag Theory, Chores and More Chores, Feed the Poor Without Diplomas, Skip School, Skip the Fun, No Sympathy, No Shopping, No More Dandelions, Telling Off the Teacher, Phone as a Hobby, He Never Reads, Give a Warning and Wait 5 Minutes, Take Your Time and Timing, Reward the Truth, A Lie is a Lie, Choose Your Battles, Deciding on Consequences, The Major League: The Big Rule Break, Catch Your Teenager Doing it Right

for Parents Too, The Basic of Decision Making, A More Simple Way to Decide, Your Head vs. Your Heart, Choose to be Happy, Before and After, It Won't Happen to Me, Real Life, Situations Before They Occur, Who Gets Hurt?, Being Perfect, Testing Out Teenager's Theories, Don't Do What I Did, Thinking it Through, Circle of Relationships

Choice About Friendships, Motivation For Choosing Friends, What Does Not Work, Who Decides?, Knowledge is Powerful, Inviting Friends Over, The Chauffeur, "One Minute Lectures" on Friends, Setting Limits with Time, Situations Beforehand, Current Situations, Parents Predict, Ask Questions, Prepare A Leader, Be Respectful, Everyone is Doing It, So It Must Be OK, You Gotta Go!, Future Neighbors, Parents Face Their Own Peer Pressure, Fake Cool VS Real Cool, The Peer Family, Being a Leader/ Being a Follower, Reinforce Positive Choices, Adopting Other Teenagers, One Minute Values, Take a Walk in Someone Else's Shoes, Saying "No" Rehearsal

Can't Hurry Love, Motivation for Love Relationships, Love and Lust, What is in a Relationship?, Rotten Relationships, What Girls Want, What Guys Want, Building Blocks of Relationships, Putting the Blocks Together, Divorce, Tell Them Your Own Love Story, The List, Dating Starts with Dinner, Working Together, Situations Ahead of Time, Grandma's Story of True Love, How Your Teenager Starts Saying "No", Love and Sex, Parents in the Driver's Seat, Sex Sells Everything, What is Parental Guidance?, Molly's Story, Media Impact, They Have Seen Too Much, Guiding Your Teenager, Teenage Sexuality, Teenagers Having Sex, When Choices Match Values, Steps to Good Decision Making, Decision Making in Risky Situations, Parenting Tips, How Do You Know You Really Are "In Love", Why Some Say "Yes', Why Some Say "No", Situations Ahead of Time, Sex Education, The Most Magnificent Christmas Present, The Pearl and Family Ring, Hot Pink Underwear, Starting Over Again, Ask Anything, What is the Script?, When Do You Say "No", What are the Results of Saying "No"?

The American Message, Escape the Pain, Face the Pain, Drink and Be Merry, Get Informed, Parent Check, Parent Values, How Do You Drink?, Reasons To Use, Smoking, The Smoking Balance, Inhalants, Offer Choices, If You're in Trouble, Phone Home, Spotting a Potential Problem, Stages of Use, Under the Influence, Look for a Pattern, Getting Help, Reasons to Say "No" to Alcohol and Drugs, Practical Solutions to Being Sober and Drug Free, Ways to Say "No", A Dozen Ways to Leave

PART 3   THE PUZZLE IS SOLVED

Foreword

In case you have not noticed, America faces a crisis of parenting: parents and teens are confused by conflicting signals at every turn. In the face of this, too many parents have abdicated parental responsibility, the results being parents on Prozac, young teens on Ritalin and older teens locked up in residential treatment centers for months to deal with diagnoses only recently invented to reflect various forms of adolescent misbehavior (Oppositional Defiant Disorder, Conduct Disorder, etc.). Noted experts are looking for answers external to the family (poverty) or internal to the child (chemical imbalance, diet, Attention Deficit Disorder, etc.) but a few are closer to the mark and speak of "a failure in family bonding".

As a therapist, nurse and marriage counselor, Annie Drake has been able to draw upon her vast clinical experience with children, teens and families to provide parents with not only hope but solutions in a practical, powerful book that empowers parents to reunite with their teens. In doing so, she has been able to avoid producing a dense academic text, glorified common sense or simple philosophical fluff. Rather, *Help Me... I Have a Teenager!!* gives the reader something much more valuable: a depth of understanding that allows parents to rebuild burned bridges. In the process of doing so she shares with the reader an old secret known to families down through the ages: teenagers are fun!

If teenagers came with a user's manual, *Help Me... I Have a Teenager!!* would be it. It provides parents with that rarest commodity, a true understanding of how teens think (Part 1) but then goes even further by translating that understanding into directions for action (Part 2) that produce results in the real world where families live. You will learn why your teen is "that way" as well as what to do about it; in the process, you will gain wisdom through understanding.

This book is a gem: a wealth of information from a working senior clinician who knows how families really work. You may be looking at the best book on parent-teen relationships written in the last twenty years. Enjoy!

Wandal Winn, M.D.
November 1998

Acknowledgments

The things in life are not what are most valuable; the people we love are. Over the past nine years many people have contributed to the success of this book; I wish to thank each of you.

Kelly, my best friend and husband. Thanks for your many roles: editor, publisher, business manager, guide and no doubt my biggest supporter. There was never a time you thought I might not finish this project, even on days I wondered if I would. To Kelsey and Courtney, my two sweet daughters. I am lucky to have the privilege of being your mother. I love you and I don't know what I would ever do without the three of you!

Tom and Marilyn, my parents, who struggled with me as an adolescent and never gave up their notion that, in-spite of myself, I would be successful. Thank you for all you have taught me.

My brothers and sisters, Ruthie Schoder- Ehri, Mike and Tim Schoder and Mary Ver Hoef, and their spouses, who have kept inquiring about my project over the years.

To Duane and Janet Drake, my dear mother and father in-law, and the rest of my family by marriage, Chris Hitchcock, Marsha Crockett, Alan and Richard Drake and their spouses. Thank you for all your support and encouragement. And I am pleased to say I did finish this, Papa, while you are still alive!

Tim and Sabrina Lamb, my treasured friends who have given me such wonderful encouragement. I really appreciate all your interest; you both have been such great supporters to me.

Dr. Wandal Winn, my colleague and friend and his wonderful wife Martha, who have watched me work on this book from beginning to end. You have given me terrific support and ideas, thank you.

Barbara Maryan, my irreplaceable office partner and friend, who was such a kind and encouraging colleague. I appreciate the time we have spent together.

Jean Kings, our precious Nana, like family, who has taught me so many valuable lessons about the privilege of being a parent and helped me discover grace. Thank you from the bottom of my heart.

Other friends giving me support and encouragement: Karen and Bill Hendrick, Pam Monday, Pastor Patterson and his terrific wife Mary, Chris Gebert and Lori and Van Woody.

Hillel Black, my editor, who is a master with a red pen and was the first person to read the entire manuscript. Thank you for all your work and advice.

To Dr. Jon Lyon, who offered his office and encouragement when I first started my parenting seminars. There is nothing like an open door and an eager audience to encourage a speaker.

Dan Miller, my cover designer, produced what I consider to be the hardest thing about the book. Thank you for your creative artistry.

People I consider mentors who have influenced my work: H. Steven Glenn, Kimberly Kirberger, Terry Hargrave, Bill O'Hanlon, Harville Hendrix, Jay Haley and Steven Covey.

The late Dr. Hain G. Ginott, the individual who has probably influenced my work with teenagers the most, lives on through his books and work. His brilliance will continue to shine.

Without the opportunity to work with such nice clients, parents and fine young people over the past 22 years, I would not have the experiences that bring this book to life. I appreciate each and every one of you for sharing your lives, joys and struggles with me. It has been my pleasure to know you and you have taught me a great deal about the love and persistence it takes to raise children.

To the many PTA members and seminar participants, who over the years kept asking me back to offer seminars and keep asking, "Where is the book?" I am glad to say, finally, "Here it is!"

Finally, I thank God to be blessed with such a rich life, a wonderful family and an opportunity to make a difference.

Introduction

Nine years ago, when I began private practice, I decided to offer parenting seminars with the goal of helping improve the health of families. In our community, most of the parenting classes offered were for parents of children from toddlers to twelve years of age. There appeared to be a shortage of education for parents facing the most difficult part of their job, raising their teenagers. Hoping to fill this gap, I developed a seven-week series of parenting seminars specifically designed for this weary group of parents. The impetus for this book came from parents attending my seminars suggesting that I write a book about what I was presenting.

Parenting, like other tasks in life, requires tools. We are all natural problem solvers. Since we were young, we have developed a vast repertoire of skills to solve problems and meet challenges. For example, when a parent tells a toddler not to get up on the coffee table, the young problem solver will find a way up by climbing and reaching.

Imagine if all the ways you have learned to solve problems in your life are tools in an imaginary toolbox. When you have a problem or dilemma in your family, you open your toolbox and try the things you think will solve or resolve the problem. One of the biggest tools we all have in our toolboxes is the "Leave it alone" tool; you just leave a problem alone and hope it goes away. Fortunately, some problems are time related and do resolve over time.

Other problems do not go away with time. When you have tried all the possible solutions and find there are no more tools left in your toolbox, you know you can use some help. In this book you will find ideas, skills, strategies and solutions that work specifically with teenagers.

As you read the stories and excerpts in this book, I hope you will hear familiar voices and be able to relate to common situations that occur between parents and teenagers. These stories come from the lives of the many teenagers and parents I have had the good fortune of working with or knowing over the past twenty years. Most of the situations or experiences presented have been altered somewhat in order to protect the confidentiality of teenagers, parents and families.

You will be most successful implementing these new skills if you understand how change works best in a family. Change that is too rapid can be fleeting. Too many changes presented by parents at once can be futile. It is common for frustrated parents to come into therapy wanting immediate solutions for the problems they face with their teenager. They have been struggling with these problems and, understandably, they want to end their difficulties quickly.

You may have had the experience of trying too many new ideas at once with your teenager. Usually what happens is your teenager looks at you and says, "So, what parenting class did you go to?" or "Hey, did you read *another* new book on raising kids?" Then your teenager goes right to work and tests the living daylights out of you until you are so frustrated you give up on your new ideas. Then you are back to square one. Your teenager still has the problem...and so do you! Failure may not lie so much in the solution but rather in how the solution was implemented.

Changes that are most likely to be successful are not rapid or complex. Rather, just the opposite works better. Slow, simple changes that occur over time are usually more effective. Take one or two ideas you like in this book and use them over two or three weeks. This period of time allows you and your teenager to become accustomed to the changes before adding any more new ones. When you find a solution that works, use it for three or four months. This is the length of time required for a change to become a permanent part of your on-going strategies and skills.

Teenagers are like snowflakes; no two are exactly the same. Children in families can have very different personalities and temperaments. With the ideas, solutions and strategies presented here, you will need to pick and choose what you think will work best for your teenager and then decide *how* to present it to your teenager. An approach that works well with one teenager may not work for another. Not all the ideas, strategies and solutions work universally with all teenagers.

Discipline, respond, critique, care and guide with love. The success of any strategy depends on how it is presented. Someone could hand an ice cream cone to a teenager and do it in such a manner that there is nothing sweet about the interaction. The love and respect you give your teenager is what you will eventually receive back from your young person.

My goal is for you to understand what is happening to your teenager, what is typical behavior for your teenager and also what is happening to you. Knowing what you might expect and what you can do about it will prepare you when problems arise.

If you cannot communicate with your teenager, even great ideas and strategies will fail. Breaking through the communication barrier is critical to your ability to help guide your teenager along the rocky path toward adulthood. I have discovered a way of talking to teenagers that is different from how I talk with other groups of people. Once you learn how this works and how to use it with your teenager you will be well on your way to a successful relationship.

Finding answers to the puzzle of adolescence requires thoughtfulness. Many parents just react when they are faced with a problem. They do the best job they can at the time. To use this book, you will need to take your time, be thoughtful and probably have a number of fireside chats with yourself.

It is not common today to hear parents raving they love having a teenager and that this is a great time in life. I would like it to become more commonplace. When parents have the tools to solve the problems and deal with everyday issues, then parenting a teenager can be a joyful experience. My hope is that by solving the puzzle of adolescence you have the opportunity to enjoy a wonderful relationship with your young person.

1

WHAT
IS HAPPENING
TO MY CHILD?

CHAPTER ONE

The Essence of Adolescence

it takes a lot of courage
to grow up and turn out to be
who you really are
                    ee cummings

The essence of adolescence is developmental chaos. With chaos comes confusion for parents. You are not alone that adolescence strikes you as a mysterious, incomprehensible condition. Your child's behavior has become foreign; what has been consistent now becomes erratic. When the day arrives your child turns into an adolescent, moods change, identity shifts, hearing deteriorates, voices rise and attitudes reverse. Adolescence can bring forth a number of new, sometimes obnoxious forms of behavior: abrupt mood swings, stair stomping, door slamming, eye rolling, intense sighs, looks to kill, shocking hairstyles and determined independence, mixed with naïve certainty on the part of the teenager.

Just as the seasons of life change, so do the seasons of your child. These new changes bring new challenges that can take any parent by surprise, leaving you puzzled with the child you thought you knew so well. As the mother of a 14 year-old boy said, "I think a Martian has taken over my teenager!" She wanted her son back. Do you wonder what are you supposed to do to tame your teenager? A change in parenting strategy is needed.

Opposition can become a way of life with a teenager. You will these kind of behaviors occur. When you want him to work hard, he will pull up a lawn chair and take a nap; when you want her to be cooperative, she'll start a fight. If you care about a good diet, he binges on junk food. When company comes and you expect polite manners, he belches and snorts . If you ask for neat clothes, she will pick out a pair of jeans that are torn and frayed.

Politely requesting an end to this obnoxious behavior is like an invitation to a showdown. In response to a kind request your teenager may escalate his or her behavior and taunt you even more. Parents easily become frustrated when their teenagers start acting like that bumper sticker that says, "Hire a teenager, they know everything!" It is not uncommon for adolescents to begin advising their parents while at the same time refusing to listen to any of their parent's valuable life lessons. Teenagers become experts, with very little expertise!

The teenager's quest in growing up is to find a new self. In this search they are no longer children yet not quite adults. Adolescents are somewhere in the middle; boy-man or girl-woman. Teenager's maturity seems to vacillate between the ages of four and twenty-four. Adolescence means teenagers start letting their personalities unravel; watch their bodies drastically change, hoping someday to become a great and notable person. There is no predictable course for the metamorphosis of personality, emotions, intellect and physical growth. Each adolescent's journey is haphazard. You cannot know exactly what is going to happen, when things change or how your teenager will react. There is a reason for these dramatic changes. This is the process of adolescence. At no other time is such chaotic and confusing behavior considered normal.

Since teenagers do not come with instruction manuals you are not prepared to know when you will need a new approach in your parenting strategy. It is important to make this change because teenagers learn differently than children: teenagers learn from experience rather than through lectures. That is why the parenting strategies that worked so well with your youngster now seem to backfire when applied to your teenager. The change needed in your parenting means learning new ways of talking to your teenager, how to say 'No' without producing an emotional explosion, disciplining in a different manner, and to discovering new ways to interact with your young person.

Most parents need some help figuring out what actually does work to successfully raise a young adult. You could try to figure out what works all by yourself. You COULD:

- politely ask your teenager to do the dishes;
- WAIT for your teenager to start;
- notice your teenager doesn't seem to be listening;
- insist a second time;
- WAIT for your teenager to leave the couch;
- give a lecture on being responsible;
- demand immediate action; watch your teenager's eyes roll;
- WAIT again for your teenager;
- yell at the top of your lungs "Do the dishes NOW!";
- watch your teenager walk away;
- find yourself alone in the kitchen;
- go find your teenager (hiding in the usual place, his or her room), threaten grounding for a week;
- hear your teenager yell back that YOU should do the dishes because they are YOUR dishes not his;
- leave before you tear your hair out;
- WAIT AGAIN for your teenager;
- note it is getting late, give up and do the dishes yourself;
- take two aspirin.

Or instead, you could read this book and learn a new way in parenting that works much better with your teenager.

What does it take to Raise a Teenager?

Some say bringing up an adolescent can drive you crazy; that it is the hardest thing you will ever do. Others say it can be the most important and rewarding time in your life. It will test you in ways you never have expected. The process will challenge your values and your ideals, put more gray in your hair and may even wear out your car tires from all the chauffeuring. You must be prepared for dramatic changes and to expect the unexpected.

It takes courage to face the adolescence of your child. You may never have anticipated that being brave was going to be a requirement to be a parent of a teenager. Throughout the rocky course of adolescence there will be days you feel overwhelmed and you'll wish you could yell at the top of your lungs, "Help me... I Have a Teenager!" Some hours may seem endless. Like other parents, you may even contemplate hiring someone else to take over your job. (The problem is no one seems to want the job!) On the bright side, not all of adolescence is difficult. Though teenagers can be ornery, they can also be sweet, kind, generous, showing great empathy and concern for others. These days bring the promise of great joy, wonderful times, accomplishments, and delightful companionship with your teenager.

It also takes a lot of love to raise a teenager. You may have thought when your child was younger that he or she would be different from other teenagers when his or her adolescence arrived. It can be a shock to witness your sweet child transition into a moody adolescent. Your teenager's moods can shift dramatically, one minute you hear loud protests and angry critiques that seem targeted right at your heart. Within the hour your teenager may smile, approach you with kind words and a laugh. "Is this the same person?" you may ask. Adolescence is filled with ambivalence and contradiction. To tolerate someone whose personality is unraveling takes a great deal of love.

It takes understanding to raise a teenager. In the upheaval of change, faced with so many unfamiliar adolescent behaviors, you may find yourself at a loss about what to do. You may not know what will calm the storm of adolescent conflict. Never quite sure what will work with your teenager, you become acutely aware of what seems to fail. Being nice can easily backfire. Pleading seems to fall on deaf ears. Nagging does not budge your teenager. Yelling fuels the fires of discontent. Demanding can start an outbreak of threats and confrontations. When parents attempt to use the age-old disciplinary technique of grounding, it accomplishes little more than grounding the whole family, now cooped up with an irate teenager. Parents need to find new ways to deal with these irritating dilemmas.

It takes patience to successfully raise a teenager. One of the first tests might occur when your teenager pulls away from you in an effort to find his or her own way in the world. You may feel sad when it seems your youngster no longer seems to need you. As much as you try to help your teenager, he or she may not give back what you want; just a little more respect, some appreciation or more time and attention. Teenagers rarely say thank you (unless you are offering money); it is not usually part of their vocabulary. They may not acknowledge their gratitude for years to come.

The most predictable thing about adolescence is that nothing is very predictable! Unfortunately, this is especially true for children in the same family. No two teenagers trudge down the road of adolescence following the same route or going at the same speed. Adolescence as a developmental stage is not permanent. Like bleeding, it eventually ends with judicious intervention, so that hopefully you do not lose the patient. This thought can help you through some of your toughest days and allow you to enjoy your teenager

What is it Like to be a Parent of a Teenager?

"This is Hard!"

What is it really like to become a parent of a teenager? First of all, you want to do a good job raising your teenager and it is hard to do so when you can't figure your teenager out. In the face of defiance, it is hard to not feel liked. Raising a teenager is hard on your blood pressure, tough on your bank account and can wear out your patience. It is especially difficult when every little thing seems becomes a contest of wills. Facing challenges is difficult work. It is also hard to know how to steer your teenager the right way in his or her complex world.

A Crisis of Carrots

Parents of teenagers say that the time of adolescence can be very challenging. Sometimes conflict arises when you least expect it. One day Joyce found her 13 year-old daughter, Katie, crying hysterically when she went to pick her up from school. "What is wrong?" she asked, wondering what awful thing could have happened as she tried to comfort her daughter. Through the sobs, her daughter told her. The crisis involved of all things…carrots! That's right, carrots in her lunch. Joyce had been packing healthy lunches for her daughter for years with no complaints. Now, carrots had created a crisis. Why was this happening, Joyce wondered? Her daughter now hated carrots. She wanted junk food like the other kids so she could fit in and not be teased at the lunch table.

Dilemmas, in need of solutions, occur when you least expect them and often when you are least prepared to deal with them. The importance of a particular issue to your teenager may baffle you, like the teenager who says she feel suicidal because of a bad hair day. No matter how insignificant or absurd the issue may seem, you must find a way to deal with it.

"I'm not confused, you are"

After so many years of parenting it can be a big surprise to find raising your young person so confusing. You may find from day to day you are not sure what works or what might be acceptable to your young person. Amy is in a quandary. "One day," she observes, "our teenage daughter says she wants to be left alone. The next day she is angry I have been ignoring her. I can't figure her out. According to her I can't do anything right."

Do you wonder what your teenager's mood will be like when your son or daughter rises for the day? Will he greet the day with an angry eruption or will he be calm and serene? If she is enraged, how long will this hostile mood last, five minutes or five hours? These mood swings confuse both parents and teenagers.

It can be perplexing trying to figure out what works to calm your angry teenager when the reasoning you try succeeds once and then backfires the next time. Ignoring a foul mood may quiet your teenager today and tomorrow doing the same thing may ignite it.

It is not unusual for your teenager to tell you he or she is not confused. According to him or her, you are! According to your teenager, you do not know what you are talking about. An adolescent is not likely to ever admit being confused. For this moment in time, he or she usually has the world figured out. Of course, tomorrow his or her ideas may drastically change. With adolescent logic, tomorrow is another day, far into the future. What is happening today is what is important for most teenagers.

Much of this confusion stems from the emotional and physical changes teenagers are going through. Since your teenager is confused, unfortunately, so are you.

"There are lots of surprises"

Adolescents thrive on excitement. The more the better, it seems for many of them. Teenagers seek excitement, even if it brings conflict. And excitement may be the last thing on your wish list. So many things seem new or novel for the young teenager. Excitement comes from trying out new ways of thinking, unusual ways of behaving or even new hair colors. Teenagers seek adventure by moving away from their families as they migrate toward the thrilling world of their peers.

One father of three teenage sons said that as soon as he walks into his house he feels like he is entering a circus arena. The kids are clowning around, balls fly through the air, music is blasting and someone is usually making loud announcements. Some of the spectators are at odds. This is his life with teenagers; excitement is the central theme for this household.

This is a Test... Only a Test

Raising an adolescent means being put to a number of tests. A test of wills. A test of authority and power. A test of opinions. Says Alice, "We have been put to a test so often I never quite know how I am doing. We just try to do the best we can with whatever crisis our kids present us."

Teenagers will test parents on anything. How you style your hair, the clothing you wear or even how you breathe can become an issue with your teenager. Challenges can come at any time and can be about most anything.

The mom of a thirteen year-old commented that her daughter seemed to have a lot of fun at the Christmas party. She said it looked as though her daughter, Nicole, seemed to be having a good time. Her daughter adamantly disagreed. She said the party was *so* boring. She demanded it would have been much better if her mother would have left her at home so she could talk on the phone. And no, she was not having fun, even though it might have looked like it (so what if she was laughing and smiling with the other kids!). In turn, Nicole's mother thought her daughter's opinion was absurd. An argument ensued over opinions and perceptions.

When teenagers oppose parents, they experience a new kind of power. They may even seem pleased when they get a negative reaction from a parent. If the reaction is great enough they feel they are winning a power struggle. The feeling is a new sense of autonomy, being a strong, unique individual. Part of the problem is that teenagers may not even be aware that the argument exhausted his or her parent.

Teenagers also test you because they want to find out if what you have taught them over the years is really worthwhile. Part of their exploration is to discover how resilient you are as well as how your ideas and ideals apply to the real world.

Too Much to Worry About

You may feel a lot of anxiety about the difficulties and situations in your teenager's world. It is very realistic for parents to worry when a naive teenager attempts to deal with the complex issues in today's world. It is not always clear what things you do and do not have control over as a parent.

John and Judy tried to control who Bonnie chose for friends, not liking how her new group of 'friends' acted. The more they demanded Bonnie drop her new buddies the more adamant she became about keeping them. They discovered they can control what happens in their home, what Bonnie's limits are, where she is allowed to go and what she watches on the TV screen. Trying to change things that you cannot can create a great deal of anxiety and stress.

You may also wonder if you are doing the best job that you can do as a parent. Self-doubt comes during times of change for anyone. A father of a fifteen-year-old son said he and his wife had worn themselves out worrying about their son, Carl. He had been using drugs and hanging around with a rough crowd of kids. Though Carl had completed a drug treatment program, this father and mother were still worried he might go back to his old habits. They felt they had to watch him like a hawk, which made them tense and anxious.

Sometimes Bad Things Happen to Good People

Some parents must deal with situations like drug use, accidents or pregnancy that bring trauma to the lives of young people. Says Jessica, "Our daughter has put us through a lot. She is sixteen and now a mother. The baby's father is not involved at all. But we are sticking together as a family, working things out. This is not how I thought it would be. But even though things have been traumatic, they are starting to work out OK."

The tests and trials in life are real. As the saying goes, "Life is not a dress rehearsal"; this is the real thing. We parents hope that traumatic things will never happen to our teenagers but the reality is that unexpected crises occur, impacting not only their own lives but the lives of their family members.

No One Listens to Me

Do you feel at times that your words fall on deaf ears when you talk to your teenager? Do you find you are frequently interrupted by your teenager who claims you are wrong and he or she is right? You are not alone; these are common complaints about communication with teenagers.

Now your teenager, an expert with little expertise, may think of him or herself as a 'professor' on adolescent life. As you know, a little knowledge can be dangerous. Your young junior or high school professor may tell you your advice and guidance is no longer needed or wanted. Reestablishing a relationship where your teenager will listen to you is critical. Finding new ways to open up communication is vital to helping your son or daughter become successful.

No One Says "Thank You"

Teenagers are not well known for being supportive and reassuring to their parents. They don't say things like: "Thanks mom and dad for doing such a great job raising me.... It was smart of you to tell me I couldn't go to the party Friday night. You know, the one hosted by the wild fourteen year-olds, chaperoned by two nineteen year old GIs. You're doing a good job by saying 'no'. Keep up the good work!" Instead you are likely to hear insults and complaints, like you are a throwback to the time when the earth was cooling. When you say 'yes' or you give in on something then you may get a big 'Thanks'. Don't despair. Your thanks will come someday. When your teenager nears the end of adolescence, around the time of graduation and is about to leave home, he or she is likely to praise your parenting efforts. Some may not show their full gratitude for your love and patience until they have children of their own. So be patient, your thanks will come... in time.

As a Parent, Will You have any Fun?

Some parents find their teenagers to be a lot of fun. Certainly not all the time, but sometimes the laughs you and your teenager share can be great. Though a teenager may look like an adult there is a lot of kid left in him or her. Teenagers love to play and laugh and many are creative and entertaining as well.

What is it like to be a Teenager?

What do you think it is like to be a teenager today? Do you think life is easy for your teenager? Do you think things are easier for your teenager than for you during your adolescent years? Does your teenager seem spoiled to you?

As I listen to parents of teenagers talk about their experiences I hear similar feelings from another group of people. Guess who? Teenagers! Listening to two sides of the story, the feelings and experiences of being an adolescent and being a parent of one may be more alike than you might imagine. This is not to say your parenting experience is similar to being a teenager or vice versa. The point is that both of you are really in the process of growing up together.

Many teenagers tell me that their life is really difficult. Some days taking out the trash may be viewed as a hardship. To others, having to take a class from a teacher they consider to be 'stupid' may seem like a monumental task. Teenagers struggle to understand the meaning of everyday life. A smaller percentage of teenagers have more serious difficulties, like failing school, becoming addicted to drugs or dealing with violence.

The world in which your youngster lives in is not the same as the world in which you grew up. They must deal with many situations that are more complex. Teenagers must decide how to fit into or deal with a very sophisticated peer group. They are a much more worldly and street-wise group of immature youth than the peer groups of past generations.

If it were possible, would you trade your adolescence with your teenager? In what ways do you think your teenage years were harder? Certainly there are many ways your teenager's life may be better than yours. Maybe your son or daughter has more opportunities, an easier life, a closer family or more chances for success. With each generation there are significant differences for adolescents. Today there are new complexities for teenagers coupled with the same adolescent confusion.

John, an adolescent, notes, "My parents think life is so easy compared to how they grew up. They have no idea how tough it is at school. The classes, the social scene and the work. Everything. I think it is really hard to be a teenager now." For many teenagers, there is pain in their hearts and confusion in their worlds.

"Confused? Who, Me?"

Though your teenager is not likely to ever admit it to you, your adolescent is often very confused. There are many choices for young people to make; how to act, how to be and how to fit in. Self-doubt is part of your teenager establishing his or her personal identity. All these things create a confusing picture.

April, a thirteen year-old, explains to a friend, "I just don't know what to do. What do you think I should do?.... I just don't know. There are so many things to figure out. I'm not sure."

Teenage Thrills

No doubt your teenager is bringing a lot of excitement into your household. Your teenager is surrounded with many fascinating people and novel experiences. A teenager's search for a new self brings mystery and intrigue. His exploration of adolescent life opens up a world that is vastly different from his childhood experiences. Many things are new and exciting. Your teenager is becoming a new person in a captivating time.

Julie, age sixteen, notes, "There are so many things going on. It is hard to keep track of everything. My life has very few dull moments. There is always something neat to do or somebody to see or talk to."

Just Leave Me Alone!

Teenagers can feel overwhelmed by school, parents, chores and some days, baffled with what to wear. Just to be asked to come out of his or her room and sit at the family dinner table may seem like a great imposition to your teenager. The way your teenager responds to simple requests, like setting the table, may seem as if you were handing him an ice pick and asking him to climb Mt. McKinley. In his or her eyes, your routine requests are impossible.

"My parents are always asking me about myself," says sixteen year old Monte. "I just don't know what they want. And my teachers are always on my case. It seems like everyone I know is asking for something. I am just doing my best and I just want to be left alone."

Are We Having Fun Yet?

Most teenagers feel their mission in life is to have fun. They love to laugh and cut up with their friends. Your teenager may avoid work because it is just not fun. Many teenagers tell their parents that they no longer can have fun with their families. They are too grown up and they would much rather be with their friends.

Unfortunately, some teenagers think what seems to be the most fun is the excitement that comes with breaking the rules or choosing dangerous activities. Many teenagers making poor choices aren't really thinking about the possible consequences. When they choose to ignore your rules, the school rules, and their health or the law, conflict is imminent.

Says fifteen year-old Teri, "We are always finding ways to have fun. Especially at school. Other people think we are really weird, but we don't care! But it is definitely *not* fun at home. My parents do not understand we are just kidding around. They take everything *so* seriously."

Am I OK?

Teenagers have a thousand worries... about hundreds of things, usually keeping these concerns to themselves. You may not know how much your teenager worries but most teenagers do worry quite a bit. Concerns range from how friends perceive them to what they will do as adults. Self-doubt is a big part of self-exploration. Another common worry is about whether they are normal or just adequate. Some teenagers are tormented worrying about the meaning of life. The questions teenagers have about themselves are very private and personal. Many wonder if the changes in their physical and emotional growth are normal. This kind of worry can flood them with feelings of insecurity and heighten their self-consciousness. With all that is happening to teenagers and around them, worry is natural.

The last thing teenagers may want to do is to risk asking someone a question and let another person in on the private world of their own thoughts. If they are brave enough to ask a question, they don't want a response that makes them feel even more vulnerable or strange. Teenagers usually want a brief, to the point, reassuring answer, not a lecture.

Says fourteen year-old Jerry, "I am always so self-conscious around the girls at school. I just don't know what to say most of the time. I am always worried if I am going to look stupid or say the wrong thing. I just wonder what I should be doing. Some days I think I should just give up and become a hermit."

Traumatic Situations

Some choices teenagers make produce trauma in their lives. Teenagers may face some of their saddest days as a result. We parents are well aware that teenagers are maimed and injured, some are emotionally or sexually abused, others die in accidents and some teenagers, tragically enough, commit suicide. Caring parents want to do all they can to prevent their teenagers from becoming one of these statistics.

Most young people are not prepared for the pain that comes with growing up and the choices they face. Life is full of problems of all sorts of difficulties and many teenagers are really surprised when they must confront a serious problem. Most teenagers have a sense of omnipotence, believing that bad things only happen to other people. This myth exists because they think since they are young, somehow, they are protected from life's mishaps. It can be a real shock to discover that their sense of immortality is really a figment of their imagination.

Fifteen year-old Kathy explains, "I just wish I could go back and be thirteen all over again. That was a bad year for me. I was so young and I didn't know what I was doing. I thought I was so grown up. I feel bad about what I did."

Julie, seventeen, says, "I just found out I have genital herpes. And I am going to have it for the rest of my life unless someone comes up with a cure. I am too young to have this happen to me. And I can't believe I got it from the only guy I was with. It is not fair. Now my life is ruined."

You are Not Listening to Me!

According to your teenager, you not only do not understand him or her, you do not listen very well either. No matter what your teenager says, if you show frustration or disagree, she or he is convinced you are not listening. If you are tired and need a break, this desire can be interpreted as not listening as well.

There are definitely times when it is very hard to listen to your teenager. Like when he just dyed his hair blue. Or when she calls you from the principal's office for the second time this month. Or when your teenager is screaming at you that he is not yelling!

Rewards

Teenagers search for rewards throughout their adolescent years. Many teenagers do not feel they have an important place in their communities. Generations ago, adolescents were vital to the livelihood of families and places where they lived. A fourteen or fifteen year-old may have helped raise younger children or become a worker on a farm to keep the family going.

Our young people today are our hope for the future. Teenagers are full of talent and energy that should not go to waste. In order to have this happen parents need to help teenagers find rewards in life by feeling good about what he or she does and find a place for them to feel successful.

You're in it Together

Though the issues are certainly not the same for parents and teenagers, the feelings and situations you and your teenager are experiencing have similarities. Remember that you too shall pass through this time with your teenager, sharing both the good times and the bad. You are in this together, as parents you are a partner with your son or daughter throughout the years of adolescence.

A Shift in Parenting Strategy

Your Choice: Parent or Friend?

Most parents would like their role in adolescence to be like a good friendship. That is understandable because we all like to be liked. However, the reality of adolescence is that teenagers need limits and guidance. Friends don't discipline their friends. Friends are equals.They listen and care. Even if a friend is heading toward a bad decision, friends may share their feelings but they don't take a passionate stand like parents do. You must make a choice, parent or friend? To attempt to be both is not likely to work. Teenagers can have lots of friends. What they need most is a parent.

Parents need to find new skills and strategies to successfully parent a teenager. You know you need help when your lectures no longer work and bounce off your teenager's ears. This new communication block is puzzling and you may initially wonder if it is you. Has something changed in the way you are saying things or is what you are asking really unreasonable? There are several things you can change to combat this problem.

Many parents try to be direct and demanding. This usually develops into a contest of wills. When the ensuing battles fail to solve the problem, many try gentleness and kindness. When this does not work the next attempt may be pleading and explaining. If the teenager is not convinced, then parents may resort to expressing their anger and frustration. If the teenager decides to retaliate with insults and attacks, a fight ensues. The intensity of the power struggle between parent and teenager seems to escalate. As a last attempt to regain power and authority, parents may resort to what seems the most powerful resource at the time. Grounding! When you are angry enough you can ground your teenager for a long, long time, weeks or even months. You might feel like grounding your teenager until he or she is twenty. As you may already know, grounding does not work very well.

This typical cycle of family fighting is one in which no one wins. In the heat of anger both parties have insulted the other with damaging name-calling and insults. You feel bad and your teenager feels frustrated and powerless. As much as you wish you could change things, you cannot take back your words... a word said is a word heard. You can say you are sorry but the damage to your teenager's self-esteem has already occurred.

What can be done so this continuing conflict ends in a peaceful resolution? You must learn to deal with your teenager in a new way. We as parents must learn an important lesson. If you are up against a rock and you respond like a rock, all you get are fragments and shale. Both you and your teenager end up with less than what you started with. You must wear the rock down by learning to be more like water. Water is quiet and sure and powerful. It flows steadily and doesn't make unpredictable changes in its course. It takes time to slowly wear away the rock.

One of the first changes you need to make involves your

parenting style. You probably give good lectures but your teenager is no longer listening. Now, your concern is called over protectiveness. Your wisdom is labeled misinformation. A great paradox is occurring here. Your teenager doesn't want you too understanding but somehow wants you to understand. He or she demands freedom but wants you to be concerned. The past is not important; they cringe when they hear, "When I was a teenager..." They don't believe you know anything about teenagers today and can't imagine you were ever young. Being compared to others or corrected makes them insecure and defeated. They don't want to be treated like a child, even though they act childish. You are in need of a new way of communicating to be able to guide your teenager.

What are all the parts of this change in parenting that is required of you? It has much to do with how teenagers learn and act differently as compared to children. Many of the strategies in the next chapters offer new skills and different ways of talking and responding to your teenager. To begin to understand the rea-

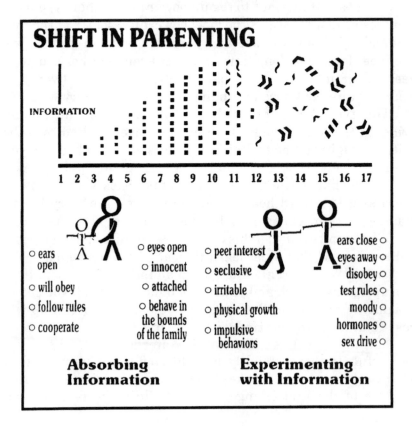

sons for this shift in parenting strategy, it is helpful to first understand the normal process of adolescence.

It is Only a Stage

The stages of development of younger children are relatively easily organized in established patterns. Their emotional and physical development is fairly predictable. We can predict that most developmentally ready two year olds learn to say 'no' to their parents. This stage is commonly known as the 'terrible twos'. During this stage parents find they need to provide their child with additional structure to ensure safety. Parents are challenged to find new ways to balance their little one's quest for independence. Throughout childhood from birth to eleven this and other stages of development are fairly predictable.

The emergence of adolescence brings great individual diversity in each youngster's developmental process. Similar to a child, in the "terrible twelve's" we can predict a teenager will assert him or herself and say 'no' to his or her parents and learn to do this in a myriad of ways. As if they had hidden radar, many teenagers will say 'no' when they detect a parent least wants to hear it. Unlike child development, there is no specific age or developmental landmark to predict just when this change will occur in adolescence. It is also difficult to be able to estimate how long a teenager's defiance may last, exactly how he or she might rebel or the way he or she will establish a unique identity. Each teenager takes his or her own independent course in development from childhood into adulthood.

A challenge from a child is different than a challenge from a teenager. When your second grader looks up at you and asserts, "I am not going to school today", a typical parent response might be "Yes, you are going to school today." He replies "Make me!" Faced with a challenge like this you might lead your protesting youngster in his pajamas to the car with his clothes neatly piled next to him. By the time you arrive at the school he has had a chance to get dressed in the car, the alternative being to go into school in his night wear. In most contests of wills, your child eventually responds by cooperating.

Now, if your 5'8", fourteen year-old asserts, "I am *not* going to school today" you face a very different challenge. No longer can you escort this guy to the car. He is too big; he could escort you instead. When you tell him, "Yes, you will go to school", he looks you in the eye and in a deep voice says, "Make me!" Now you have a new dilemma. What is a parent to do? Things have changed between you and your child. He is different. He is bigger and he is no longer a child...he is a teenager! You must find a whole new way to communicate with a teenager to meet challenges like one of how to persuade this guy to go to school.

Childhood: Absorbing Information

In childhood, behaviors associated with each year are fairly predictable. Your child typically looks to you as the center of his or her life. From birth until about the age of ten to twelve your job as a parent is to teach your child all about the world. You teach, give directions, answer questions, give lectures, teach values and ideals, provide limits and present structure. Your child listens and is in the process of *absorbing information from you.*

Through your important lectures they learn about what is safe, right and good. Your direction fills them with the vast knowledge they need to successfully grow up, why they should be good citizens, how to be a kind family member and why they should do well in school. Part of being a good parent is to join them in playful fun, share their laughter and learn as they learn.

Usually attentive, children cooperate and are fairly easy to direct because they wish to please parents. They typically will follow rules and will behave within the expectations of their family, especially if something seems important to you. Most parents find raising a child is easier and more predictable than raising a teenager. It seems friendlier too and parents may feel like it is easy to be both a parent and a friend when children are young.

The New Experimenter

Just as children want to please; adolescents want to test. Routine things like taking a shower can easily turn into ordeals as your child approaches adolescence. In the psychological development of adolescence, a teenager tends to stop absorbing information from you and now seeks to *experiment with information* instead. Teenagers no longer learn from lecture and start learning from experience. Your teenager stops relying on you as a teacher and a guide. Instead, he or she seeks to learn from the world, using resources beyond the family with the goal of becoming his or her own teacher. Trying out new things to do, usually without thinking about it, or watching others or being with others who take chances are the main ways to learn.

Billy can try shoplifting, hear about it from others who do it or stand at the side of a friend who decides to take a watch out of a store. With two of these choices, Billy might also get to learn about shoplifting from the security people in a store, meeting a tough police officer and store manager, going to the juvenile detention center and completing a Saturday course on shoplifting he is required to take. Last of all, he may learn what a hassle it is to not be able to enter that store for the next year. What an experience!

Experimenting with information requires teenagers to take all the information they have collected throughout childhood and test it. Adolescents test the "truths" of the world as taught to them by their parents. The object of the test is to find out if your values and lessons are indeed true or valuable. Watching your teenager experiment with information rather than accept information can be frightening. You may feel your teenager is unprepared or far too immature to embark on such a course of independent decision-making.

Characteristics

As your teenager becomes an experimental learner many changes take place. Here is a picture of typical teenagers: their eyes look away, they become reclusive, irritable, and they stop listening to parents. Teenagers disobey parents' wishes and requests, test the rules, act impulsively and contradict themselves. They get bigger and you look smaller. Dramatic changes in physical growth occur while hormones influence a heightened sense of sexuality.

Impulsive behavior is common, especially for the young adolescent. Instead of moving slowly or thoughtfully toward a decision, an adolescent may suddenly leap quickly to a conclusion. They commonly rely on experience to teach them how to make a decision and then they will think about it later. Your teenager's motto may be, "Act now, learn later." Learning usually occurs *after decisions are made.*

Adolescents are known to be irritable. At any given moment they may snap back at you with hostility in their voices. Many times teenagers are grouchy without any logical reason. Your teenager may get annoyed over things that may seem trivial and when you least expect it.

Hormones can turn a meek and mild adolescent into a raging emotional time bomb. Hormones have a powerful influence over mood and frame of mind. With new hormonal levels come moods with highs and lows your teenager cannot easily manage. Accompanied by a new sexual awakening, hormonal influences can lead adolescents even further from the ties of their family as they explore their sexuality and interests. Like other people under the influence of fluctuating hormones, teenagers may not always be in control of their emotions. One father said in jest that once the hormones hit, his son's brain went dead.

Physical changes impact the experimental learner. The physical changes for an adolescent can be dramatic. No longer does your youngster look like a child. What is happening to teenagers' bodies is beyond their control. Their bodies may be changing so rapidly that just as they get used to one new change, another one occurs. Rapid physical growth creates insecurity. Like the teenager that grows nine inches in a year and three shoe sizes, he now has trouble keeping his balance. As all this is happening to him, he discovers his voice is changing too. Then in the mirror, he notices sprouting facial hair. He looks like a man but feels like a boy. He is wondering who he is. Man or boy? Or is he somewhere in the middle?

A problem common for young people occurs when physical growth does not coincide with emotional maturity. For most kids a huge gap exists. With this gap, sometimes there is a long period of 'catch up' time that needs to occur. A twelve or thirteen year-old girl who physically matures early can easily be mistaken for a young woman of seventeen or eighteen. Emotionally, she may feel very much like a child. This discrepancy between physical and emotional maturation can create emotional turmoil. Now, others seek her out and treat her as if she were older, based on her looks. Though all this new attention may be flattering, her responses are immature and awkward. She is at risk of others taking advantage of her because she is vulnerable and naïve.

Part of normal adolescence is a need for seclusion and distance from parents and other family members. Teenagers begin to live in their rooms now as if they owned their own separate homes. To your surprise, you may no longer feel welcome there.

Another facet of this experimentation with information is the art of changing one's mind. Your teenager may sound so positive about a decision or choice and then within hours or days drastically change position. One day Eric, a thirteen year-old, came into my office with his father, insisting, to his fathers' distress, that he had set his professional goals on becoming a garbage man. His father had a different vision for his son, like following in his footsteps to an Ivy League school. Eric thought it made little sense to get good grades since he wasn't going to need them to collect garbage. Finally, after many weeks of irritating discussion about the pros and cons of trash, getting a BIG reaction from his father with his new professional interests in garbage he finally gave up the idea. The next week he decided to become a NASA scientist. To his fathers' delight, he resumed his math studies. Contradictions like these are common in impulsive decision-making.

Teenagers are intensely curious, interested and attracted to their friends. Part of experimenting is choosing friends and developing friendships. Learning to be a good friend is important in future roles as a neighbor, colleague, friend and spouse. Their interest in friends is most evident by their attachment to the telephone.

With growing independence from parents and family, a teenager develops new interest and fascination with his or her peer group. The world of peers can be an emotional whirlwind of adolescent energy. It is easy for the young, experimenting adolescent to get caught up in the momentum of the peer group and temporarily blinded to the important connection he or she has to the family.

Parents want to know why their teenagers are so ornery and temperamental at home with them and such a delight when they visit other people in social situations. In public, your teenager feels a need to be 'together', act sophisticated and look and talk right and be in self-control. Conflict at home is actually a compliment to parents. Home is usually the only place a teenager feels safe enough to act immature or come emotionally 'unglued'. Anywhere else makes them vulnerable to criticism.

The developmental task of adolescence is to become independent of their family and seek a unique personal identity, with the ultimate goal of attaining an adult identity. The person your teenager is becoming is very much in process during these adolescent years.

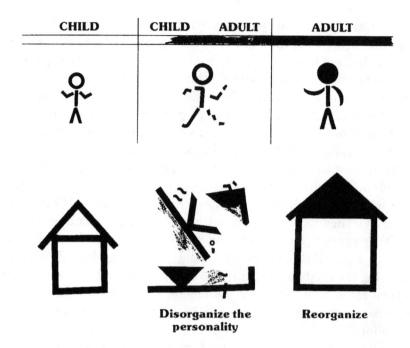

CHILD   **CHILD**   **ADULT**   **ADULT**

Disorganize the personality   **Reorganize**

Adolescence is a Process

These houses represent the personality of the person in the process of development from childhood to adulthood. The structures represent the psychological processes of growing up. To assess the personality of our young people we can imagine looking at each house individually to assess its' structural soundness.

The small house on the left is the house of childhood. The house is little, secure and close to family and friends. The world of the child is based on learning from a primary source; the child's family. Young and innocent, they are receptive to the caring and loving attention from their parents. Parents are very influential in the architecture of the house of childhood. A close, loving relationship with parents helps develop a strong foundation for the structure of their child.

The house of childhood, for most children, is usually well built, constructed slowly by thoughtful parents. When nurtured by loving caregivers, the personality structure of the house is strong and secure. The child develops feelings of safety, happiness and security.

Look now at the house on the right, the house of adulthood.

Mature and competent adults have personalities like this house; well built, a sturdy foundation and safe. Established personalities fluctuate very little. Mature adults know who they are, have clear values and are rather predictable and consistent in how they perceive things and how they act and interact with others. As children move through adolescence, parents hope their teenagers grow up to build strong psychological adult houses: becoming happy, healthy, productive, competent and loving adults.

The transformation of a child's personality into a mature adult personality spans the ages of twelve to twenty. The process begins with *disorganizing the personality* of the child in order to *reorganize the personality* of an adult. This process requires great *disorder* to complete because the teenager must become someone unique; a person the world has never met.

In the center is the house of adolescence. Doesn't this house look like your teenager's room? It looks more like a construction site, with a collection of parts and structures from both the house of childhood and the house of adulthood, in disarray. It looks this way for a good reason. It reflects your teenager's developmental stage: confusion and reconstruction of the 'self'. Your teenager's job is to take apart his or her childhood personality and to rebuild a new adult 'self'.

The teenager's house is under construction with no set architectural plan. With the mess of construction, it is hard to tell what the house will ultimately look like. Your teenager does not know either. Your teenager must take apart the house of childhood, add parts of the structures of adulthood and then rebuild his or her own house. Teenagers must take apart their personalities, contemplating the meaning of childhood qualities and the values of adulthood and rebuild to find a new 'self'. This process takes a lot of time and is unsettling, for both you and your teenager.

In early adolescence this building process appears haphazard. It becomes easier to see the probable end result by the time your teenager reaches seventeen or eighteen. You hope your teenager's house will be one with a sturdy foundation, strong, unique, resilient, warm and comfortable. The house must be sturdy enough to last a lifetime.

Unfortunately, you cannot build this house for your teenager. Much as you might want to offer architectural advice and direction, your adolescents must do it for themselves. You can love them throughout their building process, encourage them when they are trying to match the joints and secure the walls. It is best to give advice and guidance only when you are asked.

Their Rooms Are Their Homes

Now that your teenager has started the construction process in his or her 'new home' that is your young person's room, you may wonder who and how and with what frequency will it be cleaned?

The subject of room cleaning is a common source of complaints from many parents. It is important for your teenager to clean his or her own room. Once a week it is a good idea for your teenager to retrieve all the green moldy things, collect all the family towels and return other people's clothes. The best way to negotiate this task is to have your teenager set a day and time he or she will clean it (Saturdays by 3:00 p.m. is the most popular). Every couple of weeks your teenager should be able to actually find the floor and vacuum it. The rest of the time I suggest leaving your teenagers' room alone. Close the door so you don't have to look at the mess. Your teenager's room is much like a cocoon; it is here that teenagers are the closest to finding themselves.

What if you don't like the mess in your teenager's room? Ask yourself, whose mess is it anyway? The mess belongs to your teenager. And if the room is cluttered like the disorganized house, so is your teenager. And if he cannot find his clothes, ask yourself, "whose problem is this?" Remember, it is your teenager who lives here.

Just because you might want the room to look ready for the cover of House Beautiful doesn't mean your teenager will want the same thing. Your teenager will clean up and organize his or her room when your teenager is ready. This usually coincides when your teenager is ready to clean up his personality , which is when his personal identity is better defined and he has matured. One mom wanted to put police crime scene tape across the door of her teenage son's disheveled room because it looked like such a disaster area!

In this cocoon-like room more is going on than meets the eye. Teenagers are usually contemplating important things. Like the meaning of life. Who your teenager does not wish to be like. Wondering whom he or she will find to love. Facing fears and contemplating concerns. Wondering if the world has a place for him or her. Thinking, dreaming... in the process, growing up.

WHO AM I?

Adolescent Developmental Stage

It is 5:00pm and little Sam is hungry. He tells his mom that he wants a cookie "right NOW!" His mom, Sally, tells her cute four year-old that he can't have a cookie until after dinner. Instead he can have an apple, crackers or a glass of milk. Sam gets mad and decides to have a tantrum because he is not getting his way. After a few minutes, Sam realizes mom is not budging, so he gives up, stops crying and eats some crackers instead of his cookie.

It is 5:15pm and Sam's fifteen year-old brother Joel walks into the kitchen and heads toward the cookie jar. Sally says 'hi' as Joel is grabbing a fistful of cookies. She says, "Hey, Joel, please don't eat those before dinner." And then Sally gets *'the look'* and Joel says, "No, I want these now!" There stands Joel, 5'9" towering over Sally, poised with cookies in his hand. Sally tells Joel it is *not OK* for him to eat those cookies now. He sighs and with his cookies, leaves the room. What is Sally going to do? She can't wrestle Joel to the ground to assert her power as a parent. She must learn new skills to negotiate with her young adult. How, when and where to negotiate with your teenager who has grown bigger than you follow in these chapters.

Normally, children have a set of developmental tasks that progress with each year in their childhood. At each stage a child has an opportunity for a period of time to reach some level of mastery with specific developmental tasks. Parents are instrumental in helping their children with each particular developmental task, such as Sam's testing his autonomy. The emotional and physical developmental tasks are important building blocks in the development of the child.

Stages of development span a person's lifetime. These stages do not end with childhood. Adolescence marks the developmental stage called *identity versus identity confusion*. A teenager is in the process of discovering many aspects and facets of his or her young adult personality. The teenager searches to know "who am I?" Poor mastery of this developmental stage would show in a weak personal identity, being unsure or confused about 'self'.

Only for today, does your teenager know who he or she is. Teenage identity is a sure thing for this moment in time. Tomorrow brings an unknown. A lot can change for the average teenager from week to week or even day to day. Each teenager wishes to become a person others like, love and admire. Your teenager may tell you that she is vastly different from everyone else she knows. This is a teenager's attempt to find a way to be unique and special.

The Last Person on Earth

Don't be too surprised if your teenager tells you at some point in this process of growing up the last person on earth he or she would ever emulate is you. At times your teenager may seem to detest the idea of being anything like you. This is your teenagers' way of feeling *separate* and *different* from you. Not being like you means he or she is free to search for his or her 'self' without following in someone else's footsteps. One of the easiest ways to accomplish this search for 'oneself' is to be different from parents and other family members. Do not take this attitude personally, it will pass with time.

Having differences from family members helps teenagers feel independent and adult-like in their search for "Who am I?" Maybe you too thought this to be so or even said as much to your parents when you were a teenager. Let your teenager explore whom he or she may want to be, as long as doing so is safe and sound. Remember your teenager is the architect for his or her personality.

"But they all look the same," says a mother about her 14 year-old daughter and her friends. Their hairstyles may seem to be the same, their dress and their language sounds identical. In the world of adolescents, they will tell you that they each are very different. Jenny has a leather skirt with buttons and Sheila has snaps on hers. And Joe's cap is black and red and David has a Dodgers cap. So what if the skirts are the same color? So what if both Joe and David are wearing their hats backwards? Can't you see the differences? Teenagers demand, "We *are not* the same."

When in Doubt, Say the Opposite

Your teenager, in search of self, needs growing independence to test out new ideas. Challenging one's parents valued ideas is part of this process. In order to feel independent, the young adolescent needs to say or do something different. His ideas need to be different from yours. Her mood needs to be different. And your teenager must look different as well. To feel unique, the *opposite* works really well. Whatever is the opposite from you is often the easiest thing to do or say And it is convenient. And it is especially good if it gets a reaction from you!

Phil and his mom are driving in the car, the sun is shining and the sky is blue. Mom remarks on the beautiful day. Phil says, in an irritated, brisk voice, " I am *so* sick of this lousy weather. I am really getting tired of all this sun. Sun gives thousands of people skin cancer. It's disgusting! I can hardly wait until it gets cloudy and rains."

Mom falls into the trap and begins *the debate*. She tells Phil his idea is ridiculous. How could he possibly like rain? Why doesn't he like sunshine and blue skies like other people? This is a useless debate; fighting over the weather. *The debate* concerns opinions and no one is going to win. Phil is likely to think he has accomplished something by being *different* than his mom. The more his mom protests the more Phil commits to loving rain and clouds. Phil feels energized by this argument but his mom just feels worn out.

A better response for Phil's mom, one that would defuse the situation and avoid *the debate*, would be for her to say, "OK, honey, just for you, I hope it rains real soon."

Discussions like this one go nowhere fast. If you and your teenager are having arguments over minor things like the weather, whether it is responsible to eat beef, what are the right kind of shoes to wear, it is best to *stop* until you understand your teenager better. These debates can be endless as well as useless. Let your teenager feel different from you... he or she needs to feel independent and exploring the opposite can accomplish that.

Let your teenager share with you his or her unique and intriguing ideas during this exploration for 'self'. Remember a teenager will test a variety of ideas, dress styles, personalities, attitudes and hairstyles before settling for an established sense of 'self'. Accept that some days it is truly a mystery 'who' your teenager might possibly become.

The Spotlight

For the young teenager the rapid passage from a child's physique into a young adult's body creates self-consciousness. When teenagers no longer look like children, but still feel very young, many feel as if there is a spotlight shining upon them. Being in the spotlight produces feelings of insecurity with teenagers wondering if they are normal or like others.

Your teenager may tell you she could *never* be seen in a certain discount store, either alone or with you. It just couldn't happen, it would be far too humiliating. Why? Everyone would *see* her. *Everybody would know.* A teenager's belief is that if she did go into that discount department store, certainly *everybody* at school would know she "discount shops!!" She would be embarrassed beyond her wildest dreams. Even sitting in the car in the parking lot would be out of the question.

In the spotlight young teenagers believe everyone is acutely aware of all the changes happening to them. Those pimples on their face flash like neon lights. Everyone notices his or her large feet. Their clumsiness is obvious to all. New curves and the shape of their bodies draw everyone's attention. Young adolescent girls will dress to cover and hide their developing breasts and body. Boys, too, experience embarrassment thinking others will notice how they are developing into young men.

When teenagers think everyone is watching it is best not to debate what is actually happening with them. Just respect their discomfort and feelings of self-consciousness. They are uncomfortable with the changes that are occurring. These developmental changes can make them feel out of their control. Physical changes bring expectations about growing up. Your teenager is not alone thinking he or she is being watched, their friends probably think they are being watched too.

In time the spotlight fades and your teenager will no longer feel this way. As your teenagers becomes more comfortable with their physical and emotional development they will become more secure. Your teenager will eventually go into the discount department store and realize that quite frankly no one really cares if he or she is there or not. Your teenager may even run into a friend or two.

I am the Center

Your teenager may seem and act self-centered as he or she questions a new identity.

The adolescent identity search requires much introspection and serious contemplation about one's 'self'. With a focus on 'self' the importance of others can seem secondary. It is not that teenagers do not care about others. They do care. It is just not as obvious now. Your teenager, especially during the early adolescent years, must contemplate all the possibilities of the illusive question, "Who am I?" Until they figure out themselves they have more difficulty reaching out and helping others. Putting the puzzle together well is important. How a teenager solves it will determine the quality of the rest of his or her life. Setting up situations or teaming up with your young teenager to help others promotes this behavior that may not otherwise occur.

The Mood

Jennifer enters the den; her younger brother and sister grab the remote control and run for cover. She begins to scream, "I am going to kill who ever changes my show!" She finds her brother and sister behind the couch and explodes, yelling and cursing. Her mother comes in and demands she stop yelling. She screams at the top of her lungs, "I'm *not* yelling!!" Then she continues: "I don't get any respect around here and these kids are driving me *crazy*! I wish you would sell them!" The children flee from the room. Even the dog runs away. Jennifer is on a hormonal rampage.

A half-hour later Jennifer's mom enters the den. To her delight and astonishment she sees Jennifer on the floor with her brother and sister playing a board game. Jennifer sees her mom and smiles.

One minute they are happy, the next they are hostile. The erratic moods of teenagers baffle parents. It is not uncommon for a parent to react and respond in a like manner to a teenager's sulky and irritable mood. Sometimes you just want to scream or tear out your hair with this kind of frustration. Your teenager's mood can really test your patience and rattle your nerves.

Much moodiness seems beyond your teenager's control. Moodiness and impulsiveness together can cause the teenager problems. A teenager may be surprised at what he or she says on the spur of the moment. What was said may have been rude, embarrassing or hurtful and the teenager must accept the fact he or she did indeed say it. After your teenager has insulted you, you might hear your young person say, "I can't believe I said that!"

Most likely you will not be able to change the mood of your teenager but there are some things you can do to help quiet one. For instance do not engage in a discussion when he or she is irritable. That means a parent does much more listening than talking. Keeping a respectful distance can also be helpful. Handling a hostile teenager is a lot like approaching a porcupine with his quills up. You need to approach slowly or you could easily get hurt. Accept that your teenager's mood is irritable, angry or sullen for now. Food is a lot like love; feeding your teenager can help soothe combustible moods. It helps to remember, like bad weather, moods will pass so be patient.

Include your teenagers *mood and all* in family activities no matter how they feel. If you tell your teenagers you will wait to include them when their moods or attitudes change, you could be waiting months. I think leaving your teenager out of family activities is a very poor message to your young person. It can make them feel they are no longer important or significant. Go together on family outings and vacations, have dinner and plan activities for the whole family. You may notice that many times changing the scenery softens your teenager's irritable mood. Activities have a distracting quality. This really applies to any family member having an emotional struggle.

How do you get your teenager to come along if he refuses? First, tell your teenagers the reason you want them to join you is because they are an important part of the family. You can't all be together unless your son or daughter is with you. Then you need to believe that your teenager will come... *in time.*

Then you will have to wait. Let's say you are planning on going out to dinner and your teenager is in a foul mood and announces he is *not* coming. First, tell him he is important and the family can only be complete with him. Then wait for him in the car. In time he'll come. Teenagers are curious, social creatures. He will be peering out the window wondering what you are doing sitting in the car. Remember if his feet are moving and he gets in the car that means he is coming. You have achieved success. Even if he is angry. Even if he is hostile. Even if he seems miserable. Remember, *in time,* his mood will pass.

Most importantly, do not reprimand someone because of his or her mood. Or draw too much attention to your teenager's "attitude", as long as his behavior is not rude. That is not what loving someone is all about. We all have bad days. Teenagers, especially, seem to have an excess of bad ones. You don't want others to give up on you just because the mood you are in might not be easy or convenient. So to the best of your ability, accept your teenager, mood and all.

The Costume

I have seen some of the most remarkable styles of adolescent clothing come in and out of my office. On the streets, I am always intrigued by the new fashion trends of our youth. Some teenagers are unmatched in their creativity with their dress. Many of them could outdo Paris designers. When I see teenagers with wild outfits or radical hairstyles, I just imagine them in costume. Every day could be Halloween in my office!

Many parents become really upset with hair color, hair cut, hair length and style of dress. Style choices can attract a lot of attention. With any unusual dress your teenager is probably just trying to be recognized as *unique and different* from you.

It is easy to forget not to judge a book by its cover. It isn't fair to teenagers to react to them because of how they are dressed. So, if her hair is an odd shade of chartreuse or he is wearing enormous shorts, large enough to fit a person weighing 250 pounds, ask yourself, is this a really big deal? Remember that the costume usually does not reflect the real young person, except for that moment in time.

I don't think the garb teenagers wear matters and needs to change unless it is indecent, rude, gang related or derogatory to others. If a colored bandana represents a gang or T-shirt graphics are indecent, you will need to say no. When teenagers dress in extremely radical ways (or gang related ways) it is usually an indication these young people are in need of a great deal of attention, which they are seeking from their parents. When a young person is wearing rude or indecent clothing, it is a parent's job to make sure they change it.

What your teenager wears, as with his or her mood, will pass through phases, throughout the years of adolescence. Radical styles are *not* likely to be permanent. However, it is more than reasonable to tell your teenager he or she cannot wear their unique dress out to dinner with the family, with company, to church or to grandma's house.

One day I was having some car trouble, so my two little girls and I had to wait in the service center while my brakes were being repaired. When we entered the small waiting room there was only one place with enough room for the three of us to sit. On the fourth chair sat a young man, about fifteen, sporting a Mohawk, dangling pierced earrings in one ear, a ponytail trailing down his back, wearing a leather neck choker with silver metal spikes, a black T-shirt with a skull decal and of course, in the middle of winter, shorts (this was typical clothing for teenagers on a cold snowy day in January). And he was, as you might guess, plugged into his set of earphones.

I walked up to the empty seats and sat down. My youngest little girl sat right next to him. While we waited I began reading aloud one of my favorite children's stories <u>Stega Nona and the Magic Pot</u>. It is a story about a wonderful woman who has a magic pot which teaches a young man in the village a lesson in respecting others' things. As I read I noticed he took off his headset and was listening to our story, occasionally checking out the pictures. A couple of times I smiled at him. He smiled back.

Later, he and my little girls made hot chocolate together. If you just looked at us it would not appear we had much in common. But we did. He seemed like a nice guy who still had some kid in him as he listened to our story and shared hot cocoa with my little girls.

I always try to compliment teenagers on what they are wearing and their individual expression. If I am not keen about their new style of dress, I go for color compliments. I am sincere and respectful in what I say to them. So I might be impressed with the shine of his high top black leather boots or the shade of burgundy in her hair. Many teenagers have gone to a great creative effort to dress for the day. The person in transition is who is important to me, not what the person is wearing.

The Rule Breaking Challenge

Irritable moods will pass. Your teenager's dress and style choices will change. Friends will come and go. Over-reacting is not usually productive or necessary, though that is much easier said than done.

However, when faced with rule breaking and negative behavior a parent needs to be responsive. Thoughtfully and calmly reactive. The change in parenting style needed means you take time to respond and evaluate your strategic options in order to deal with negative behavior.

If your teenager calls you an insulting name, swears, throws something or hits a brother or sister, this behavior goes beyond mood and should not be excused because someone is expressing his or her 'personal style'. If this happens parents need to respond in some way to let the teenager know this behavior is not acceptable. No matter his or her mood. Even if your young person insists the behavior fits his or her new tough style. Behavior is where parents need to draw the line and give a teenager a consequence for his or her chosen action. Many undesirable ideas and opinions may be tolerated during the maturation process as long as the behavior that accompanies it does not infringe on the rights of others.

How Does Your Teenager Think?

Have you ever wondered how your teenager thinks? A number of parents have asked me IF their teenager is thinking at all. Have you noticed when you ask your teenager why he or she did something, all you usually get is a shrug and a "I dunno". Do you wonder how your teenager interprets the world? How do teenagers perceive things the way they do? Why does your teenager criticize what you do? How do you help your young person think through issues rather than make impulsive decisions?

To better understand the process of adolescent thinking let's look first at how a child thinks. On the next page is an outline to follow.

There are two parts representing children's thinking. One is the "C" which represents the *child* part of their thinking. The second is the "P" part, which depicts the *parent* part of their thinking.

The *child* or the 'C' is playful, impulsive, demanding and wants immediate gratification of needs and desires. You hear the 'C' loud and clear when your five-year-old demands to go outside after dark. You tell him he cannot go outside because it is too late to play. This kind of answer makes the 'C' angry. The result is often a temper tantrum. He is not getting what he wants and battles to get his impulsive need met. The 'P' tells the child he

How Teens Think:

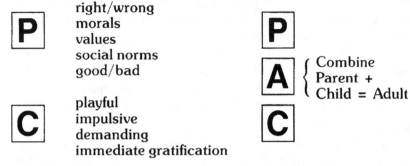

Child   **Teenager**

cannot win. He cannot have his way; it is not safe to go outside alone after dark. The 'P' reminds him that mom and dad are in charge and eventually, he must give in. In time, the 'C' gives in. He recognizes you, the parent, are in charge. He gives up and does not go outside to play.

The 'C' in him needs both structure and limits. The 'C' cannot be wild and have all his impulsive needs met. The balance of limits and restraints make up the other part of the child's thinking, the *parent* or the 'P'. This is the part of the child's thinking that is the most mature. You develop the 'P' by teaching your child about the world, what is right and wrong, what are good and bad, social and family norms. The child *absorbs* the information from a parent, which is registered in the 'P' part of the child's knowledge base.

The thinking process of the child is relatively simple. Over time with maturation and cognitive development, the child's thinking becomes more sophisticated. The complexity of children's thinking changes from concrete thinking to more abstract thoughts.

As the child grows into adolescence there is an additional element that develops in his or her thinking. Below is a diagram of the maturing adolescent thought process:

> *P   (parent)*
> *A => combine Parent and Child= Adult*
> *C   (child)*

What we call the *adult* begins to develop in the adolescent, represented in the diagram by an 'A'. The job of the new Adult or the 'A' is to begin to independently make decisions balancing issues between the Parent or the 'P' and the Child or the 'C'. This 'A' is very immature and impulsive in most twelve or thirteen year olds. By seventeen or eighteen the 'A' part of their thinking has matured, becomes quite stable and more adept with decision-making abilities.

The 'C' part of the teenager's thinking changes as the adolescent does. The 'C' of the adolescent is now playful, but the environment for play is very different from childhood. New friends and a new social world offer more sophisticated ways to have fun. Teenagers with a budding curiosity about relationships, language, sex, alcohol and drugs are intrigued with what is happening around them. There are many opportunities and choices about ways to have fun on the playground of adolescence.

The 'C' in the teenager is still impulsive and wants immediate gratification of needs, wants and desires. In the young teenager, the 'C' is just as demanding, only interests have changed. Now with the addition of powerful hormones, new sexual interest and drive, impulsiveness takes on a whole new context.

The Parent or the 'P' remains intact, even though at times it seems absent. You may wonder, especially in early adolescence, if your teenager remembers any of your lectures and teachings on values and morals. The adolescent continues to put in new material into the 'P' part of his or her thinking, not only from family but from peers and society as well.

The 'A' or *adult* emerges to help create a balance between the impulsiveness of the 'C' and the wise guidance of the 'P'. The 'A' has the job, in a sense, of making choices for the teenager, deciding between having fun or doing what is best and right. What the 'C' part wants to do is sometimes in direct conflict with what the 'P' thinks the teenager should do or what the right thing is to do.

In young, immature teenagers, the 'A' decisions lean much more toward the needs and interests of the 'C'. The 'C' is very curious about the new things surrounding young adolescents. It is a whole new social world in middle school or junior high. The 'C' is impulsive and wants to join in all the fun and excitement, without heeding the consequences. The impulse is driven by a strong need to feel important by fitting into a peer group.

As time passes and new learning experiences occur, the 'A'

becomes wiser about choices. While the 'A' is young and immature, you need to provide plenty of structure and limits for your
teenager. As teenagers mature, it is easier to allow them to make
more independent choices and take on more responsibility for
themselves.

Here is an example of a young teenager's thinking process of
the C, A and P:

John is fifteen. He is with his friends who have decided at the
spur of the moment to go to a party. This is the party his parents
would not let him attend. To make this decision he _briefly_ thinks
about his choices.

The 'C' says: "John you gotta go to this party. You can't miss
it. The guys will think you are a jerk if you don't go. Everything
will be fine, just fine."

The 'P' says: "This is not a good idea. You will lose your parents' trust and respect by breaking this rule. And if you get caught
it might mean *Big Trouble*. Don't go!"

His friends have little patience so this young 'A' must make a
choice quickly. So with great impulsiveness he simplifies his
choices. His choices are to fit in and have *fun* or the possible *big
trouble*. So the young 'A', feeling lucky, quickly decides and the
answer is "Go!" Fun won. John quickly forgot the warning of the
'P'.

And away goes John.

At the party he feels a little guilty. Then he sees *her*. That girl
he is so attracted to. Suddenly, the guilt is forgotten and he feels
great satisfaction. His 'C' is very happy with his choice.

It is getting late. His buddies are ready to leave. Outside, the
group heads to the car with the sixteen year-old driver, Matt.
But Matt is staggering to the car with a beer in his hand. John is
faced with another decision. The 'C' says, "Everything will be fine,
go! Hey, everybody else is going." The 'P' warns of danger: "This
is a serious situation, it is not wise to go." The 'P' warns him to
think carefully. If John would listen long enough the 'P' would
suggest getting his friends together and taking away Matt's keys
because friends don't let friends drink and drive. Making the
wrong decision could mean *Big Trouble*.

John's 'A' must decide what to do. And fast. Again, there is
not much time to decide. There is much at stake; his reputation
with the guys as well as his safety. The other side of the issue is
that he has already broken a rule and the trust with his parents

by going to the party. The pressure is on again and he must make another decision.

Situations like these are tough for a teenager, especially a young teenager who feels vulnerable and unsure of himself or herself. In an effort to ease the discomfort associated with the decision young adolescents feel pressure to decide quickly. He feels the pressure from his peers because he wants to be included. The group provides a false sense of reassurance and security. The young teenager rationalizes if others choose to do the same thing it must be OK.

It is now 1:00 AM and John's parents get a call from the police. Guess what? Matt did drive, with John in the car with his buddies. It was a really exciting ride... until the police officer pulled the car over. John never took the time to think of this possibility. It was a shock to him as well as to the other teenagers in the car. Oh, no... *Big Trouble* happened.

His parents wonder what he was thinking about when he decided to get into a car with an intoxicated driver. John did not think about the possibility of being pulled over by the police. *Big Trouble, Big Lesson.* The young 'A' is now more aware of how serious his choices can be. He is also more experienced and hopefully more mature. The 'Child' is humbled. The 'Parent' is justified.

Who Makes A Real Difference To Your Teenager?

Who really counts in the life of your teenager? Who can influence your son or daughter the most? When the going gets tough for them, whom do they *need* the most? Lets start with a multiple-choice question for you. Please choose one answer.

Q. Who is the most significant and influential person(s) in your teenager life?
    a. Peer group
    b. Friend
    c. Boyfriend or girlfriend
    d. Coach, Teacher or Club leader
    e. Parents

Let's look at all the possible answers.

CHOICE (a) Peer Group

Does your teenager let the peer group influence his or her choices, interests and behaviors? Will your teenager do almost anything to fit into a group? Will your young person give up favorite family activities to join his or her friends?

A teenager's peer group can exert a great deal of pressure. Teenagers feel a strong need to fit into a group, to feel included and be recognized. Some peer groups can exert a positive influence and support your young person as he or she makes good choices. Today, our young people are far more sophisticated than a few generations ago about drugs, alcohol and weapons, all of which are more easily accessible. The peer group may be much more knowledgeable about sex, diverse life styles and deviant behaviors than your adolescent peer group was. Your teenager can be exposed to vastly different temptations than adolescents dealt with in the past. The choices for our young people today are more complicated, at times more dangerous and occasionally even deadly.

CHOICE (b) Friends

Does your teenager seem to put his or her friend before you and the family? How many hours on the phone does your teenager spend with a friend? Does he or she have a friend with whom he or she must do everything?

Having friends is important to all age groups, especially to teenagers. There is great security in being able to talk to someone who is changing as much as you are. With friends, teenagers don't feel so isolated, odd or unusual.

Your teenager may have just one good friend or be very social and have several friends in several peer groups. When you do not like new behaviors in your teenager, look for the influence of new friends. Friends can be powerful and persuasive.

CHOICE (c) Boyfriend or girlfriend

The third choice is the influence of a boyfriend or girlfriend. Falling in love can make your teenager behave like a very different person. If your son or daughter does not have a boyfriend or girlfriend he or she may feel driven to get one. Relationships are very important during the adolescent years. Once your teenager has a boyfriend or girlfriend, you and the family go on the back burner of importance.

Having a boyfriend can make a drastic change in your daughter's behavior. She may give all her attention to her relationship and give up time with her friends, family and homework. You may worry if you do not like her choice in young men.

Your son may finally change his personal hygiene habits when a new girl is on the scene. He may actually care about wearing clean clothes, brushing his teeth, and looking neat and well groomed.

CHOICE (d) Coach, teacher or club leader

Does your teenager have a significant adult relationship with a teacher, coach or youth group leader? Sometimes an adult, other than a parent, who takes an interest in your son or daughter, can be very influential. It may be the teacher of a class your son or daughter takes that he or she really loves. It may be a coach that takes an interest in the athletic abilities of your young person. For example, Chris's mother is nagging him daily to do his ninth grade homework, without much success. One day Coach Reed calls to remind Chris to do his work, so he can keep up his grades to play football. Then, Chris does his work! The coach is better able to get her son to do his homework when the same requests by his mother have been ignored.

CHOICE (e) Parents

You may think I added parents last to the list just for fun. Do you think you could ever stand a chance in a popularity contest with all the other people on this list of choices? Teenagers are notorious for notifying their parents that they are no longer important or needed in their lives. These messages are clearly sent with their attitudes and their behavior or your teenager may tell you, straight out, you are no longer important.

Which of these answers is correct?

Believe it or not the answer is *e*. You, the parent, are the *most significant and important person* in the life of your teenager. Parents are the only people who remain a constant throughout the years in a young person's life. Only you will love and care for your teenager no matter what happens. A teenager's peer group will change throughout adolescence. It is unlikely your son or daughter will have the same boyfriend or girlfriend over many years (most love relationships last an average of about three weeks in middle school). Friends will come and go. Teachers and coaches may only be involved for part of your teenager's adolescence. Unlike all these other people, parents are a constant.

Parents are usually the only people who know their children through all the seasons of their adolescence. They stay with their offspring from the day they are born until the day they leave home, even in the most unpleasant and trying times.

When your teenager has a broken heart, whom do they need? It is your shoulder your teenager wants to cry on. No one can love your child the way you do. Your love and caring is just as irreplaceable during adolescence as it was through childhood.

Even though friends are important, the family is essential. So go ahead and take your teenager with you on those family outings, camping trips or dinner out. Insist your adolescent join the family for meals, mood and all. Though he or she may never admit it, on these outings and gatherings, your teenager can be having a great time.

Kerri is fourteen. She tells her parents she *hates* camping because she detests dirt, she can't use her hair dryer and it is a huge waste of time out of her important social schedule. Every time the family talks about going camping, she adamantly repeats her distaste for joining the group. In spite of her complaints, her parents insist she come along, telling her she is part of the family and they cannot leave her behind (even though she pleads she has friends with whom she can stay). After a recent camping expedition, where she complained most of the time about how stupid it was to take a trip to the lake, she called a friend as soon as she got home. Mom overheard her saying, "I had the most awsome time at the lake. The weather was great, I got a tan and I met this really cute guy who was camped next to us. He was to die for!..." Kerri did not thank her parents for taking her. The next camping trip, oddly enough, she did not complain as loudly.

You are the Balance

When the influence from a powerful group of peers is negative, parents must provide the balance for their teenager. This is especially true when other teenagers hurt your teenagers' feelings or say derogatory things.

Thirteen-year-old Stacie came into my office with her parents. Her biggest problem this year was a severe case of acne.

She was devastated and thought she was the ugliest person on earth because the kids at school had fun calling her "pizza face". She said she would never return to school she was so humiliated. Her mother said a wonderful thing to her. She smiled and said, "Honey, I think you are beautiful!" Parents can be the mature and loving balance that help their teenagers deal with negative and painful words from others.

While your teenager is in love he may say his girlfriend is the most important person in his life. After the break-up however you might hear him say the biggest mistake he ever made was to date this girl. The love and care that is constant for a teenager comes from that young person's parents and family.

Your teenager may go through periods of needing to make new friends, or losing old ones. During these changes an adolescent's family is a vital source of stability. When friends are not around your teenager always has your family. When she feels left out from peers, you and the family can help her feel loved and cared for.

Because of teenage instability, your son or daughter needs you to be consistent and reliable. You are very important for his or her security. You are the one who can give consistent loving care and attention and you provide the balance for the complex world that surrounds your teenager.

What Motivates Your Teenager?

What motivates a teenager today? Teenagers like to be recognized and validated by others. This makes them feel important and significant. Getting attention, being liked, and being accepted are important motivators for young people. Validation is especially critical at this stage in life when they are feeling so vulnerable about themselves.

Teenagers are motivated by curiosity, which leads them in many directions, learning something, getting to know someone, or discovering something important. The world of the adolescent is filled with intrigue and mystery.

When a teenager's need for love, recognition and acceptance are satisfied in their relationship with a parent there is less need to seek a friend or peer group to provide these primary feelings of significance and importance.

> **#1   TO BE LISTENED TO AND TAKEN SERIOUSLY**
>
> **#2   TO FEEL IMPORTANT, WORTHWHILE AND**
>
>   **SIGNIFICANT**
>
> **#3 TO HAVE MEANINGFUL ROLES**

According to H. Steven Glenn, author of <u>Raising Self-reliant Children in a Self-indulgent World</u>, there are three basic needs in the development of a self-reliant young person[1]:

The most common complaint from teenagers about their parents is that they do not feel listened to and taken seriously. Understandably, it is difficult to listen to your teenager when she has just tattooed her arm, when his hair covers his face or when your young person frequently changes what he or she has to say. You may have difficulty paying attention when your teenager defends radical ideas, especially those beliefs you oppose or even abhor. Your teenagers' voice may sometimes be so loud and angry you feel you cannot hear yourself think. It is hard to listen when your son or daughter's moods and ideas seem so negative, and even wrong to you.

It can also be very hard to take all this change in your young person very seriously. It is difficult for your teenager to move on to other things if he or she stalls in trying to convince you that his or her ideas are worthwhile and valid. What teenagers have to say today is all they have to say (and all they know). Tomorrow is a distant day, with more to learn and experience.

Adolescents need to take themselves seriously for their personal growth and development. If you are not able to listen and give credit to your young person's ideas then he or she will be persistent trying new ways to convince you.

Many parents are under the misunderstanding that listening to their teenager means *agreeing* with them. Sometimes you must agree that the two of you disagree on a subject. Nevertheless, it is essential to listen even if you do not agree. If you won't listen then teenagers won't believe they are important and worthwhile to you. The next best thing to having a parent listen, is to have friends who readily agree with anything your teenager is saying. We all liked to be listened to and taken seriously at any age.

The second basic need is to feel *worthwhile, significant and important*. Isn't that what most people want out of life? Any person feeling that he or she is worthwhile to others is most often a happy, contented, capable, competent and loving individual.

This is not something your teenagers can provide for themselves. The significance of who they are and what they do comes from the feedback of others. It is *critical* the feedback comes from the people the teenager loves the most, you and other family members. Taking your teenagers with you on family outings or anywhere else helps them feel included and important. Remember to include your teenager, regardless of his or her mood or attitude. Your teenager does not want to be left out. Most importantly, find a reason to smile at your teenager every day. To do so you may have to resolve current problems and find successful ways to talk to your teenager.

The third basic need is to have a *meaningful role*. As your teenager hears that he or she is important to you, it is *only* believable if his actions make this a reality. For example, consider a teenager, doing little to nothing, spending his time at home on the couch watching endless TV. He has parents continually say to him that he is a terrific guy, a bright and talented young man and that he is important and valued by his family. If this young man does poorly in school and does little or nothing at home, how can he believe this is true? I don't think he can. What he does in the world does not validate what he hears from his parents. With hard work on his schoolwork, participating in family chores and activities, involvement in community, church or extracurricular activities in school like sports, this feedback from parents becomes *believable*. His actions and accomplishments confirm what his parents encourage him to believe about himself.

It does take more than *words*. To feel good about him/herself a person needs the partnership of *words* and *action*.

For years I wondered why so many teenagers were working. What motivates them? Money was the first thing that comes to mind. Paychecks were initially motivating but the novelty was often lost after the first four or five were cashed. Many of these young people already had plenty of money from their families.

What seemed to motivate these young people was something far more valuable than money. For many the incentive is being recognized by others. Someone would smile and say "Thank you". I think of a fifteen-year-old who walks a woman and her children to their car carrying their groceries. He opens the door, loads the groceries and then she smiles at him and says "thanks". This interaction makes this young man happy and proud with himself. He believes he has value and worth and a meaningful role. A *meaningful role* is an essential part of motivating young people and encouraging positive self-esteem.

Our communities are not set up to readily provide our teenagers meaningful roles, as they were generations ago. Two generations ago, a fourteen year-old working in the family may have meant the survival of a crop or helping rear a younger child. Meaningful roles were readily available. A teenager was a valuable asset to the family and community that had an abundance of meaningful roles available.

Now parents and communities struggle to find things their teenagers can do. Our teenagers have so much talent and energy that can be valuable to our families, our businesses and our communities, but without roles and opportunities this talent is wasted. The challenge for you is to find something your teenager can do with his or her talents, interests and energy that helps him or her feel busy, productive and therefore valued.

The Circle of Influence

Here are two circular charts. Each chart can be divided into many different slices. The size of each slice of the pie is relative to

A teenager must be motivated first in order to make the best choices

Q. What used to motivate teens?

Relatives •

Peers •

Society •

TV   Teachers
         Coaches

• Family & extended family

• Parents (home)

• Church

Radio

Q. What motivates teenagers today?

Radio •   • Computer

TV •   ●   • Media/Video

Peer • •   • Working Parents

$ •   •   • Drugs

Job   Sex

• ↑ Time Alone

its importance. The pie of life changes with time. How your teenager's pie pieces are divided today is likely to be quite different from how it will look in a year's time.

With each generation we can expect changes in the pie chart of life of a teenager. Look at the top example of what motivates teenagers. This is a pie chart from the late 1950's and 1960's.

The things that may have influenced you as a teenager may be very different from what motivates your teenager today. Take peer pressure for example. A thirteen-year-old's peer group today is far more sophisticated than it was for most eighteen-year-olds in the past. Drugs are different, social expectations change, risks like AIDS make choices more serious and general knowledge is different.

Extended families of yesterday are not like they are today. In the past the extended family was an important resource for many struggling teenagers. A teenager, frustrated with how he or she was treated at home, was able to walk to grandma's house after school or spend some time with an aunt or uncle. These other adults were available and involved in a teenager's life. Having a choice of adults who care, a teenager could seek someone other than a parent to get his or her basic needs met for feedback, support and encouragement.

In the past a parent was likely to be there when a teenager got home from school. Teenagers were not usually left alone for long periods of time without supervision. One parent, typically the father, was working outside the home and many mothers remained with the children.

In the past, the American family had a much lower divorce rate, so there was greater family stability. The work ethic prevailed in marriage as well. In spite of marital conflict, there was more social pressure for parents to stay together. If a couple survived a difficult marriage, sometimes that relationship improved by the time the children left home. Working parents, single parent families, divorced and diverse 'family' groups now replace the 'Parent At Home' section. The American family is indeed fractured and still changing.

There were fewer outside distractions to take members away from family activities. The family spent more time at home together. Before many of our modern conveniences, there were more chores around the home to do so that less idle time was available.

Church and other places to worship were another important influence in the lives of teenagers in the past than for many families today. Religious education gave parents additional support by teaching values and morals in developing faithful, altruistic young adults.

Though class sizes continue to grow, generations ago communities were closer knit. It was typical for teachers to know you, your brothers, and sisters, your parents and members of your extended family. Coaches often had a smaller group of kids to coach and there was less competition so everybody interested could make the team.

The number of teenagers in high school and middle schools today is probably significantly larger than when you went to school. Today the collective sophistication of the peer group is very different. As our society grows more complex, so do the issues for our young people.

Communities were smaller and people knew their neighbors. The community played a more active role in raising young people. If Mr. Jones saw Billy Smith steal something in a store, he was likely to intervene and reprimand Billy. He would likely know Billy's mother and father and call on them to discuss the matter. Society was not so complex, less violent, more predictable and less sophisticated. Communities brought together interactions with teenagers and adults.

Television and media was not like it is today. Though media can offer wonderful education and information, evil and the anti-hero were not glamorized, as it is today. Graphic information about deviant adult behavior was not as accessible to impressionable children. Some of what your children see today on the screen and on covers of magazines was considered pornography in the past. Children and teenagers learned about the adult world from others around them or by reading books and a much more benign media. Too much mindless media can squelch the imagination and creativity of children and teenagers.

The content of songs on the radio in the past was what we might call 'mild'. The music had a different context and therefore a different influence on young people. Watch a music channel on TV from the eyes and ears of your child and take note of how it may influence your teenager today. Popular music of the past did not lure young people with explicit sex and violence as it does now. One of the most significant differences is the 'We' generation of the past versus the current 'Me' theme in songs. As you listen to oldies you hear lyrics about the songwriter's concern and interest in another person, like "Oh, Donna" sung by Richie Valens and "My Guy" sung by Mary Wells. The singer sings about the attributes of a special man or woman they love or admire. Today, many of the popular songs have self-centered lyrics about the singer, his or her needs and wants. Songs commonly include violence, sexual abuse and derogatory messages to others.

When you take a look at the lower pie chart of today's teenager things look different. Compare machines to people. Most remarkable is how much modern technology has influenced our youngsters. Media like radio, TV, video, computer, computer games and advanced computer networks begin to replace people. In the age of rapid technological advances we need to take a long, thoughtful look at how it influences the rearing of our adolescents.

Drugs and alcohol may be far more readily available to your teenager. And many of the drugs to which your teenager has access are much more powerful and dangerous than those that were available during your adolescent years. Most teenagers have access to most any drug and alcohol they might want. Unfortunately, this is also true for many children in elementary school.

Money and jobs may have a different place in your teenager's life than in past generations. Many young people seek work outside the family to earn money for themselves. A working teenager must balance time between work and school. It may be the first time a teenager has had to work hard since most children and teenagers do fewer chores today. Some adolescents don't know how to work hard because life has been too easy at home.

The issue of sexuality is different too. The age of AIDS demands a new kind of mature thinking about sex and adolescence. Ask yourself what does the media tell your young people about sexuality and sex? Are these messages what you want your innocent youngsters to learn? Every parent needs to think about this. The influence of the sex drive is very powerful. That drive, coupled with the permissiveness and moral irresponsibility portrayed in the media, opens the door for very early interest and experimentation. With the emergence of AIDS, experimentation may have deadly consequences.

The most significant pie piece is Time Alone. Time alone and idle time was a very small piece of the pie of the past. Teenagers were much busier and more involved, with more active roles in their families, with sports or activities taking them into their communities. Teenagers today, left alone to raise themselves, tend to develop chronic boredom and depression and become our young people at risk.

How much time does your teenager have without a parent around? How much of that time does he or she spend alone? How much time with friends? When young people spend a lot of time alone, boredom sets in. Teenagers are usually social people. Unsupervised hours offer the opportunity for your teenager to be involved in activities, such as drinking, drugs and sexual experimentation, that you may never know about if you are not around.

Jason and Andy are friends. They are twelve year-old friends and live in the same nice neighborhood. They have gotten to know each other well this year riding the bus. Both have similar family situations; both have an older sibling in high school as well as two working parents who do not arrive home until late. Jason and Andy started spending the time together after school, even though they were not allowed to have their friends over while their parents were away. For the past six months, Andy and Jason have been up to all kinds of things. They call their friends, go through their parents drawers, watch all kinds of movies, get pornography off the computer and check out what is new in Andy's brother's room as well as Jason's sister's room. Worst of all both the boys have started drinking and smoking. They sneak liquor from both houses and have been getting drunk for the past three months on a daily basis after school. They cover up their drunkenness by being 'tired' when their parents arrive home and 'sleep' in their rooms. It took three months before one of the parents became suspicious and checked their liquor supply. They were shocked to discover what had been happening.

How much time does a teenager need on an average with a parent a week? Here are some choices:

a. 15 minutes
b. 2 hours
c. 8 hours
d. 15 hours

In these important formative years, teenagers need as much time with parents and other adults as they did when they were toddlers. Teenagers need at least fifteen hours with their parent a week. This does not mean you have to be talking together during this entire time. To accomplish this your teenager needs to come out of his or her room, be in the same room with family members, without a TV on or earphones on.

There are so many productive things teenagers could be doing with their idle time. With parent's help, young people can find any number of positive things to do, like being involved in community activities, sports or special programs. Without this kind of encouragement and guidance the average teenager is likely to choose to do nothing rather than choose something that requires effort. A bored teenager is dangerous for he or she is most vulnerable to the pressures in our society and more easily influenced by his or her peer group. On the other hand a busy teenager is a happy teenager.

There is not much we can do about technological advancements and social changes. Change in society is a given. This is the world we all live in. However, you *do* have some control over what happens in your family, what your children are exposed to and how hurried your son or daughter is to grow up.

Fill in an empty pie chart for your teenager. How much does he allow his friends and peers to guide him? How much of a role does media play in her life and learning? How many hours a week does your young person spend watching TV, videos, computer games or other multi-media? Who are the adults that are important and have an influence? How much time alone does your teenager spend each day? How productive is your teenager? What would you like to change in your teenager's pie of life?

Who Influences Young People?

Values are what we believe in. What people value influences the way they behave, what they say as well as the way they think. Every family has their own set of values based on their religious, moral and ethical beliefs. Teenagers, experimenting in the world, begin to look at and compare other values that are different than those they learned in their family. In the process of becoming a young adult, adolescents evaluate values that arise from four main sources.

Peer Values

Peer groups provide great diversity in young peoples' choices and behaviors. Some groups of teenagers are great role models; they are productive and active in their school, involved in athletics, music or other activities. Unlike this group, other groups condone breaking the rules and pushing the limits. The collective conscious determines values in a peer group. Without your involvement, an immature group may become a powerful influence over your teenager. Ultimately, your son or daughter must decide what is right and wrong and what is best, apart from his or her peer group.

Social Values

When you look at society through the eyes of your teenager, what kinds of messages are sent? When your teenager reads a newspaper, watches TV, sees a movie or drives in traffic, social values abound. Do social values support a 'Me' centered message or a 'We' centered one? Does our society offer our young people models of moral excellence?

What can your teenager draw from society and its directives? Social values may imply that young people to be mature should be wealthy, thin, drink and smoke. This is the kind of pressure that sends a message to teenagers to grow up fast. Another popular value along the same lines is, "if it feels good, do it".

Classic Values

Classic values are the beliefs of right and wrong, good and bad that have remained unchanged over generations. These values endure in spite of what is currently popular or interesting in society. Classic values tackle basics like lying, cheating, fidelity and being self-serving and stealing. Classic values have a history and can be found in many sources, history, and books, the Bible, stories, our constitution and film.

Family Values

Family values are what you teach and what you live, not necessarily in that order. What parents talk about and what they do become the basis of family values. What parents teach or emphasize is what becomes most important in the eyes of children and teenagers.

Family values may be closely tied to religious beliefs, which can be an extension of the family teaching. The most powerful influence comes from what is taught and lived by parents in the family. For instance, if parents teach their children they should not tell a lie and when a friend calls and mom tells her son to say she is not home, she teaches her son it is OK to lie. These values becomes a foundation for the next generation.

When children in a family are allowed to fight, bicker and argue with each other, the adolescents are likely to do the same with friends, boyfriends, girlfriends and eventually their spouse. What they learn at home becomes what seems 'normal'.

What Does Parental Guidance Mean?

The most powerful balance to the social pressures affecting your teenager is *you*. You can be the balance to the complex issues of our society with your guidance. A commitment to guide your teenager is essential.

Parental guidance is another way of saying protection. My idea of *parental guidance* is this: If you can look at the world *through the eyes of your teenager*, to find out what he or she sees, hears and experiences, you have a better chance of slowing down your teenager's world. When your teenager is not so rushed to grow up, he or she is not as likely to be overwhelmed by difficult situations or issues.

Parental guidance requires effort and participation from you because most teenagers are vulnerable to influences around them. You *first* see or explore what your teenager is interested in (i.e.: a party or movie) and *then you decide* if your teenager is ready for what he or she wants to experience. If you do not feel your young person is mature enough you say, "No, not now..." and evaluate it again when your teenager is older and more mature. If you think your teenager is ready then say yes. Then discuss your teenager's experience with him or her afterward.

Parental guidance is very important when screening media for your teenager. Media is one of the most powerful influences on our children and teenagers. Begin with the TV, movies and video (computer games too) in which your teenager is interested. Parental guidance means *you watch* a TV show, movie or video *first, without* your teenager. After viewing the movie, TV show, etc. ask yourself, "Do I want my teenager to *look like, talk like* and *behave like* these people?" If you do, show it to your teenager. Teenagers naturally model what they see and hear, especially attractive young adult actors and actresses. If you don't want your teenager to *look like, sound like* or *act like* the people in the film or on the TV show then tell them you don't think this kind of entertainment is a good influence for them and *DO NOT* let them watch it. And say to your teenager: "No, I don't think this _____ is good for you right now."

One of my favorite stories concerns a mom who took charge of what her children were watching on TV by coming to work with the television cord in her purse!

As you start your *parental guidance* viewing, don't be surprised if there are very few films you want your teenager to see. I think there are very few PG and PG13 movies that are good for our teenagers (or children) to see. R rated films are rated for mature adult viewers.

If you don't like how your teenager acts toward you or others, tune into whatever your young person is watching or listening to. This could be what influences your teenager to model his or her behavior from. When parents set thoughtful and careful guidelines and limits, they create safety and security for their adolescent.

How teenagers discriminate is very different from adults. Though they may think they know a great deal about adults and adult issues, there is still a lot of naive 'kid' in our teenagers. Their ideas about adulthood are not always accurate. Teenagers are not always able to differentiate a realistic portrayal of adulthood from one that is mostly fantasy when viewing TV or movies. The ideas movies and television offer put a lot of pressure on your teenager to act like an adult and grow up fast. The industry is not interested in offering entertainment that is beneficial to children and teenagers.

Adam is fourteen years old. In 1995 he saw a film (rated R) portraying a woman who houses a famous author in her remote cabin, after he is injured. She becomes obsessed with him. In order to keep him at her home, she takes a sledgehammer and breaks his ankles. After Adam told me how 'cool' this movie was I asked him several questions, to fully understand what he watched.

First, I asked, "Do you think there are people in the world that take sledge hammers and break other people's legs?" He replied, "Sure." Then I asked him if very many people did this in the state we lived in? He answered "yes." Next I asked him if people in our city did this to one another? "Yes," he replied confidently. Then I asked if there were people on his street that did this? And he said, "Probably." My last question was, "Adam, is there anyone at home who would beat you with a sledge hammer?" He looked at me seriously and said "no".

What your young person hears influences the way he or she thinks, speaks and behaves. What your teenager sees guides how he or she will think and behave. Your teenager is impressionable so what your son or daughter experiences, you cannot take away. It is learning for better or for worse. Some of the limits you set may postpone an experience until your teenager is older and more mature and more capable of handling a situation, film, show or task in life. Once your teenager and children see or hear something that is not good for them, you cannot take it away from them; it is etched in their minds.

TV Impact

Turning a TV set off is much harder than turning one on. Do you know why? Advertisers and producers spend billions of dollars to get our attention. Their concern is not the impact of the content on children and teenagers. If sex sells, sex will be in every commercial and show possible. If violence attracts viewers, it too will be peppered throughout TV and movies. The world is not going to slow down for your young person.

One way to get some control over the influence of TV is to decide how many hours of TV are good for the kids and family. Get the family together on Sunday night and highlight the shows everyone will watch for the next week. You may have to practice a new skill... turning a TV off! If your teenager and children have their own TVs, your ability to monitor what they watch is seriously compromised. Consider reducing the numbers of TV sets in your house. So parents can watch, you can tape your shows and view them later.

After hearing my idea on 'Parental Guidance' one family decided to take all their TVs out of their home for a month. Initially the kids went through withdrawal and were unsure what they would do with all their spare time. Dad, too, had a hard time figuring out how to relax without watching sports (Being a couch potato is quite boring without a TV or a movie). Within a few days the kids were less traumatized and started finding projects and playing outdoors. By the end of the month, it was the teenagers who decided *not* to bring the TV back. This family had so much fun playing games, talking and spending a lot more time together that they decided they were better off without the television.

My ideal for media viewing for our children and teenagers would be program and channel blocking so that only those shows acceptable for children are accessible when the TV set is turned on. And filmmakers would offer two versions of a film, the original and an 'edited family version' for young people under the age of seventeen. When your family goes to the theater, the children can see the edited version and adults could see the original film. You might even choose to see the edited film yourself, without sexual content, foul language and violence. This kind of editing may make the film more enjoyable for you as well. When you choose videos you could have the option of the 'original' or 'family version'.

The Parent Source ... Saying 'No'

As difficult as it might be, the responsibility of slowing your teenager's world is *yours*. You must decide what your teenager views, what he or she does and what he or she learns. Setting limits may seem a burden, but you are essential in guiding your teenager. No one is going to be as concerned or as committed to your teenager as you. No one is a better advocate. No one is a better guide to the adult world. No one can love and care like you do. No one can replace you.

Setting limits is a key to teenagers' success. Knowing how to say 'No' to your teenagers so they don't get angry and hostile is essential for parents. The best way I have found is this: "I have to say 'No' because I love you too much to let you do _____. If I didn't love you I wouldn't care if you lived on the street or ever came home. But because I love you my job as a parent is to decide what is best for you." Here is another script for saying 'No' that applies to something you think your teenager can do later in life; "I have to say 'No' for now because I think you are too young. You will be able to do _____ when you are older and more mature." When both parents are in agreement the 'I' can be substituted with 'We'.

You must be committed to doing the best job you can do to raise your teenager. To do your best, everyday. You must insist on ears being covered at 10 degrees above zero, wearing clean clothes, watching good shows and being kind to others. This is your commitment to do the best job you can with the most important job you will ever have, raising your children.

Pass the Baton of Responsibility

Teenagers are in training for the run of their lives. Each young person needs a coach (parent). You are the best coach your son or daughter could have. Without a coach, a teenager is likely to fumble and fall learning how to run. Without coaches, teenagers are likely to produce mediocre results. They cannot learn enough of what they need to know from only their fellow runners. To be successful they need someone who is older, wiser and more objective, committed to coaching them and cheering them on. When they fall and get hurt, they need their coach to help them up, brush off the dust and show them how to get back on the track.

Teenagers need your love, understanding and recognition. Your young runner wants you to be proud of his or her efforts, slow to point out errors and encouraging with mishaps. Your runner needs you to be honest about his or her poor efforts and at the same time kind and forgiving. There will be times when you will be reluctant to have your son or daughter run on their own but you must pass the baton of responsibility to your teenager. Your teenager needs to prepare for running in life in the years ahead.

Your runner does not want you to be afraid. He or she is fearful enough. Your runner needs you to be strong, confident in your ideas and ideals. Your runner never wants you to give up or leave the track. He or she needs a smile everyday. As a good coach you must be persistent, positive, never letting your runner settle for anything less than his/her personal best. You are the key to your teenager's success!

How do You Talk to Your Teenager?

"It seems your teenager not only knows just how to
push your buttons but he can light up your whole panel."

When Their Ears Close Up

Mark is thirteen and seems to live in his own little world. One Saturday morning in June his dad, David, finds Mark in his room and asks him to come out and help with the yard. Mark has always seemed to be a good helper. Outside, David waits twenty minutes for him. When he goes back inside he finds his son still on his bed in his room, staring into space. He asks Mark why he hasn't joined him. Mark says he doesn't know what David is talking about, apparently he never heard him. Showing his irritation David explains how he knows he did hear him. He reminds Mark again to come outside and help. Under his breath Mark sneers 'later'. His father tells him, "Now! Not later!" His son seems to have become deaf to adult voices. As Mark's father leaves, he wonders what kind of game his son is playing.

Often when you try to communicate with a teenager this communication puzzle may sound familiar. What has gone wrong with Mark's hearing is a common adolescent problem called a *selective hearing loss*. This phenomenon occurs in adolescence when the teenager 'selects' whom he or she will and will not listen to. And parents are usually not on the 'listen to' list, unless you are offering food or money.

The acuity of your teenager's hearing is never in question when the phone rings. Your teenager can even catch the phone on the first ring as well and will have no trouble hearing friends at the door. The puzzle with *selective hearing loss* is how you can you get through this hearing block so you can be heard?

Selective Memory Loss

Often accompanying a *selective hearing loss* is the *selective memory loss*. Your teenager has great difficulty remembering after you asked him four times to put away his clothes. He has no problem remembering his friends phone numbers, what he last bought at the store or how many times he thinks you have nagged him in the last week. Another common example of lost memory concerns homework. Your teenager may say he or she 'just forgot' about that assignment due tomorrow. Funny how certain things can just slip their minds! Breaking this 'attention gap' in order to open up communication is essential to helping your teenager become prepared for adult life.

One of the important changes in how you communicate with your teenager begins with your approach. Your attitude about your teenager succeeding is crucial to your ability to keep their attention while you communicate.

To break through the selective hearing loss begins with your belief in your teenager capabilities. *Teenagers will rise to their parent's level of expectation.* What this means is that whatever you think your teenager will do or become, is likely to be conveyed in all you say to your young person. If you believe your teenager will never make much of himself or herself, your son or daughter is likely to prove you right. If you can believe the notion that your teenager will become a success, in-spite of your adolescent's antics, you are likely to see your son or daughter turn into a winner.

For example, lets say you get bad news your son or daughter is in the principal's office. It is important that you tell yourself you believe your teenager will be a success in life, in spite of these kind of temporary setbacks. Then when you talk to your teenager, your belief that your youngster will succeed will be conveyed. He will hear through your words, that *in time* you believe he will become a success. When your belief in your teenager is unshakable, eventually your teenager will give in and believe you. Then he or she will do a great job growing up as a young person. This notion is a basic change in your thinking necessary for successful communication with a teenager.

When I was in elementary school I got off to a slow start by spending a good part of second grade pretending how to read, rather than actually reading. My mother discovered this one day when she asked me to read <u>Dick and Jane</u> to her. I 'read' the story in my imagination about how Dick and Jane thought they might like to go on a picnic, taking their dog Spot along. My mom was pretty shocked I didn't know how to read but never made me feel like something was wrong with me. Instead, over the years as I struggled in school to learn phonics and catch up in my reading my parents told me I was very smart even when I got a 'D' in phonics. When I was frustrated my parents said, "You can do it." When I compared myself to other students, who could read much better than I, they told me, "You'll catch up... we know you can do it." They never gave up on this notion that I was going to be successful. It was their belief in my capabilities that led me to be successful.

Responding to Issues

One day fourteen year-old Julie walks down the stairs sporting a leather miniskirt that has fifteen holes in it. When her mother sees the skirt she knows she needs to respond to what Julie plans to wear to school. She says, "Julie, that skirt is one you are welcome to wear in your room but it is definitely *not* for school." Then her mother witnesses *the teenage tantrum*. Julie starts yelling at the top of her lungs as she stomps up the stairs, yelling her mom she is the most out-dated parent in America and doesn't know what she is doing. She slams the door, walks in her room and throws open her closet. Standing in front of a closet full of clothes, some still with tags, she screams, "I have nothing to wear!" Finally after loud crashes from her room, she comes downstairs wearing something more appropriate for school. She slams out the front door without a goodbye.

Two days later to her mother's surprise Julie is sneaking quietly down the stairs. Guess what she is wearing? The same skirt! So again, her mother tells her she cannot wear it. Again, Julie erupts, stomping up the stairs, blaming her mother for her misery and telling her *everybody* at school wears skirts like this. Her mother is unprepared for this kind of emotional tornado at 6:30 in the morning.

Four days later, the morning Julie's mom has a pounding headache and feels awful, is the day Julie has chosen to attempt to wear the skirt again to school. Feeling exhausted, when her mother sees her skirt her she looks the other way, just too tired to respond. Guess what Julie thinks? Bingo, she just won! Because her mother did not respond, she is convinced mom has changed her mind and now her inappropriate skirt is OK! Mom is back to square one, starting the clothing battle all over again.

With adolescence come many battles. The 'teenage tantrum' is the kind of response that is typical when you set limits. Unfortunately, tomorrow you may be faced with more of the same: another skirt or shirt that is just as unacceptable.Though parents grow weary setting limits and monitoring their teenagers, the battles persist. Frequent testing is probably the most exhaustive part of parenting. When you do not respond to an important issue, by neglecting it, you may be reinforcing it. You must be constantly aware of what your teenager is doing and deal with any test presented to you.

Testing the rules includes tactics aimed at manipulating you to change your mind, your ideas or your ideals. Challenges take many forms. If you have a teenage son, you may be have to respond to a rude message on his T-shirt, how low his pants ride or whether he has showered in the past four days. The tests vary, but undoubtedly, your teenager will choose to do something you are likely to detest.

Goals for Your Teenager

We all want our teenagers to be self assured, happy and to become capable and successful young adults. We wish our children to be even more successful and find more meaning in their lives than we have found in our own. This is what drives you as a parent to work so hard with your young person. And also why it is easy to feel crushed with failure when their teenagers make mistakes. Perhaps there is no greater pain for a parent than to watch your child or adolescent have to suffer.

In the adolescent process teenagers often want to test your family values. Against your wishes your adolescent may want to test things that are important to you like your traditions.

Fifteen year-old Stan announced to his mother Judy, he is opposed to Christmas tree cutting and has decided to boycott the annual tree shopping. He said the family tradition was 'stupid' and refused to go with them this year. Judy, his dad and two sisters were sad when they left without him and he was not included in their annual tradition. While trimming the tree, Stan sat on the couch wearing his 'Save the Rain Forest' T-shirt. Still bewildered, Judy left all his ornaments under the tree. Something magical happened in the night... the ornaments ended up on the tree!

Challenges like this can be very shocking. The question most parents ask is, "Where do you draw the line?" A teenager may find he or she gets a big reaction from parents as they begin to test and present challenges. One of the most promising things about rebellious adolescent behaviors is that they are not likely to be permanent.

Teenagers also may test your views with religious and moral values. Much of what our society presents, especially in the media, may directly contradict what you believe is right and wrong. Your teenager is working on establishing his or her own sense of morals, what he or she does or does not believe in.

From simple to complex, your teenager may surprise you and put you off balance with their adolescent antics. If you value cleanliness you may find their rooms would not pass local health standards. They may decide not to shower and find out how long it takes for others to notice. If you care about good table manners, you may hear slurping, belching and snorting at the dinner table. And the noises may be loudest when you have dinner guests. If you appreciate the quiet of your home, you may come home to blaring music with high pitched screams from your teenager. If you treasure neatness, you may find your teenager wearing torn and sloppy clothes combined with hair falling over their faces. They may refuse to pick up their own clutter and ignore your requests for cleaning it up. Many times your teenager will challenge values you hold most dear. We all have buttons to be pushed and pet peeves. It may seem like your teenager has an undercover informant to help them find out what annoys you the most.

6 Steps to Having a Civilized Conversation

I discovered years ago that I talk to teenagers differently than I do any other group of people. What works for children does not always work with an adolescent, especially one who is rebelling against authority figures. As you are well aware, pleading, threatening, yelling and screaming prove futile. You need to find a change in the ways you talk to your teenager. Here are six steps to help you have a civilized conversation with your teenager. Using a new approach takes patience but as you know, continuing what does not work is destined to fail.

The first three are *Emotional Climate, Setting the Mood* and *Location*. The best communication begins when you pay attention to the next three steps before you begin talking with your teenager.

Communication ➞ HOW?

3 Things to Start With:

☒ Emotional Climate

- High    YOU   TEEN
- Medium
- Low

☒ Location
- Set the mood
- 2 places not to talk

☒ Time
- Relaxed vs rushed
- How much time?

Step One: Emotional Climate

Emotional climate is the emotional state based on the responses of people who are interacting. Emotional climate is like an 'emotional barometer' with a continuum ranging from high to low. Each person brings his or her own emotional climate to each situation. It is important to assess both your own emotional state and that of your teenager's *before* communicating.

A high emotional state is usually driven by feelings of anger and frustration, natural feelings when a person feels hurt or disappointed by a real or supposed injury or insult. Anger is a common emotion you often confront during adolescence.

Imagine what you would do in the following situation producing a *high emotional climate.* A mom wakes up one winter morning to a snow storm. She leaves for work late and hits bumper to bumper traffic, arriving twenty minutes late to the office. When she arrives at work she discovers three of her co-workers did not show up for the day. Only a few minutes after she settles into her office, her boss shows up and he is angry about some missed deadlines. In a panic, she works all day, right through her lunch break. Feeling frazzled, she leaves from work twenty minutes late and is greeted by more snow. On the slow trek home, things get worse, she gets a flat tire! She has to stop to change it by herself. Exhausted and cold, she finally walks into her house an hour and a half late. She is immediately surrounded by her children yelling, two are angry about dinner being late and her teenager is demanding help with his homework. In this high emotional state who wouldn't blow up at the kids?

What does a *high emotional climate* for a teenager look and sound like? You might see any number of behaviors, depending on your teenager's personality, such as yelling, screaming, swearing and *'the look'* with eyes like daggers that could kill. Other teenagers may be demanding, threatening or start crying, hysterically. Angry teenagers are well known for stair stomping, door slamming, punching others, throwing and breaking things or attempting to kick holes in walls and doors. A teenager may yell directly at you or just holler in general. The less verbal teenager in a high emotional state would be quietly angry, giving looks that if read properly would say, "I hate you" or "I'll get you!" Other non-verbal signs are clenched fists, turning his or her back, a stiff posture, general pouting, refusing to do what is asked, refusing to listen and occasionally smiling or laughing at you. Teenagers are likely to retreat to their rooms, slam the door and blast their most hostile music which seems to match their foul moods.

Whenever you or your teenager hit this high emotional state, you only need to remember one thing... *do not talk*. This means you *do not talk* until you or the other angry person has calmed down. Just imagine a red light flashing that reminds you *do not talk*. You may need to introduce one idea by saying you are giving a time out signal or one statement like, "I'll talk to you later. If I talk now I will just yell." Then, *do not talk,* leave. Even though your teenager is likely to continue ranting and raving, it is important that you remain silent.

When someone is enraged, they are not rational. Engaging in further discussion with them is like pouring gasoline onto a fire. The conversation then explodes. When we try to communicate in a *high emotional climate* we are emotionally volatile and if enraged anyone can behave irrationally. With two people yelling, the discussion escalates. Most people say hurtful things they wish they hadn't said later on. We yell and scream. What people hear in a *high emotional climate* is the anger, not the real issues.

What would be best for this mom in a *high emotional state* is to wave hello to the kids, say she has had a horrible day, go lock herself in the bathroom and take a 15 minute hot bubble bath. After she gathers herself, she joins the children to begin dinner and help with homework. Most of us wouldn't think to do this and would probably react like most human beings, by yelling and screaming back.

Another reason not to talk, is that it does take two people to have an argument. When you leave and your angry teenager is alone, he or she may have a difficult time staying angry without you as a target to argue with. Walking away can also help you not to talk and will diffuse the anger. When you walk away and leave your teenager, he or she has only the refrigerator to yell at.

An example of a situation creating a *medium emotional climate* with the same mom. Mom arrives late to work due to snow conditions. Two people do not show up at her office and she is behind with her deadlines. Her boss walks into her office upset about the deadlines but understands the blame is not all hers. She works hard all day, skips lunch and, when she leaves her office, it has stopped snowing. She hits bumper to bumper traffic for a slow drive home. She is tired and frenzied when she walks into her home thirty minutes late and the kids are yelling, demanding dinner and one needs help with his homework.

In this *medium emotional climate* this mom is less likely to get irrational with her anger and start yelling at her children but this day would definitely be stressful for most of us.

An example of a *medium emotional climate* for your teenager is when he feels pressured about getting an answer from you about going out with his friends. He might be intense, have a tense posture and raise his voice when he talks to you. He demands that he get an answer *now* about going out with his friends (who are waiting outside for him). He may quickly react to anything you say but he is not kicking, swearing, throwing or slamming anything.

Another example of a teenager at this medium level is a daughter on the couch who won't let anyone sit near her. She yells at her brother if he comes near the TV screen she is watching, sternly warning him to leave the set alone. She is likely to ignore any request to move or to do anything else. If she gets up she is irritable, growling, sighing and talking under her breath. Pouting and refusing to talk can accompany this level of emotion.

Most teenager's emotional states usually range between the medium range of emotion to the high range. Not all their moods are irritable, sometimes they just have a lot of energy and are busy and preoccupied. They can be laughing, teasing or joking on this level. Teenagers have so much energy, both physical and emotional, at times they are not sure what to do with themselves.

Finally, here is an example of a *low emotional state* for a mom of a teenager. It is a peaceful Saturday morning, the sun is shinning, the birds are chirping. Mom is sitting on the porch, with the morning paper and she is sipping a great cup of coffee. She feels relaxed and calm. Classical music plays in the background and the children are sound asleep. This emotional state is what we adults strive for as often as possible in our lives. In midlife, we like to be relaxed and have things be peaceful and calm, contrary to your teenager who is full of energy, excitable and wants life action packed.

A *low emotional state* for teenagers is different than for adults. When this level occurs usually one of three things is usually happening.

1. Either your teenager is sound asleep,

2. he or she is sick or

3. your teenager is clinically depressed.

Most teenagers have far too much energy to stay on this low emotional level for long. The typical teenager doesn't have much interest in being serene, peaceful or calm. On the contrary, teenagers think this calm relaxed state is only for old people (like their parents), not for the young and the restless.

Communication with your teenager in a low emotional state doesn't usually work well. For instance, your teenager cannot hear you when he or she is sound asleep (it can be nice because you don't get interrupted!). When teenagers are ill, it is a great time to be able to hug them and comfort them but it is not usually a good time to have an in-depth conversation.

If your teenager has grown quiet, reserved, sullen and pensive and this mood lasts over an extended period of time you might wonder if he or she is depressed. They may still laugh at a joke but they respond in a quiet manner. This low emotional state can be a sign of serious problems that are unresolved or your teenager may be clinically depressed. Professional help may be necessary for lingering depressed moods.

The best time for you to communicate with your teenager is when you are between medium and low emotional states. In contrast, your teenager is better off communicating with you when he or she is in medium to medium-high range. When your teenager moves into the high emotional range, just remember: *Do not talk*. When you have had enough stress and you get to the high emotional range, walk away, write a note, leave the room or just listen.

Your Anger and Your Teenager's

An angry adolescent can be a lot like a porcupine. When a porcupine is angry you may find if you get too close it's quills will strike and it hurts you. The best thing to do with an irritated porcupine is to respect their nature, back up, be quiet and stay away until the porcupine settles down. Then, you can try to get closer. Each porcupine is different and takes it's own time to settle down.

Everyone gets angry about something. Anger is expressed in four main ways.

1. The first and most common is with our mouths. We scream, yell and say things in the heat of anger that we may later regret (one mom called this "machine gun mouth"). You may be surprised at the words that spring out of your mouth when you are in a highly irrational state. Family members are usually on the receiving end of your verbal abuse.

2. Other people express anger with their fists. They throw objects, grab someone, slam doors or pound their fist on the table. Those around them may need to learn to duck a punch or move to avoid a flying object. Others get far away.

3. A third way to express anger is through one's feet. A person may kick, fling his feet, stomp the floor or pound up stairs. Other expressions are running or walking away from those around them.

4. The fourth way, that adults are usually better at than kids, is to repress one's anger, becoming a human volcano. In time this pent-up anger and hostility, is likely to explode. Some people will say "Nothing is the matter" but inside they are fuming. People who internalize anger are prone to depression, pouting. Others become adept at inciting anger in others by refusing to do things, not hearing or attending to others, acting in a passively aggressive manner. Usually one small thing will make them explode, bringing out the old angry issues.

If talking to an angry or upset teenager does not work, what does? It is easy to say, "just stop doing something that is not working," but in order to stop you need to know what *to do instead.* Many adults think their children should be able to sit down and talk out their anger. Most people, especially teenagers, are not likely be able to discuss anything rationally until *after* their anger has subsided. Fighting occurs when one person is ready to deal with an issue, the other person feels off guard and their emotional level moves to *high.*

Of all the ways to express anger using your feet is probably is the best choice of these four. This way of dealing with anger is best for maintaining family peace and self-esteem for both you and your teenager. I encourage parents when they loose their cool and they are ready to scream and yell at their children, to *walk then talk.* When anger hits *high,* parents learn to "zip their lips" and head for their front door and take a brisk 5 minute walk. Upon returning most of us will be rational enough to not be careless and scream and yell at our children. Teenagers and children can learn how to control their anger using parent's responses as an example.

Taking your anger outside, getting fresh air and most importantly walking off the adrenaline that has built up in your system from being angry, helps you stay in control and spares the members of your family. The fresh air oxygenates your brain and will help you feel better. As you calm down, you become more rational. Only the trees will have to tolerate your angry verbal abuse.

With *walk then talk* as your way of controlling your anger, you may find that when you leave your house in order to regain your composure, your teenager may pay more attention to you, even in your absence. For example, if you are angry your teenager is not doing the dishes, instead of yelling, you can announce why you are angry and you're taking a time out so you won't yell. You may return after a 5-minute walk to find your son or daughter has actually started the dishes. The best part is that most of us won't yell or scream or belittle others after we have taken our anger for a walk.

Once you are using the *walk then talk* method of control yourself, your children are likely to follow in your footsteps. When you ask your teenager to walk, after you have walked, he or she is more likely to cooperate. Teenagers don't feel they are the only ones who need to control their anger. He or she will model after you.

How does your angry teenager take a five minute walk, you may wonder? Once you are willing to walk it can become a family rule that those who are angry and ready to yell, must take a walk. One way is to hand your teenager's coat to him or her, head them toward the door saying, "Please take a five minute walk to cool down," and then walk away. You need to *believe* your teenager will walk and give him or her plenty of time alone to start to walk. If you get resistance, another option is you can walk with your teenager. Try saying, "Please come with me, we both need a walk." Then walk out of the house. Keep walking, eventually, you are likely to hear some footsteps behind you. On your walk it is best *not to talk*, just walk briskly for five minutes or until you and your teenager are calmer. Managing one's anger is not meant to be punitive, rather it is meant to be positive in order to not hurt others.

Walk then talk anger management works for all members of the family. In some circumstances it may not be safe or easy to walk around the block. If this is the case taking laps around the house for five minutes can accomplish the same thing.

This approach to dealing with anger teaches family members to be more patient and accepting of others. Anger is a normal and expected response when things get difficult or frustrating. Knowing a way to act rather than just reacting helps keep family peace.

Years ago I worked with a young man named Kurt. At the age of fifteen he was well known as one of the 'tough guys' at school. He was very hot tempered and others in school knew that if they teased him, he would most likely explode. The kids at school had him pegged as a 'hothead'. He would be verbally abusive to both teachers and students. He would easily get into fist fights when he was taunted by others. Because of his temper, he was spending days out of school, time in detention and he was not doing well in school.

In the course of my work with Kurt, he decided to try another way to deal with his anger rather than yelling, swearing and punching others. It took almost six months until he could walk away from other students that found sport in teasing him. He also found he could walk out of classes that frustrated him, before he was ready to explode. One day he proudly told the story of a group of guys in a car that stopped him on the street. All three of them were walking toward him, anticipating a fight and one of the guys had a baseball bat. Kurt looked at them, turned and briskly walked the other way. He felt proud of himself and more empowered as a person. He had learned that fighting did not really solve anything. Using his feet helped him get the adrenaline out of his system and be able to think through situations.

Another strategy for reducing the aggression and hostility of an angry teenager is to try sitting with him or her on the floor. This is best for a medium to medium-high emotional states. Try doing this when two of your children are fighting. Sit both of them on the floor of your living room and let each talk, one at a time about what they are fighting about (oldest always goes first). You will watch the children and teenagers visibly settle down. If you sit on the floor with them you will notice how you calm down as well. When you are angry standing allows you to posture in an angry way. When you sit it is harder to maintain an angry stance.

On the emotional continuum at the medium-high level of emotional strain, good communication is difficult at best. When you feel you have reached a low emotional level, successful and positive communication is likely to happen. This is the time you are likely to have the most success. When you wish to communicate with your teenager, try doing an emotional level check on yourself and your person.

One way to help you remember not to talk when your teenager is in a high emotional state is to imagine you see a *red light* flashing. When the red light comes on it tells you to *stop, count to ten, do not speak.* This is not the time to communicate with words. When anyone is at a high emotional state they are not rational. They usually have so much adrenaline in their systems they are not thinking or acting rationally. Only when they have calmed to a lower level are they even remotely close to being able to speak without yelling and fighting.

Your job is to wait until the mood of your teenager subsides to a calmer, less volatile level. Think of these volatile moods like dark, cold and stormy weather. The mood, like the weather, will pass and better weather will follow. Some people calm down in minutes, others will take hours or even days. During this wait, you can certainly look them in the eye or watch them to make sure they are doing safe things. But this is not the time to begin to have a meaningful dialogue. Not talking can calm things down. It does take two people to have an argument. So your teenager may be talking or yelling but you do not need to respond to him or her. *Count to ten.* This pause is crucial to thoughtful parenting. A ten- second pause will allow you to evaluate the advisability of responding.

Teenagers at a medium level may be irritable and demanding. They may appear rushed and have a hard time listening to you. Intense and pressured they are loud but they usually are not yelling. You might see clenched fists or rigid body postures but they are not kicking or hitting anything. An example would be a teenager saying: "Mom, you have to tell me about going to the movie NOW! I can't wait for an answer later! I can't!"

At this medium level it is helpful to imagine a *yellow light* has just come on. Your response and reaction should be to proceed with caution. Imagine the yellow seems to be getting more orange as your teenager's mood is escalating into the high range. This is not the best time to engage with your teenager. A waiting period could be very helpful.

Most parents strive for low emotional climates. This is very conducive to rest and relaxation. When you are at this pleasant level and your teenager is somewhere between medium high to medium low, imagine a *green light*. This is a good time to converse with your teenager.

The following are combinations of emotional states where verbal communication is *not* productive:

1. You are in a high emotional state and so is your teenager.
2. You are in a medium emotional state and your teenager is in a high emotional state.
3. You are in a low emotional state and your teenager is in a high emotional state.
4. You are in a medium-high emotional state your teenager is in a medium-high emotional   state.

Communication works best when:

1. You are in a low emotional state and your teenager is in a medium to low state.
2. You are in a low emotional state and your teenager is in a medium to medium-high emotional state.
3. You are in a medium emotional state and so is your teen ager.

Step Two: Location

There are two places *not* to have conversations about 'hot' family issues. In these locations no matter what you talk about will result in an explosion. You may be able to predict a fight when you say the 'N' word (no) to your teenager. You also know if your teenager is irritable, talking about easy things will turn into a shouting match. These two places are where family members typically try to resolve their conflicts. Both places tend to increase tensions rather than provide a neutral place to discuss and resolve issues. These two places might surprise you. One is *your home* and the other is *your car.*

Your car is a poor place to engage in an emotionally charged conversation. Someone who is driving cannot concentrate well when his or her attention is split between a heated argument and what lies ahead on the road. This is especially dangerous if the driver is your teenager! Talking in the car lends itself to poor eye contact as well. When 'car battles' occur both passengers and other drivers are at risk.

Your home is not a good place to deal with conflicts because your home is the one place that should be a haven from the hectic pace of the world around you. It is where the most important people in the world reside your family. Most of us wish to relax, eat and sleep and enjoy the company of our family at home. When we deal with conflict in the home, we lose our safe haven.

When you try to make changes in your home you may find a lot of resistance to your efforts. Conversations are likely to become less volatile between you and your teenager when you take them outside your home. You may find the conversations are not as intense when walking around the block, sitting on your back deck or out having an ice-cream together. Places away from where we live offer us neutrality, we are not as likely to fall into the programmed roles or patterned behaviors we would at home.

Your teenager is not as likely to get loud, yell or act out in a public place. They need to look 'cool' when they are away from their home because their social world puts pressure on them to be sophisticated and grown up. You may find you too are calmer and better able to listen to your teenager than you would be at home.

Step Three :   Setting the Mood

The mood of where we talk can also have an effect on how well our conversation goes, especially with our teenagers. Setting the mood is helpful for the conversations you have at home. Try to create an atmosphere that quiets your teenager before you try to communicate. You can do this with lighting, sound, smells and location.

A mood change can be influenced with something as simple as moving to a room in which you normally do not have discussions or sitting on the floor. Dimming the lights changes the mood or you might try candle light at the evening dinner table. One couple told me they really got their children's attention when they set a different dinner table. They lit candles, put on a linen table cloth and the best china. Mom and Dad even dressed up for the occasion. The parents turned on classical music and the menu consisted of hot dogs and chili! The kids were guessing it was some special occasion they forgot. Mom and Dad said it was just for fun. The kids had a great time at their special Wednesday night supper and had some great dinner conversations.

Music, a powerful way to enhance our moods, can elicit a full range of feelings and moods. It can be soothing, stimulating, even depressing. Rock and roll and jazz can prove invigorating. For starters try classical music for dinner. When a teenager is in a moderate to moderately high emotional state changing the mood with lighting, the room, and music can soothe his or her mood.

Light and sound can distract all of us. Music and colors can soften and lighten moods with those people to whom we are conversing. Altering moods can make your teenager conducive to listening to others. Remember the last candle lit dinner you had with your spouse, with good food and good discussion, unlike the usual discussions you have at home. Changing your environment can be meaningful and memorable for you and your teenager.

Setting a Mood and Location Menu

- Sit on the floor
- Dim the lights
- Talk by candle light
- Candle light dinner in middle of week (linen table cloth, fine china, candles, etc.)
- Watch the sunset together
- Watch the sunrise together (only for early rising teens & parents)
- Sit on the back porch
- Sit on the living-room floor
- Play rock and roll and bake cookies
- Sit in the dark in their room (with your teenager's permission)
- Go for a walk
- Go out for coffee or a soda together
- Prepare a favorite food and sit together to eat it
- Play fun music while you do chores
- Scent the house with new fragrances like peach, apple and cinnamon
- Turn out the lights and sit in the moonlight
- Use full spectrum lighting in the winter months
- Sit together in the shade in the summer

- Lie on pillows and talk
- Tell jokes
- Sit in a tree house
- Walk in the rain under umbrellas
- Sit together under the stars
- Sit by pumpkin light
- Go on a run together
- Play catch or tennis
- Play a board game or cards
- Sit in the family hot tub
- Walk in the snow
- Sit on the beach
- Play musical chairs
- Go skiing
- Go sledding
- Watch the rain, snow, sleet together
- Sit in the yard at dusk

Step Four: Time and Timing

Are you relaxed at home? Do you usually feel rushed or hurried around the children? Are you frequently feeling pressured for time? You need to think about this before you talk to your teenager. If you are in a hurry you are not going to be able to give your teenager the time he needs to communicate with you.

If your teenager is in a hurry you can fall right into the trap of responding in an angry or intense way, which usually starts a fight. You also may feel pressured into making decisions with haste. Feeling rushed, not relaxed, is not your best time to communicate with your teenager. You may make decisions with your young person you will later regret.

Hurried times create situations for your teenager that have an advantage. If he or she catch you off-guard or rushed, you may make decisions that are not really what you think is best. So your teenager may not like it when you find a way to not be so rushed.

When you are feeling relaxed, you are not pressured to do

anything else except have some time with your family, it is prime time to parent your teenager. When you are relaxed as a parent you are at your best when you can give your teenager your full attention.

The Time Delay

Working on timing can reduce conflict and significantly improve communication with a teenager. Though parents become accustomed to responding immediately to issues with younger children, one of the important changes in parenting has to do with taking your time to respond.

Time delay is a strategy whereby you delay a conversation with your teenager until a specific later time. A conversation can be delayed five minutes, two or three hours or even overnight. Doing so accomplishes several things. Your teenager will not be used to this way of responding. But once he or she learns how you delay a conversation your young person will become more comfortable with it.

First, the *time delay* allows your teenager a chance to calm down while waiting. You both have time to get prepared for a confrontation. Secondly, an amazing thing can happen during the *time delay*. Your teenager will actually *think* about what he or she wants to say to you. That is exactly what you want; instead of acting on impulse, we want teenagers to think first. Parents, too, will have time to think about what we want to say with a *time delay*. If it is a passionate issue for you, you may find yourself in a calmer emotional state if you can wait 30 minutes or more. Learning to wait can also teach your teenager patience, thoughtfulness, discipline and self-control.

For example you are cooking dinner, the phone is ringing, Spot needs to go out and your teenager is demanding to talk to you about going out with friends right *now*! You may respond, "I would like to listen to what you have to say and I can't right now. Lets talk about this right after dinner at 7:00 in the den." It is important to tell your teenager both where and what time you want to meet. Explosive issues that typically turn into a fight need to be scheduled out of the house, less critical issues can be dealt with at home. Most teenagers feel respected and cared about if you are honest about your need to have time to listen to them.

There are some things you can't *time delay* of course, like a medical emergency or a fire in your home. Usually the rest of the issues can be delayed for a period of time. If your teenager really needs your help and says, "I can't wait!" it is best to stop what you are doing and meet with your young person immediately. Sometimes dinner will be a little late or a few other things are postponed. Even a *time delay* of five minutes can help an anxious teenager start to relax and talk more calmly.

Most teenagers learn to handle the *time delay* well, knowing they will get a chance to talk in a meeting later. Teenagers can anticipate when they get a chance to talk to you and can rely on you to follow through and be ready to listen.

Timing with an Irritable Teenager

It is not uncommon when out of the blue your teenager becomes angry, irritated, upset or demanding. Sometimes your teenager's reaction is an over-reaction. Like the teenager who started uncontrollable sobbing because of a 'bad hair' day. Her mom thought she looked fine, not much different from other days, her teenager felt this was the worst day of her life. When your young person's issue and reaction seem abnormal, beginning a debate only makes it worse.

Offering rational ideas to an irritable teenager only escalates his or her anger. When you receive this type of response, the reason may not be important; your teenager may be overwhelmed with emotion. He or she may feel hopeless because of a friend's mood or not wanting to be seen in the family car with you. The change needed is to recognize that timing is critical to be successful in the conversation. What you can begin to hear are the hormones.

Here is a way to reduce the volatility of these discussions:

Teenager:	Irrational statements, increasing anger
Parent:	One attempt at a rational response
Teenager:	More irrational statements, louder, more intense.
Parent:	PAUSE.....become SILENT and just listen
Teenager:	Louder continuation of irrational statements, more anger.
Parent:	continue to pause and remain silent. Listen until the intensity starts to wane.
Teenager:	eventually tires of talking and being so intense.

Parent: ONLY AFTER THE TEENAGER IS QUIET,
            say something that acknowledges their complaint
            and then change the subject. Plan to bring up the
            conversation at a later date.

Timing can help you and your teenager especially when your
teenager's mood is hormonally influenced. Let it subside on it's
own without responding. This allows your teenager to vent, and
when they are through you can go on to another conversation
that is more rational. You may notice how calm your teenager
becomes, after he or she has had his or her emotional venting,
when you change the subject.

Time Together

How much time do you actually spend with your teenager
during a week? Most of us could count the time in minutes. Time
to many of us is a precious commodity. Most adults complain
they never have enough time. Many teenagers complain they have
too much time. To really communicate with your teenager you
must have time to sit down and listen.

Years ago it was popular parenting idea to value the 'quality
of time' versus the 'quantity of time'. This fad helped busy parents think if they spent a meaningful five minutes a day with
their children, it was enough to do a good job raising them. Though
this idea fostered more thoughtful parenting and parents tried
harder to do a good job in a short period of time, their children
were often shortchanged.

In our fast paced lives, many teenagers and children have
been lost in the shuffle. Contrary to popular opinion, teenagers
need a lot of time with their family. They also need a lot of supervision. So the *quantity* of time is even more important than the
quality of time. If you are silent or just in the house together, it is
better than leaving your teenager alone and unsupervised.

Your time may be in great demand. To find the time to talk
you may have to juggle all your other priorities. A hurried conversation can be like a verbal ping pong game. It may take days
to get to the bottom of the real issue between two people when
they are rushed. Sometimes, with your teenager, all you may
achieve when you are too busy, is a fight. Parents need to take
time to think about a teenager's situation and request.

How do you create more time? With our busy schedules and

commitments, finding more time may seem like trying to get blood from a turnip. It is important to look at what is important to you. What are your priorities? If the answer is your children and family, you may have to give up some things until your children are older. It helps to have a family meeting and gather everyone's ideas on creative solutions to making more time. It may mean creating new schedules to find more time to be together. If it is important to you, don't give up searching until you have found a solution.

After coming to my seminars, Lisa explained to me how their family found a creative way to spend more time together. Her husband, Jason, is a contractor in his own business. Days would pass that the children would not see him. He would return home very late and leave in the early morning during his busy season. Lisa realized their teenagers especially needed more time with their dad. So she decided to make a point of having dinner together. But dinner was not eaten at home. The picnic basket, cooler and the kids went to the job site. There on the floor of a house under construction or in a nearby park the family ate together. When dad was between jobs and on holidays, they all went out of town to avoid the telephone and spend extended time together. This is an example of a creative solution.

Another family had so many sport commitments with soccer, basketball and volleyball in the evening they could not all be together for dinner until the weekend. So they decided to wake up bright and early and have breakfast together every weekday morning at 6 a.m. This was the only time they were all together at home during the week.

One of the biggest time consumers in our families today is the television. If you want more time together just try turning off the TV for about a week. You may find you have a lot more time available for family activities than you thought. You will find you have time to talk, listen to music, play games or go outside. Without TV no one is distracted.

Time alone with your teenager is important too. Have you taken your teenager out on a 'date', just the two of you? These are very special moments for a parent and adolescent. One teenager told me her favorite memory was when she was thirteen and her dad took her out to dinner while her mom was in the hospital. Her dad hadn't remembered that occasion until she talked about it. He had no idea the importance his daughter gave to the time he spent with her.

One family set up a special shopping day for each of their three daughters. This developed out of a financial strain of buying clothes for three girls at one time. So when there was money for clothes it was one of the girls 'special day'. This day was named 'Stephanie's day' and mom took her out to lunch and then the two went shopping. She showed her sisters what she got when she got home. Each daughter felt special on her special shopping day. Her mom said these were her favorite days with her girls because she could pamper each one individually.

The old saying that 'time is money' means that time is valuable. It is most valuable to your children and your family. When most people face the end of their lives they don't have regrets they didn't spend more time at the office but they wish they had spent more time with the people they loved the most, their families.

MENU FOR CREATIVE TIME SOLUTIONS

- One parent working, one parent is at home
- Both parents work half time or job share
- Create a work schedule so one parents works, the other parent is off (shift work)
- Hire a senior citizen to come into the home until you are home
- Parents take one day of the week with other neighborhood children for after school care
- After school activities without TV
- Kids come to the office
- Schedule in Family Night, turn off the TV, phone off the hook, front door locked.
- Gather together for dinner, at a hockey game, at mom or dad's work or 9 p.m. at home
- Change the workplace to home
- Hire a teenager to drive children to after school sports and activities.
- Reduce activities outside the house, maybe only one per season
- Get up early to all have breakfast together

- Vacation together, at least once a year
- Twice a month have a family exercise day
- Breakfast together three times a week
- Dinner has passed and you are gathering at a late hour, have dessert together
- No TV days

Listening VS Hearing

What is the difference between hearing and listening to someone? You can be doing many tasks at the same time and *hear* what a person is saying to you. So while you are trimming the hedge or preparing a meal you may indeed *hear* your teenager talking to you. But you may not be able to repeat back to your son or daughter what they have said. Understanding comes from listening to a person, not just hearing them.

When someone is really listening to you, you know he or she is paying attention to you and to what you are saying. The person listening may be telling you what he or she heard you say and then respond. The listening person may be nodding his or her head. Besides using your ears, the most important part of listening has to do with someone's eyes. When the person is looking at you, you know they are attending to what you are saying.

To hear someone requires much less energy. You can hear someone talking while you are doing the wash, looking the other way or paying attention to two other things. You can be walking out the door and be able to hear someone else. Although you are aware that the person is talking, you may not have any idea of what he or she is really saying. When you are only hearing someone, not listening, you are only partially paying attention. Teenagers can get really angry when their parents only hear them and won't take the time to listen.

Listening to a person requires more than just being near the person who is speaking. It requires two important things, your eyes and your ears. You must take the time to look your young person in the eye. If you don't have time to sit with your teenager, look him or her in the eye and be able to listen, then it is best to postpone the conversation to another time. This, by the way, is the one of the biggest complaints from teenagers. They want so much for others, especially parents, to believe what they say and think is important. And if you don't listen to them, with your ears as well as your eyes, then your teenager will not believe you take them seriously.

Looking into the eyes of your teenager is an easy way to feel close to your son or daughter. Many teenagers shy away from those hugs and kisses you used to give when they were younger. To teenagers, going through drastic physical changes means dealing with new sexual feelings. A hug or kiss from a parent can feel very uncomfortable. A smile in your eye can be your way of showing them how much you care and how important they are to you. Listening requires one more thing. You must stop talking.

Step Five: 3 Communication Rules

There are basic rules to our communications with others, whether you are aware of them or not. Our rules guide us with an expectation of how a discussion should proceed. These rules influence how we respond to and approach others, both within our families and outside them. Your rules of communication, especially in your family, guide you in how you live and interact with others.

It is important to understand your own set of rules of communication because they will influence how you interact with others. The goal of these rules is to create peace within your family, for each member to feel loved, respected, listened to and recognized.

RULE #1   No two people feel exactly the same way.

RULE #2   No two people think exactly the same way.

RULE #3   Everyone has a right to his or her opinion, **with out** *interruption.*

No two people feel the exact same way.. How a person *feels* comes from his or her background, his or her personal history, perceptions, beliefs as well as many experiences. The way a person *feels* is based on what he or she has learned as a child, teenager or adult. Your own feelings are derived from your experiences growing up as well as the experiences of your life. Impressionable experiences that have moved you are lasting. Frightening experiences can influence how you feel about a situation or a person. Things that have hurt you keep you cautious. Powerful experiences that taught you about love will always be tender and precious. Your life experiences have been how you have learned about yourself and others, and are the basis of your own personal worth.

Your experiences make you the unique person you are. No one else will have a life like yours. Even brothers and sisters living in the same family will each have a different family experience. Each person reacts and responds differently. Feelings, being male or female, experiences in life and how you think influence your personality. No two people, even if identical twins, will have the exact same experience in life.

Now there certainly can be many areas of agreement with feelings and thoughts between two people. But for one person to have the full spectrum of thoughts and feelings identical to another person is highly unlikely.

I don't think how a person truly *feels* can be completely understood or fully judged by another. A person must decide about the *value of his or her feelings* for him or herself. It is up to each individual to know what they believe is right or wrong, good or bad and what is acceptable and what is not. Others cannot comprehend how you might feel useless you can tell them and they can understand the context in which you live your life.. No one knows exactly what it is like to walk in your moccasins.

No two people think the same way. I don't think how someone thinks can be completely understood by others. How someone thinks is a product of his or her history, experiences, beliefs and the things that have moved him or her. Understanding how someone may have been influenced to think begins with understanding the context of that person's life or experience.

Like yourself, your teenager's thinking is unique to him or her. As your young person approaches adulthood, his or her thought process develop and mature.

I have never met two people who think and feel exactly the same way about anything, especially members in a family. Most couples fight about how the other one feels and thinks. Intense feelings erupt when one family member wishes another to think and feel the same way. Like a wife who says to her husband, "I wish you would love my mother like I do!" She wishes her husband to have the same feelings for the people in her family. The wife's feelings and thoughts are a result of the experiences in the family in which she grew up. The husband has developed an acquired relationship with his wife's mother through marriage. When they first met they were strangers with no common life experience.

Differences in both how someone feels and thinks can be the basis of passionate debates between people. Men and women typically think and feel differently about issues. So do parents and their children. So do people with different cultural backgrounds. People who stand next to each other and witness a car accident report different stories of what happened. What they experienced can be very different as well. Sometimes two eye witnesses have stories so different you wonder if they were at the same accident scene.

The third rule is about being heard. Opinions, based on feelings and thoughts, are again unique and individual. Just like fingerprints, no two are the same. Opinions are different from facts. A fact is something that actually happened and can be proved which is different than something that is believed. An opinion is a judgement but not necessarily a fact. Opinions, like thoughts and feelings, vary greatly from person to person.

"Uninterrupted" means there is enough time for each person to share his or her unique ideas or opinions. No matter how young or old he or she is. No matter the color of a person's skin. No matter his or her culture or creed. Each person is different and deserves the opportunity to be allowed to speak.

I have found most people have a unique and original way of perceiving the world. It is normal to guess how someone thinks or feels. People can surprise you when you hear how they think in unique ways. For example, you and ten other people are enjoying a sunny day. I ask each of you to describe the exact color of blue of the sky and write it down. I think there is a very good chance you would receive eleven different answers. We might read a variety of descriptions ranging from 'sky blue' and 'powder blue', to 'light blue', 'frosted royal blue' and 'robin egg blue'. A color-blind person may write the color 'gray'.

Each person has a unique view of the sky. Now if we had an ornery teenager in our group, he or she might tell you the sky is "pink with purple Polka dots".

I don't think there is one correct answer or that one answer is better than another. If I want to start a fight, I could correct each of you, telling you one answer is right and the others were wrong.

Being judgmental about the "truth" of others' opinions is usually a futile task. Even with scientific proof a person may continue to believe his or her own interpretation.

I hope there is room for everyone to have a chance to share his or her opinions of what he or she believes. Each family member would feel respected and recognized for his or her own view of the world. This kind of respect is basic to how we love others and how we are loved in return. Each person in the family is recognized for his or her individual viewpoint and ideas.

Though a person may choose to act according to his or her feelings, thoughts and opinions, behavior is different. Behavior *is* right or wrong and good or bad. That is why we have laws that set limits on people's behavior. Behavior may infringe on the rights or lives of others. Behavior is also evaluated by others based on what our society believes is right or wrong. Each sane person knows what is right or wrong, whether they choose to admit it or not.

The Power of Influence

You may find you have never felt so passionate about wishing to change someone's ideas or feelings than when you are faced with differences between you and your teenager. This may be especially true when your teenager presents radical ideas.

Out of passion for our own ideas and feelings we can step into a position of being 'forceful' in an attempt to control or change another. Though this wish is usually well-intended, it is usually counterproductive.

One could spend a lifetime trying to change another's feelings, without success. Forcing change upon another by telling that person, "How you *feel* and *think* is wrong..." does not allow for productive change. Nor does fighting over the "truth" of a feeling or idea. Direct confrontation does not allow for the power of *influence.*

The power of influence occurs when one person shares his or her feelings and thoughts with another, allowing the other person to think about the ideas you offer (or feelings you have). This is a *non-defensive,* non-controlling way of dealing with each other. The person hearing your thoughts and ideas is respected and recognized for his or her own ideas and feelings without demands to change.

The ideal way to communicate in families occurs when each

person is allowed to express his or her feelings and thoughts without interruption and without interjecting your own feelings, demanding that your teenager or any one else must change his or her ideas.

Step Six: The Talk Timer Method:

Solutions to Interruptions

Most of us interrupt because we are afraid if we do not express our ideas at the moment we will forget them. We also insist because we feel passionate about what we are saying and therefore it is important we express our view immediately. Sometimes it is the loudest or most demanding person who dominates the conversation. Some feel interrupting is the only way they can be heard.

So what can you do *instead* of interrupting? The best way I know of how to have a civilized conversation is to work with timing. The *"Talk Timer"* method uses a timer. (You may find a *"Talk Timer"* minute timer attached with your book). If you do not have a *"Talk Timer"* you will need to get a portable minute timer, otherwise all your conversations will need to be around the stove. Here are three things you will need for civilized communication in your family:

WHAT YOU NEED:

1. A *"Talk Timer"* (or minute timer or watch timer with an alarm)
2. A pad of paper (for each person listening)
3. Pencils or pens

Step One

Everyone who starts as a 'listener' gets a piece of paper with a pen or pencil. Then the minute time is turned to *three minutes* as the first person speaks. After the timer rings, or runs out of sand the next person speaks, while others write ideas on paper. The timer is passed back and forth between parent and teenager. Parents are always in charge of the timer as well as monitoring who is speaking. Conversation ends when the topic of discussion is resolved or one of the parties is tired and wishes to rest.

Here is the Talk Timer method of communication between you and your teenager:

Who starts? **Your teenager *always* starts** (they really love this part). Your teenager begins with conversation because you must first listen to your young person before you are ready to respond.

Begin: Parents turn the *Talk Timer* on three minutes. The first *three minutes* your teenager talks. He or she needs to be stopped only if he/she name calls or insults another. During this time parents or other listeners *do not talk*, instead the listeners write down ideas on paper so you won't forget.

Three minute timer rings: Teenager stops talking. (If sharing paper, the tablet goes to your teenager. The listener keeps the paper you wrote your ideas on for reference)

Time is started for the parent: The next three minutes are for you to talk and share your ideas and feelings while your teenager listens to you. Using statements that start with 'I' rather than 'you' are most productive. "I feel _____ or I think _____" rather than "You always _____ ."

Three minute timer rings: The parent stops talking. (The paper and pencil are passed to the parent)

Three minutes for the teenager: Conversation goes back and forth until the conversation is over.

A few other rules to follow:

1. If things get out of hand, the parent needs to be a referee and intervene, take a break or begin again another time.

2. If more than two family members are part of the discussion then the timer is passed from child to child (oldest children always first, then proceed by age hierarchy) and last to parents.

Paper and pencils need to be provided for all listeners not speaking. If the person speaking does not need the full time he or she may pass to end his or her turn early.

Using the *Talk Timer* method is the basis of productive, civil and courteous communication. It creates 'respectful waiting' which is the way most people converse in business transactions, in the workplace and in successful relationships. This way of having a discussion is not usually utilized in families.

The timer makes conversation predictable for those talking.

It should eliminate interruptions and stop fighting. Most teenagers like this method because they receive their parents' full attention. Your teenager will love to know he or she will be heard. Parents also like it because they get 'air time' without getting cut off or ignored.

This method works when all members of family enter into discussions. You should find it difficult to fight with this kind of communication structure.

Listening to your teenager's ideas on life is not as neutral as his or her opinion of the color of the sky. Parents may become very emotional when they hear the way their teenagers feel or think about issues today. For instance, you may not like how nonchalant your teenager seems to be about drinking and driving. This attitude really pushes all your emotional buttons. Then you find yourself back on that soapbox, lecturing to a deaf audience. Try to stop and listen. In time, teenager's thoughts, feelings and opinions are likely to change. Ideas modify, feelings fade and thinking gradually changes. Over time, your teenager may give up more radical notions as his or her ideas become more like yours.

Respecting how your teenager thinks and views the world can make a big difference in how good your teenager can feel about himself or herself. A good way to respond to an unwelcome notion is to attempt to understand what has influenced your teenager's thinking and feeling. It may be a class, friend or something they saw or read. If you can locate the source, you can discover how long this new notion has been important to your teenager to explore. Sometimes the radical idea is just to be different.

I think it is vital, through love and respect, for parents to tell their teenager they view things differently. Keeping these differences free from demands, threats or an over-reaction, can allow you to talk freely and can result in your influencing your teenager.

The Value of Behavior

To allow your teenager to discuss his or her developing ideas tells you about the issues, expectations and dilemmas he or she may face. With this information you can certainly influence a person with your opinions though each individual has to decide for himself or herself. Radical opinions do not always lead to radical behavior.

It is important to let your teenager know when you disapprove of his or her choice of behavior and why. Your teenager's behavior deserves your full attention and reaction. That is why you provide consequences for behavior and choices (see Chapter 3).

A teenager can present thoughts that worry us, like suicidal wishes. Some thoughts and feelings do require intervention. Most people will contemplate the idea of self-harm at some time in their life. Such desires expressed in notes, words or gestures demand immediate attention. Teenagers crying for help usually provide 'clues' and are asking parents to act and assure their safety. Professional help and a safe place may be necessary. Always err on the side of being over-reactive with suicidal talk and writing. It can save lives. Thousands of teenagers die of suicide each year in America over the past decade.

Faking an Opinion

Telling your son or daughter that you have an opinion different from how you really feel does not work. This 'reverse psychology' isn't honest or sincere. When teenagers know parents do this to try to change them, they are likely to teach the parent a lesson instead by doing exactly the opposite of what parents want them to do.

It is better to accept your teenager's opinion as well as to acknowledge that you have a very different opinion. This allows your teenagers to be free to have their own ideas. What you offer is a chance for your young person to hear how a more mature person feels about the same idea.

What works best is for you to allow your teenager to have his or her opinion *and* for you to let your teenager know where you stand, based upon your values. This way your adolescent is given what he needs in order to change his own thinking while being given the chance to listen to you. The result; successful communication between parent and teenager.

The Eye Hug

Sometimes it seems like you are the last person on earth your teenager wants to hug and let alone be given a goodnight kiss. But there is something you can do to feel close to your teenager when they become uncomfortable with hugs and kisses. The eye hug. You can hug them and show how much you love them by looking into their eyes. Now when you try this, your teenager may look away. Don't worry. Persist in your eye hug. The important thing is that they will feel your love and caring. Hey, you can sometimes even get an eye hug back.

Keep in mind, in transition from childhood to adulthood, teenagers usually become uncomfortable with parents touching them. This is because of their development as a sexual person. So when hugging and kissing is not comfortable for your teenager, try some of these ideas.

The Foot Massage

One mom shared the idea of giving a foot massage to her teenager. (You could probably use one right now for yourself!) The foot rub puts you and your teenager at a comfortable distance from one another. It allows you to touch your teenager in a positive, neutral way. See how calm your teenager becomes. It can help you have a great conversation with your teen. Especially if no one interrupts you, the lights are soft and the music soothing.

Neutral Touching

You can touch your teenager's heads, if she (or even he) is not into their "dos"(hairdos) too much. Also neck and shoulders are neutral areas. Put an arm around their shoulder. A pat on the back. Try reaching out and touching their arms. Not hands. You might want to offer a back rub. If your teenager accepts, then you have another way to touch them. Some teenagers are comfortable with a handshake. You may have to readjust so that your touching is comfortable to your teenager rather than what is comfortable to you.

Hugs for Comfort

When your teenager is upset, sad, tearful, it is best to try to hug and comfort them. During this kind of stress, human touch is so healing and nurturing. During difficult times you may find your teenager snuggled up next to you and you can have close physical contact like when they were younger. Pushing physical contact that makes your teenager feel uncomfortable may distance your teenager from you and create more conflict.

Social Distance

Recognizing social distance that is comfortable for your teenager may take some getting used to. If your once cuddling child, now a teenager, shrugs you off or becomes tense when you touch them, they may need more distance from you to feel at ease. Also, how close you stand to your teenager may also change over time. If you stand too close you may notice he or she becomes tense and steps away.

It is important to realize this is part of the phase of adolescence, not necessarily an established fixed pattern that won't change over time. Notice when you teenager approaches you how far away he or she stands. When you are walking together you can begin to gage what is a comfortable distance as your teenager chooses his or her distance from you. As you walk with your teenager the outdoors creates a feeling of more space for both of you and may ease and calm your teenager .

Remember, it is important not to get too close when your teenager is in a highly emotional state. This can really intensify their emotional reaction. It is best to give them lots of time and room to cool down. Or the opportunity to take their anger for a walk.

How Do You Talk to Your Teenager?

"How do you talk to teenagers so they will listen?" is a frequent question. Parents look into their tool box of solutions in search of how to improve communication. When you have tried every tool that has worked for the first twelve or thirteen years and nothing seems to work, great frustration sets in.

For many years I found I talked to teenagers differently than other groups of people. What follows is the *new approach in parenting strategy* I have discovered works well with teenagers.

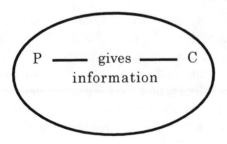

Let's compare how we learn to talk to our children first (see the diagram above). In the beginning we learn to teach our children by talking to them. We *give information* and our youngsters *absorb* what we are teaching. Each of us gets reinforced in our giving information as our little children seem to be attentive and say things like "uh huh". They register what we are teaching them about life and living. Because of the way children learn, you, like most parents, become good at lecturing during the first eleven to twelve years of their lives. Communicating with your teenager is very different.

No Lecture Method

With the emergence of adolescence, your lectures, once considered important and worthwhile, begin to fall on deaf ears. The process of adolescence is to think and respond to the world by experimentation. This is like living life on the edge. Not knowing what is coming next can be a scary thought for parents. What you have found is probably what I have discovered...that lecturing to your teenager does not work. You need a shift in your parenting strategy to change your approach.

I do not lecture teenagers. What works well is actually to reverse how we talk to them. In the *No Lecture Method,* instead of you lecturing, your teenager lectures you! If you think this ideas sounds preposterous, listen. Before you do that, hang in here and give this idea a chance.

The *No Lecture Method* is not that you now have become the child and your teenager has become the parent. Nor does this mean you gave in and that you have just lost a power struggle with your teenager. Rather, you discover what your teenager understands from all the lectures you have provided for those twelve formative years. This is not to say you can no longer impart your words of wisdom to someone who still needs some good words of advice. Your teenager becomes more open to communication by becoming the lecturer. As your adolescent turns into the lecturer, you will see how you will be better able to communicate with your teenager. Only if you open up communication do you have a chance at influencing their thinking and behavior.

If I tape recorded your lectures and played them for your teenagers they would likely say, "Oh, yeah that is mom's lecture # 101 on sex and drugs." Or "This is dad's talk # 214 on how to tell a lot about your friends by how respectful they are to other adults." Another, "I've heard this one a million times, do your homework so you'll grow up and get a good shot at success in life!" And then the teenager adds something like "How boring" or "This is so stupid" or "Really". Or the infuriating eye roll. Your teenager knows your lectures. Even though they may choose to break your rules, they usually can repeat what you would say to them verbatim.

The key is, if you can get your teenager to turn this process of education around and you can get your young person to lecture you, you have the beginnings of your teenager teaching him or herself what you want them to learn! What a great deal. And this can be energy efficient for you if most of the time all you need to do is to listen.

Now for the listening part. Listening is a skill. You may find yourself out of practice since you have gotten so good at lecturing. By listening to your teenager you have a good chance of getting to know him or her. At least who your teenager is today. For tomorrow, as you know, your teenager may change.

So here is how you start the *No Lecture Method*. This is very much like a spiral as you can see in the diagram on page 115.To start the process, the first thing you do is *ask a question*. Next, wait until your teenager responds. Sometimes a response is a grunt, a shrug or an, "I don't know." That is OK, this is a response. Some teenagers just jump right in and start telling you about their answer to your question.

After your teenager has responded the next step is for you to *ask another question*. Then your teenager responds again. Followed by you asking still *another question*. And the process continues very much like a spiral as each question feeds a response or answer.

Your goal is for your teenager to tell you your lecture or idea. For a quiet teenager, it may be easy for you to try to answer for them. It is critical that you *wait* for a response. A question posed needs to be less than three or four sentences. Optimally, it is one sentence. An example: Parent: "What do you think about your friend being picked up for shoplifting?"

The question posed replaces a lecture on why your teenager should not shoplift and should reconsider the friendship or what would happen to them if they would ever do such a thing. You will have to refrain from telling them they would be sorry for a long time, not be able to shop in the store or go to the mall for at

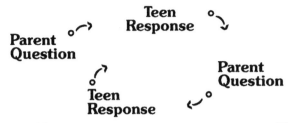

TEENS

"No Lecture" method

GOAL: Teenager answers your questions. You gain more information about your teenager.

★ FEEDING QUESTION ⟶ CHANGES ANSWERS

least a year. Instead, ask questions like, "Why do you think a teenager would want to do such a thing?" or "What kind of reputations do kids who shoplift get, at school or in stores?" and "How could others, like a coach, trust a guy who shoplifted?" You wait for a response from your young person. Let's say this is what you hear next from him or her: "I don't know".

The infamous answer, "I don't know," is typical. Depending on the question, "I don't know" can mean a number of things. You will need to decipher what your teenager's answer might mean.

If you have asked your teenager if he will go into the restaurant with you and he says, "I don't know," that almost always means "yes". If he meant "no", your teenager will definitely tell you so. For more difficult questions like, "What were you thinking when you told off your teacher?" and you get an, "I don't know" that has a different meaning. This is the safest way to answer a question if your teenager is unsure of how his or her answer might be accepted. Or you'll be given this response if your teenager doesn't know what answer you are looking for and he or she doesn't want to fail any of your 'tests'. It is important you do not get mad if he or she doesn't know the answer. The "I don't know" can mean "I don't know what you want to hear" or "I am afraid to tell you" or "I don't want to get into trouble with my answer" or "I haven't thought about it" or "I feel so many things I don't know how I feel" just for starters. I suggest you let your teenager answer "I don't know" and then find a different question to ask.

What you do next with the *No Lecture Method* is to ask another question that may get a different response. For example: Parent: "It really bothers me that your friend is in trouble. I would like to know if that bothers you?".

It is important you look your son or daughter in the eye to be both serious and loving when asking a question. We need to be reassuring with our posture that we are not leading an interrogation. It is also crucial that you *stop talking* after you ask a question to leave a pause for an answer. Even if that pause lasts a long time. It denotes our seriousness and concern if we wait.

This style of communication can be very awkward for you. It takes time and discipline to have this work successfully. Remember to give communicating this way lots of time and practice. And sometimes all your patience. Let's say the next response from the teenager is: "Yeah, I guess."

The parent responds by asking another question. The communication spirals as the parent keeps asking questions, teenager answering. Communication has been started when your teenager starts beginning to lecture you, informing you and sharing his or her ideas. Remember, if your teenager is lecturing you, he or she is really lecturing him or herself.

Here is an example of how a *communication spiral* in the *No Lecture Method* goes: I had a fourteen year-old young man and his mother in my office. During the session he mentioned one of his ideas. He thought it was "really stupid that we have so many police." He went on to say all they did was chase speeders which he thought was a waste of time and money.

Another thing that irritated him was he thought there were far too many traffic lights. His mother interrupted him and told him she did not want to be bothered with this silly, ridiculous notion of his. Unlike his mother, I did want to hear from him. His mother's approach of lecturing him on why his idea was ridiculous only encouraged him to hang onto it. It certainly got a *big* reaction out of her. I wanted to get this teenager to talk so I asked him to tell me more about this idea of his. Teenagers tell me a number of very unusual things so I am not as shocked or angered by 'unique' thoughts and opinions.

So I asked him a question: "tell me more about what it would be like without police or traffic lights"? You would have thought I handed him a one hundred dollar bill if you could have seen his face! With this question, he sat up proud and straight, smiled broadly. He eagerly began to tell me about his plan. He said, "It would be so cool. Everybody could cruise around as fast as they wanted to around the street. Any speed you want. There would not be any cops to stop you. It would be so much fun!"

Ok, so here we are. He's got an idea. A little radical? So what I did is to pose my next question. I said, " With everybody speeding around, how would you drive on the streets so no one would run into each other?" He replied, "Well.....uh.... what you do is make all the streets one way so you wouldn't run into anyone else. We could get rid of all the traffic lights too!" So I asked another question, "Let's say I am driving around at high speeds on these one way streets and I want to go to the grocery store. How do I get off the street?"

"Hmm...(long pause). Well, we could build ramps off all the streets. So all you would need to do is to ramp off wherever you wanted to go. See, you could speed in the middle lanes and get off on the ramps." He was really revved up about his ideas now. His ideas were building great momentum.

So here we are ramping on and off, driving at high speeds in the city. To help him test out his notion and find holes in his theory, I needed to ask another question (not give him a lecture). "How would you get to your house in your neighborhood?"

He replied, "Well, we could make all the streets one way. All you would have to do is to ramp off to your house." He is able to begin to think about how his ideas might work by answering my questions.

At this point I was trying to think of how to ask questions so he would begin to see this might not be such a great idea. He was really excited! So I asked, "What would you do if while everybody is driving as fast as they can, ramping on and off, someone robbed your house? And there are no police. What would you do?"

Long pause. "Wow, I don't know...well, ah, all the neighbors could get together and find the robber," he answered confidently.

"Ok," I said, "what if a whole bunch of robbers got together, while everyone is ramping on and off, and robbed the whole neighborhood?"

He readily replied, "Well, we would call in the National Guard! The National Guard would straighten this out right away."

He looked at me a little startled. He said slowly, "You know...

this isn't such a good idea is it?"

I told him I thought there might be better ways to find ways to drive a car fast. And he was very creative thinker. He agreed.

The critical part of the *No Lecture Method* is the teenager talked himself out of his idea. His mother could have easily told him it was a poor idea, which she did as often as he brought this idea up. She had never heard his entire ideas out because she thought it was so preposterous. Now after hearing it, it was no less radical than she thought. But he needed to figure this out for himself. My questions were helping him find *holes and gaps in his logic.*

Asking your teenager questions is a respectful way to communicate; taking your young person seriously is far more important than how seriously you take the subject matter. Sometimes when you take your teenager seriously they do not view themselves in the same fashion. When you become less over-reactive to your teenager's ideas, I believe you tap the power of communication that can lead to change. Sometimes you may end up having a great laugh with your teenager. You will find your communication can really change if you start to *listen through* your teenager's ideas and notions. As you cut them off or resist hearing their opinions it can encourage them to cling to their ideas for a long period of time out of rebellion or anger.

When I ask questions, I try to pose a few ideas that the teenager may not have thought about yet. I am looking for the teenager's ability to *critically think* about their idea. A more mature person is the only one who can provide the teenager with questions that help them evaluate their ideas. A more mature person might ask a younger person, "What would happen next semester if you fail math?" or "Do you think if you told your friend you are sorry, you could be friends again?" A peer usually does not have the life experience to know how to pose the most helpful questions.

In this question exploration, parents can cover every aspect of their lecture they would like to give. The difference is that your teenager lectures you on their ideas. Just your questions can plant the seeds for change.

Dealing with a major topic will take more time with spiral communication. When you address topics you are very concerned with such as drinking and driving, sex, drugs, violence, law breaking, etc. you may need to have a number of communications on a subject over a long period of time. Like the young man who feels drinking and driving is a symbol of being a man. A parent tackling this concept with their son could take twenty different discussions over a month before handing him the keys to the car.

Your teenager will feel valuable and respected when we listen to them. You as a parent have the ability and wisdom of asking questions so that irrational ideas or misconceptions becomes more apparent to the teenager.This is not a communication method that will always produce a change in the teenager's thinking but it can open up valuable discussions.

Ruining a Perfectly Good Conversation

With the *No Lecture Method*, there is one thing that a parent may do that will ruin the success of a great conversation. If at the very end when the teenager gets an "Ah ha" (he or she decides to change his or her idea), a parent says these words... "I told you so" the conversation may be worthless. The teenager is likely to get angry and decide his or her idea is a great one after all and hang onto it for a long time. "I told you so" is a power move that destroys a good conversation.

Here is another example. Let's say a child is stuffing his mouth full of Oreos, opening wide. His mother addresses this rude behavior and says, "Please don't chew with your mouth open." The child says, "OK, mom." And then closes his mouth.

Here is the same situation with a teenager stuffing Oreos into his mouth, opening wide.

Mother: "Do you and your friends eat like this in the cafeteria, with your mouth wide open, stuffed with food?".

Teenager :"Not very often".

Parent: "Would you stuff your mouth with food like this if you were on a date?".

Teenager "No way. That would be really gross... The girl would never go out with me again!"

Parent: "I would really appreciate it if you would not do that here".

Teenager: "Yeah" (mouth closes)

Once you have gotten enough of your lecture back or the behavior has stopped it is best to stop the conversation.You have now caught your teenager in his own logic. He has given you reasons to stop this behavior. Once you have made your point with your questions, leave your teenager alone to absorb your questions. Instead of ending this conversation with, "I told you so," your final sentence can be to say "thank you".

This kind of spiral conversation led by the adult allows the teenager to begin to look at a parent's point of view while they respond to your questions. Your question leads them to think and compare. This method also allows them to change gracefully and with fewer demands and direct attention. A basic premise for you to remember is that your teenager may be very good at talking to friends and on the phone but not to you. It is not that they cannot or do not want to converse. So allowing them to converse about issues in a lecturing format opens up communication. The end result of the spiral communication in many cases is a change in thought or behavior.

A teenager presents herself early one morning sporting green hair. Her mother, though shocked, posed questions for her: "I didn't know you were going to dye your hair green. Is it close to St. Patrick's Day?"

She waits for a response: a shrug from her fourteen year-old. Then the mother asks, " How long to you plan on leaving it this way?"

Her teenager replies, "I dunno."

The next question: "Is this permanent or temporary?"

Teenager replies, "It will last for two to three days and it is no big deal."

Then mother says, "As you know we are planning on going to our favorite restaurant this Saturday. I expect you to re move the dye from your hair before we go."

So when we begin to ask questions our kids start to respond to us. This situation could have easily blown up into a big fight based on a number of assumptions a parent could make about green hair. Or a lecture on hair dying or responsible behavior. Our assumptions may not always be accurate. But we don't know why their hair is green and we don't know for how long. I think the best approach is to discover what your teenager's ideas are all about before reacting. No doubt these ideas may sound simple but they are rarely easy. So give your teenager the benefit of your doubt before you react to the situations they present to you.

Let it Be

A father and his fourteen year-old daughter, Shannon, were driving together. A top ten song came on the radio by a singer who was a girl of fourteen who had made it big in music. Shannon commented that how this singer looked and so*unded* made her seem much older than fourteen. As dad listened, Shannon said, " I don't think fourteen year-olds should be allowed to be movie or music stars." Dad asked why. Shannon explained, "They are not old enough to make their own choices, at least the right ones." These kinds of statements are golden moments, when the teenager reaches an important conclusion all on his or her own, without prompting from you. When these profound statements occur, it is best to not comment. Just let it be.

How to Say No

Telling a teenager "No" can be a very difficult thing for a parent. Sometimes your teenager gets so mad you will try anything to quiet the emotional explosion. The parent saying "No" can feel like the 'bad guy' and may say "Yes" just to avoid the hassles. If you change your mind after your teenager tantrums what happens is teenagers knows they got their way. The next time you say "No" you may see the same behavior because in the end you changed your mind.

It is essential to set limits for your young person. If you don't do it, no one else will. The responsibility for raising your young person falls on your shoulders. Setting limits helps your teenager grow up slowly, not hurried.

Here is how to say "No" to your teenager without having an emotional explosion. Begin with, "No, I love you too much to let you do _____ ." Tell your teenagers if you didn't love them they could live in the mall, you would never care what time they came home or what they did. It is because you love your teenager you must say "No". Otherwise, you would be failing as a parent. Don't be too surprised after you start saying "No" this way; your young person will beg you to stop loving them so much! So in spite of what "everybody" is doing, you need to love your teenager enough to have courage to say the 'N' word.

Another way to say "No" is to say why not. This goes over much better if you have taken the time to hear your teenager out. Listen to the reason why your fourteen year-old wants to go on a weekend camping trip, without any adults. Even though you know right away you are going to say "No" to this adventure, it is important to hear your teenager's idea and request. (This is a good way to open up communication between parent and teenager.)

After you have listened (and asked a few questions) then take some time to think about what your young person is requesting. After you have taken a long pause, even as long as a day, then you can say why not. Explain to your teenager why you don't think it is a good idea. One of the best reasons is that you saying why not is because your job is to be a good parent and decide what is best for your children. And why not is also based in your values and beliefs. Even if your teenager gets mad at your decision, stick to your answer.

A third way is to say, "Not now." That means "no for now". The reason is usually you do so because your teenager is trying to grow up too fast. If a fourteen year-old asks for a 12:30 p.m. curfew, what will he want when he is fifteen? Then what will he want at seventeen? Tell your teenager you are not saying "No" forever. You will seriously consider saying yes when they are older (and wiser).

When your teenager erupts into an emotional volcano, you should note one thing. You are probably right on track saying "no". That emotional response is your teenager showing you how immature they really are. If your teenager loses control this easily at home, why would you send him or her out of the house behaving this way? As a parent, you won't be popular but you need to keep your teenager close to home.

A response from a mature teenager when you say "No" is when you hear them say, "Hey mom and dad could we sit down and talk about this..." There is no big emotional eruption, no tantrums, no door slamming, foot stomping or yelling, "I hate YOU!" at the top of their lungs.

Negotiate, Negotiate, Negotiate

Conversations with a teenager can sometimes seem like holding peace negotiations with warring countries. After asking questions and listening to answers if you think what you are hearing from your teenager has some merit, it may provide an opportunity to allow your teenager to experiment with his or her new idea.

Your teenager may actually have a reasonable explanation about why you should allow him to drop band class. You may be able to negotiate with him that he will trade the class for athletics so he can try out for basketball. He may feel both activities require too much time for him to keep his grades up. Your daughter may negotiate starting her own business instead of getting a job to pay for her car insurance. Her business idea is to collect manure and sell it to local gardeners. Her new business, Callie's Cow Pies, may seem a little shaky but you negotiate to give it a try for three months and then if it fails she can find a part time job.

Words Can Hurt

Words are how we learn about ourselves. Children rely on parents to give encouragement and care with their words. Teenagers, as well, are vulnerable to what others say to them. When parents or peers are angry they can say words that are cutting and cruel. Once a word is said you cannot take it back.

Not only are your words powerful but so is your voice. For instance, if your dog walks up to you and you say sweetly *and* softly, "You are such a little brat. I wish I never got you," your dog is likely to happily wag his tail. Now if you use a cutting and cruel voice to your dog saying, "You are the sweetest little puppy ever", your dog may withdraw and look hurt. Not only what you say but how you say it makes a big difference.

The words from peers can be very influential in how your teenager views him or herself. Teenagers wish to fit in and seek to be accepted so negative words can make them feel left out by the peer group. What is said as joking or teasing can be cruel and unforgiving. Just walk through the halls of a junior high or high school and listen to the derogatory statements and teasing you hear tossed around you. During the vulnerability of adolescence our kids need us to build them up when their peer group or friend tears them apart. You are a key influence in helping your teenager deal with this kind of social pressure. What you say and how kindly you treat your teenager is important as a counter to how his or her peers treat them.

Words from Parents

Words that hurt our kids are more likely to come from parents than from anyone else. The words that come from parents that are painful can stay with children a long time. For some, a lifetime. You are so significant to your children. They learn from you. They rely on you to love and encourage them in their life. If you find yourself losing faith in your young person, they too are likely to lose their confidence in themselves. When your teenagers are going through so much emotional change, they need you to be reliable and loving in the face of their turmoil.

When you call your child a negative name, like "stupid", "liar" or "incompetent" your young person will remember that remark Will they ever. And they will come to believe you. And another thing about words is that once you speak them you cannot take them back. Once they are said and heard they are permanent. You might find yourself saying you are sorry or you didn't mean what you said. But the words spoken are many times believed, especially by teenagers. When I see teenagers in my office, sad and dejected, it is not usually over loss of a peer group or a boyfriend or girlfriend. It is usually over the feeling of isolation or dislike from their parents. Though you might feel unimportant, your teenager is well connected to you. Words from parents are more powerful than from anyone else.

A number of adults have told me of what was painfully said to them by one of their parents when they were young. Even as adults they can recall something that was devastating to them. Even exact words. Those words are etched in their mind and heart.

Angry Words at Home

Many families seem to believe it is OK for members to be verbally mean and cruel to one another. We see such behavior on television, in movies and in many homes across America. We have grown accustomed to parents and children screaming and yelling "shut up" at one another, calling each other derogatory names. Getting angry seems to be a commonplace occurrence. Parent and children bantering using belittling words as weapons, verbally abusing each other.

The odd thing is that we are kinder to strangers on the street than we are to the people we love the most. We wait for strangers at traffic lights, wave them across street, stand patiently for them in lines. We do not yell and scream at them, calling them horrible names. I think we have got our ideas about how we treat family members backwards. I think we ought to be kinder, more caring and loving to people in your family than we are to strangers on the street.

Using the notion of how we treat strangers, you can tell your children they will no longer be allowed to be unkind to each other. And if they insist on being verbally abusive to you or someone else in the family you will put them in the car and drive to the nearest stranger. Then you can let them out at the stranger of your choice and they can be mean to that person. Now if you actually get this far, your child or teenager is not likely to be rude to a stranger. This action makes a strong point about how serious you are about being kind to one other.

If you have a temper or lose control of your anger with the people you love the most, put on your hat and coat and head for the front door. Take out your anger on the pavement or hurl it at the nearest tree. Once you have gathered yourself, return to your family.

Words can Encourage or Discourage

Adult, teenagers and children who feel good about themselves produce great results in life. If a person has a positive sense of themselves, generally positive things happen in their life. They feel confident in their sense of themselves as a unique and valuable person. They like who they are and what they do.

Encourage success in your children. When your teenager is feeling low you can change this mood with words of reassurance. This gift you give is priceless. And nobody does it better than you for your teenager. You will find that saying "I am proud of you", "I like you", "I love you", "I will always be here for you", "I believe in you" or "I think you are very special" are the basis of building high self-esteem in our children and teenagers.

Opening up your communication with your teenager is a prerequisite for giving encouragement. If you cannot break into the deafness and distance between you and your teenager, you cannot start to give them the loving promotions and positive responses. Once the communication is working and your teenager is talking you have a great opportunity to say positive and loving things. The loving things you say will be remembered for many years to come.

Words Focused on Actions, Behaviors, Events

In a well meaning attempt to build self-esteem in our teenagers we can get caught in rather general statements that our young person has a difficult time believing. For instance, if a parent says to a teenager, "You are always so responsible", the teenager might think, "If only she knew what I did last night! I skipped doing my homework and I forgot to feed the cat." Sometimes these general statements create guilt and disbelief in our teenagers. Rarely is a teenager "always" anything... always responsible, always caring, always kind, always conscientious or perfect in one particular way. Another reason your teenager may not believe you is because last week you might have been commenting on how irresponsible your teenager was.

Teenagers react well when your responses are based on events or acts. So when you see your teenager either do something positive or acting responsibly, then you can comment. For example, if you saw or heard your teenage son run after his little brother in the street and move him to the roadside you might tell him, "John, I am so proud of how you took responsibility today for your brother. You taught him an important lesson. Thank you." Perhaps John then compliments himself because he has pleased his mother by his behavior. He feels important. He acted responsibly today. He has confidence he can do it again. Teenagers build up themselves based on our feedback about their actions.

Another way is to comment when your teenager does not do something negative. If you walked into the living room hearing an argument between Jeff and his younger brother and noticed that Jeff did not bop his brother Jimmy on the head like he usually does, you might comment, "Jeff, I really appreciate you not hitting your brother on the head when you are mad at him. That took a lot of self-control." Jeff then may say to himself, "I pleased my father. I acted with self-control. I did a good job. I am proud of not hitting my brother. I can act that way again."

Comparing your teenager to others is not helpful either. Like, "If you were only more like Bill next door. He is such a great student." You might hear this angry response: "Why don't you go adopt Bill?" Though you were well intentioned, this response usually backfires and your young person feels rejected not motivated. So when we as parents focus on actions and events, actual situations, our teenagers are able to hear us and respond. They can correct their problem behavior or compliment themselves on a job well-done. Your praise turns into self-praise.

Personality and Character Attacks

There are things that parents can be heard saying to their teenagers out of great frustration. Like, "you are an idiot" , "stupid", "irresponsible" , "delinquent", "lazy", "rude" or "inconsiderate" to name a few. They feel demeaned and begin to believe they are worthless if told often enough. These names, spoken in frustration, really hurt our kids. Parents think saying these names will motivate them to stop their imprudent behavior. Many parents attempt this 'reverse psychology' in an attempt to motivate their teenager. The reason why this usually backfires is that teenagers believe what you say about them.

When called stupid regarding homework your teenager may say to himself, "She thinks I am stupid. Well, I'll show her. She hasn't begun to see stupid." Then he fails three of his classes instead of one. He tells his friends at school his parents think he is stupid. A teenager will prove you right every time.

This negative commenting is fear based and does motivate some people, primarily adults. For instance if a boss came in and told his employee that he was a poor worker and sloughing off on his responsibilities, he would give work his full attention out of fear of losing his job. He would be motivated to prove his boss wrong. Teenagers react in an opposite way. They may take what you say, especially the negative comments, literally. A teenager may say to himself ,"OK, so they think I am inconsiderate. I'd better start working on that inconsiderate behavior. I'll get them!" They attempt to prove you right and make you pay for hurting them. Then everyone loses. So instead of ripping our kids apart with our words we want to build them up.

Behavior and the Person

When you don't want to damage your teenager's self esteem and your son or daughter makes poor choices, you need to find a way to discuss negative behavior. Separating behavior and the person's character is the best way. Here are some examples:

"That was a foolish behavior"
"That was an inconsiderate thing to say (or do)"
"This is irresponsible behavior"

"That was really a poor choice"

By addressing your teenager's behaviors and choices this way, your disapproval is easier to be heard by your young person. This way you say the behavior or choice is stupid, not that your teenager is stupid. This helps the teenager own his or her behavior or choice while not degrading his or her sense of self.

You can tackle most of their poor choices and behavior by making statements like, "I think not doing homework for three weeks is a very irresponsible behavior. I think you can do much better." This is a much better choice than, "You are an irresponsible idiot. What do you think you are doing?" With this approach your teenagers may now say to himself, "My dad really thinks I have great potential to work hard and pass my classes. Maybe he is right and I can." In time your young person may surprise you and show you that he can do what you think he is capable of. The behavior you may address are good grades, taking out the trash, controlling angry outbursts and picking positive friends.

Sometimes when a mistake is obvious, taking your time and not saying something negative, your teenager may say negative things about him or herself. If you don't get angry and belittling over a 'D' they got in a class you may find your teenager does it to himself. He says, "I am stupid...I can't do anything right...I'll never make it." You can then help your teenager differentiate between how they behave and who they really are.

"You" Statements

There is not a better way to start a fight than to start a sentence with "You...". Saying the word "you" to others is like pointing your finger at the other person. Pointing a finger towards someone can intimidate them or make them defensive. "You" statements rarely work for anybody, not kids, not teenagers and not in marriage. "You made a mess.." "You always do that." "You are so irresponsible." Can you hear the finger pointing? Most "you" statements are derogatory. They also can become a launching pad for a lecture or a fight.

So what do you do instead? Use of "I", or "We" statements can be very powerful in getting our teenager's attention without making them defensive. "I" statements are usually clear and not pointed. Here are some examples:

"You" Statement	Solution Statement
"**You** are always late."	"**I** do not appreciate it when you are late."
"**You** are so irresponsible."	"**I** want to count on you. I need you to do your chores."
"**You** never listen to me!"	"**We** do not approve of having your friends over when we are not home"
"**You** live in a pig sty."	"**I** want to see your room clean."
"**You** did this..."	"**The** living room is not for playing with the ball."
"**You** are acting like a mad man."	"**I** can't understand you when you are yelling. Please take a walk and calm down."

These solution statements make it hard for your teenager to argue with you. When you address actions and behavior specifically, without generalizing to your teenager's personality, your teenager is better able to understand the problem and does not feel a need to defend themselves.

"You" statements tend to be too general and can feel like an attack to the young person. "I" statements are clear, concise and less intimidating. They are heard best if they are short and to the point. Kids feel more respected with these statement and are more likely to follow through.

When you say, "I want the TV off in ten minutes and the dishes started", try walking into another room. You leave your teenager alone to think about what you have said. Initially, your teenager may think, "Hmm, no lecture? And she is gone. She seems serious... maybe I should do the dishes?" When you walk back in you may find your young person at the sink.

Take yourself seriously, say your solutions statement once and leave your teenager alone to think about what you have to say. You may be pleasantly surprised how they respond to this kind of request. Leaving the room can get a lot more attention than arguing. Without a disagreement, your teenager cannot wear you down.

Questions?

A critical change we parents need to learn is how to ask teenagers questions. This may feel a little rehearsed until you begin get better at asking questions. Here are some key words for questions:

Please note the "why" word is crossed off. To start, let's take these words and make them into questions for your teenager.

HOW
WHEN
WHO
~~**WHY**~~   **FOCUS ON:**
WHERE   **OTHERS**
                     SOCIETY
DID YOU...   **SITUATIONS**
WHAT

"**How** did it happen that you got in the car with Alex, who was drunk?" (wait for a response, maybe a shrug).
"**What** were you thinking when you decided to go the party you were not allowed to attend?"
"**When** did you leave the party and get into his car?"
"**Who** was in the car with you? I understand there were seven of you."
"**Who** asked you to go driving with Alex?
"**What** did you think when you saw Alex holding a beer, walking to the car?"
"**Where** was it the police officer stopped you on the road?"
"**Tell me** what happened when the police officer pulled Alex over? **What** did you do?"
"**Did you** think that you might get stopped when you were in the car with a drunk driver?"
"**What** did you think when we didn't come down to the police station for four hours after you called?"

These questions are *open ended* questions and are difficult to answer briefly with "yes" or "no". Open ended questions require a more detailed answer from your teenager.

"Why did you do that?"

Now we come to perhaps the most commonly asked question with a teenager... "Why did you do that?" We pose this question when we want others to explain the one reason something happened. We expect adults to be able to explain why they did something. When we ask children, "Why did you do that?" they can answer and give a single reason because of how simply they view the world. For instance, when you ask a five year old why she let the cat out, she might say she thought her kitty wanted to catch a bird.

Unlike children, the most common response to the "why" question from a teenager is "I don't know". Teenager don't think about the world in a simple way. The problem with the word "why" is that teenagers don't understand the complexity of their behavior or the consequences that may follow. They are learning about their lives at that moment, or the hour or the day, mostly through experience. They don't usually understand thinking about something in depth before they decide to act. Especially young teenagers, who many times impulsively leap before they think what might happen to them. Because they tend to believe things will always turn out good for them, they do not have to think through things much. The "I don't know" is because the question is far too complex. "Why did you do that?" is mind boggling for most teenagers.

If a teenager could possibly answer the question "Why?" this is what they might say in response to the question, "Why are you acting so rude?"

Teenager: "Well, I've got these raging hormones. Every time I look in the mirror I see a different guy. And there is this gorgeous girl at school I am madly in love with. I am really upset she likes this other guy. He is so lucky and I am so bummed. I feel crazy when I am near her. I am feeling pressured. I have three zits on my face that are so embarrassing and I am worried about my grades. And my voice squeaks at the most embarrassing times and also I'm worried I don't have a clue what I will become as an adult..."

This might only be the tip of the iceberg of a teenager's feelings! They can go on and on with worries, fears and concerns. Most cannot begin to put into words how they feel like an adult can. This is probably the reason they spend so much time on the phone with their friends, sorting out all feelings and issues of their lives. There is comfort with someone who is just as confused about the "whys" of life.

Until your teenager hits the age of seventeen or eighteen you should try hard not to ask why. You'll have to practice the other ways of asking questions with your teenagers to improve your communication. Asking "why" will only leave you and your teenager more frustrated. If you do catch yourself asking "why" just say oops and restart your question with any of the other words listed here.

For example:
"**When** is it OK for kids to tell their teachers off in school?"
"**Who** at school is dressing like this?"
"**Who** is "everybody?"
"**Where** were you when your friend was shoplifting?"
"**What** is happening in your history class?"

Our goal with our questions is to gather information about our teenagers and what is happening to them. As you begin to use these questions, you will find the conversation changes and you may find *The No Lecture Method* becomes much easier as you use these questions as well.

Lying "Did you..?"

A way to encourage our children to lie is to ask a direct and pointed question that only has a "yes" or "no" answer. This kind of question is usually started with "Did you...?" For instance, "Did you take the money?" With this *on the spot* question your teenager has two choices. To say "yes" or "no".

Answering "yes" means to most kids that they will definitely get into trouble, right away, if they admit what they did wrong. So when they are feeling backed into a corner with this kind of question, many times your child will be inclined to lie by saying "no". With the lie, they are off the hook for a short while. Perhaps forever, if you do not find out.

Usually your child or teenager has said "no" to avoid conflict. Saying "no" does buy you some time so you don't have to deal with the situation, like homework or chores. If they said "no" as a way to avoid getting in trouble when they did indeed take the money, if asked again, they again have to lie to cover up the first lie. The catch is if they decide to admit they did take the money now they will also have to admit that they lied about it too. So their situation worsens with the lie. Consequences may be more serious and they are in their situation deeper.

What works to help our children and teenagers to be truthful is to start questions with, "Tell me about..." So you could say, "Tell me about the missing money." Now your teenager must think. He or she cannot lie and give you a quick "no" to avoid the missing money issue.

Another example would be to state, "I would like to know about the dishes in the sink". This way of asking is less pointed than asking, "Did you do the dishes?" This way of asking gives them an opportunity to explain themselves and their situation. It also is more respectful to be less pointed. They are more likely to think about what you are asking rather than have to give you a quick answer to cover for what they might be doing wrong.

Here are some more example of solution statements for typical "Did you" questions.

Q. "Did you do your homework?" becomes "Tell me about your homework.".

Q. "Did you do your chores?" becomes "Tell me about feeding the dog."

Q. "Did you skip math class today?" changes to "I got a phone call from school telling me you were not in math today."

Q. "Did you break my favorite cup?" becomes "Look at my cup. Tell me what happened."

Focused on Others

To successfully gather information, ask questions that are focused on others and society in general rather than your teenager. For instance, "Did the whole class say rude things to your substitute?" Or ask your ninth grader, "How many of the tenth graders smoke marijuana in the parking lot at lunch time?" With these questions focused on other teenagers, your son or daughter will not be under a spotlight. Teenagers do especially well explaining about what others are doing. From their explanation, they can apply what they learn from other people to their own lives and decisions. It is easier to see the picture if you are not in the frame.

One Minute Lecture

Though we have talked about letting your teenager feed your lectures back to you, there are plenty of times your young person needs information guidance from you.

What works well is the *One Minute Lecture*. Your task is to condense your fifteen minute lecture into about a minute or less since you no longer have the luxury of a lot of time to impart everything you want your kids to know. The goal is to get your teenager's attention in that first minute or before your adolescent will block out anything you say to him or her.

Once you have given your *One Minute Lecture* then you can pose a question for your teenager's response.

Here are a some ideas on phrasing your *One Minute Lectures:*

* **Topic #1:** Teenagers having sex. *One Minute Lecture:* "Dad and I don't think anyone who is fourteen years old is mature enough to have sex. There can be serious consequences like AIDS, Herpes, pregnancy. But most of all relationships usually don't last long and kids can feel bad about themselves and they feel used." *Question:* "Do any kids at your school feel bad if they have sex when they are too young?"

* **Topic #2:** Failing classes. *One Minute Lecture:* "If you choose to fail your class you will have to look at the option of summer school. Mom and I know you are capable of doing anything you put your mind to. And you can learn anything in school. We will not support your failure. If you fail now, you may choose to fail with other things in your life. We know you're a winner." *Question:* "Can you get into college if you get D's and F's in your classes?" or "Can you be promoted to 8th grade if you flunk 7th grade."

* **Topic #3:** Having friends over to the house when we aren't home. *One Minute Lecture:* "We don't think it is a good idea to leave you with your friends in the house alone. We know you can be responsible for yourself but we don't expect you to be responsible for your friends. Without an adult here your friends might decide to try things that are not acceptable with our family. It is a great opportunity to break the rules and nobody may find out. We love you too much to leave you alone." *Question:* "How many kids do you know who can do whatever they want after school?"

Notice how these questions include both parents as a parenting team by using "We" or saying "Dad and I". When you and your spouse can say things together, you become much more powerful with your teenagers. Teenagers have more difficulty splitting the two of you with your differences. If you and your spouse don't agree on issues and feel differently, you need to compromise on a message you can both give to your teenager. When you share your values also tell your kids *why* it is important to you and what happens to others. Your task is to do this briefly. Adding a question at the end also gets results in responses from your teenager.

For shorter subjects you can condense your ideas in one or two sentences:

1. "Dad and I want the whole family at dinner on Sunday. Our family isn't complete without you".

2. "We don't think smoking is good for your health. It is a bad habit to start because you could get addicted to nicotine."

3. "We don't think it is good for teenagers to spend the whole weekend together. We like having time with you every weekend. You can see your friends other times, like school, and you can talk on the phone."

It is a good idea to begin to prepare *One Minute Lectures* on everything under the sun that is important to you and pertinent to teenagers. Here is possible subjects:

- Honesty
- Consideration
- Being trustworthy
- Being loyal
- Being considerate, respectful
- Being a good friend
- Being kind
- Treating brother/sister well
- Having the courage to say "no"
- Making your own decisions when with friends
- Being independent

- Doing what is right
- Handling your anger
- Taking care of yourself
- Integrity
- Being dependable
- Showing pride in yourself
- Valuing/Managing money
- Courage
- Responsible choices
- Being a leader
- Sharing
- Being peaceful with others
- Caring
- Value of virginity
- Self worth
- Value of working hard
- Helping others who have less
- Receiving respect from others
- Having good fun
- Alcohol or drugs
- Being a good citizen

Situations Before They Happen

It is far better to discuss *situations* with your teenager before they might occur. You may need to look at older teenagers to figure out what issues your teenager may face in the coming years. If your son or daughter can describe how another teenager would respond, he or she will be better prepared when he or she has a similar experience.

Here are some examples:

Question #1 : What should a teenager do if he were at a party, someone handed him a drink and it was laced with LSD?

Question #2 : What do you think a girl should do if a guy she likes starts to call her nasty names, thinking he is being funny?

Question #3: Do you think teenagers can be good friends with others who drink and smoke and not be influenced to start using too?

Now don't be afraid to ask your teenager questions for which you may not have the answer. Your job is to present the possible situations and then through discussion and thoughtfulness work out the solutions together. After discussing these situations you may find your teenager is more savvy when they go to a party and someone hands him a drink. He may look around and see if other kids are getting spaced out. They might decide to make their own drink so they know what is in it. Or when they are in dating situations, so that they do not allow themselves to be put in vulnerable situations. If you discuss situations *before* your teenager is in them then they have a much better chance of moving successfully through them.

Do's and Don'ts

Here are some do's and don'ts that improve communications that work well.

* **Do** use positive words to encourage your kids. You could also use positive words to encourage each other, to encourage yourself. Doing so makes you feel good. Work on replacing negative words with positive words. Everybody will benefit.

* **Do** use a positive approach to behaviors. We tend to scream and yell because we don't know what else we can do. Later you will read a chapter on rules and consequences filled with strategies that replace screaming and threats.

* **Do** spend some time each day listening to your kids. I think teenagers need anywhere from ten to fifteen hours with you a week. Sound like a lot of time? You need to tend to the garden you have. You have only so many days with your teenagers. Remember the moment will never occur again.

***Do** say please and thank you. Add kindness to requests. If you say "please" and "thank you" often you get "please" and "thank you" back. As often as you say those I think they are returned to you. In time. They are basic to a respectful interchange between any two people.

***Do** compliment your son or daughter on a job is well done. When we feed compliments to our teenager they begin to believe that they are capable and worthwhile. A job well done is different for a thirteen year old than for an eighteen year old. And also we have different expectations for a teenager who is just learning about doing a good job verses a hard working young person. If you look hard enough you can find something positive in the efforts of most teenagers.

*Do STOP, count to ten, take a deep breath, leave the room, leave the house before you let your angry words fly at others around you. You do not want to yell. You want to postpone hot issues and conversation leading to arguments. Hot issues with high emotional climates are like fire and dynamite. This is the time to stop communication to have successful communication.

*Don't nag or compare. Comparing your teenager to other kids like the youngster down the street or someone else on the football team isn't helpful. Teenagers don't like to be compared to other teenagers because they are striving to be unique and individual. Like diamonds, each is unique in pattern, shape and clarity. Nagging is not a productive way to motivate a teenager.

*Don't yell, scream or threaten. It hurts you and it hurts your kids. All it does is make a situation worse. If you can cool off, then you are more ready to communicate and your teenager may follow your example.

*Don't use words that attack, belittle, degrade or intimidate.

IDEAS

Here are several ways you can improve your relationship with your teenager.

* SATURDAY MORNING BREAKFAST Every Saturday morning Jim would take one of his three teenagers out to breakfast. Without fail, every third week one of his kids could count on having time alone with their dad. He remarked the best discussions he had with his teenagers were on these Saturday mornings. When they ran out of things to talk about they would randomly pick a new topic, like politics in America., freedom of speech, current events like legalizing marijuana. This father has wonderful memories of being with his teenagers. Time alone with each family member helps build a positive relationship between parent and teenager.

* FAMILY NIGHT Another idea is the concept of Family

Night. Teenagers usually balk at this one. They may say, "Oh, no, not family night! You guys can have it without me!" It is essential that your teenager join you so that your family is complete. You should find a comfortable place for the family to gather, somewhere comfortable in your house, where there is no television and offer sweet treats to eat. You can discuss everyone's dreams and wishes, plan where to go on vacation or how to divide chores or how to make your family better. I recommend the discussion be fairly structured. Take all the phones off the hook, put a sign on the front door telling friends to come back in an hour. Put on some enjoyable music. My favorite is classical. Sit back and enjoy your family.

* DINNER TOGETHER Today's typical American family is always on the go, especially with two working parents and active children. For a family to function well all members need to gather together. Having dinner together can become an important tradition. Your children may complain but the more often you dine together the less complaining you'll hear. It makes everyone feel important to be included.

The Scott family had so many commitments during the dinner hour that they used to meet at 7:30 or 8:00 PM every weekday so the family could sit down together. The members who had dinner earlier ate dessert and their youngest, Sarah, was usually in her pajamas.

* CHORES TOGETHER I think many of our teenagers do poorly with their chores because they are lonesome. Teenagers are social beings and don't like being alone. One dad found his son sitting near the snow shovel without beginning his chore. Quietly he got another shovel and walked out, said "hi" and started shoveling. Soon his son was at his side shoveling too. That night, they enjoyed being outside together.

* DINNER DATE Credit goes to The Bill Cosby Show for the idea of the dinner date. Portraying a father of a teenager, Bill Cosby insisted the young man who wanted to date his daughter would need to come to dinner to meet himself, his wife and the family. He felt if a young man was brave enough to confront the family test he was a good candidate to date his daughter. If a young man refused to come to dinner he was lacking respect and should not date his daughter.

* WALK AROUND THE BLOCK As suggested previously, if your teenager is angry, hostile or just down right annoying, a walk around the block can really evaporate his negative mood by decreasing his adrenaline as well as adding fresh air to his brain. Go with your teenager, let your son or daughter vent frustrations and problems. Be a good listener and when your teenager has settled down then you can talk to him or her.

* FOOD   Feeding others is one of the most nurturing things we can do. At home, with our kids, relatives and even at the office. It is one of the most welcome gestures of friendliness. Offering food is usually readily accepted by teenagers. It has a quieting and soothing effect and the chewing may help open up their ears! It may seem like they are only coming for your food. But they are also seeking your company even though they are not likely to tell you that.

* COMPLAINT JAR   One young teenager proposed setting up a complaint jar to collect complaints from any family member. When one of the parents noted there was a paper in the jar, the family would sit down and discuss the complaint, seeking a solution. All family members participated in the discussion. One complaint noted the two parents were talking about their work too much at the dinner table. They also complained there was too much talk about work and about money. The parents like to know what is bothering their children.

* OUTINGS   Teenagers love to have fun. Take teenagers on vacations, weekend get-a -ways, camping trips, cross-county ski trips, company picnics and just for starters to the bowling alley. Don't leave them behind even if they insist it is humiliating to be with the family. When you return home they may not hail a great time, but they usually will rave to their friends.

* WRITE A LETTER   When things seem to be going poorly write your teenager letter. Depending on the topic, you may ask your teenager to respond by writing back. Your teenager can read what you are saying over and over until your thoughts sink in. It is not surprising to know teenagers keep most of their letters, especially from parents. Sally wrote a letter to her daughter Jenny, it read;

Dear Jenny;

It has been great to have you home this weekend. We really enjoy your company.

Since school begins tomorrow, I need you to finish the two jobs you promised to do this weekend; your laundry and the cat box.

I love you,

Mom

I have great confidence that parents can have wonderful relationships with their teenagers. And teenagers can learn the most important lessons of their lives living in and loving their families. When you have discovered an open way to communicate with your young person, you can begin to enjoy the kind of relationship you want. Before you know it, your young person will be waving goodbye, leaving you behind. And you are going to miss them. Your finest, most precious hours are now, not tomorrow. The best time to start communicating with your teenager is today.

CHAPTER THREE

Who is in Charge of the Rules?

"You're grounded!"

Parenting a teenager means you have to know how to handle your son or daughter when she or he decides to break your rules. When your child was three she could readily tell you "No" and with opposition you could then steer your youngster in the right direction. Now, in adolescence, your teenager has a mind of her own and has become adept at how to say "No way" as she heads off in her own direction. Oppositional behavior can begin when your adolescent refuses to do chores, ignores homework or generally defies everything. Your experimental learner needs an important lesson from you; it is not a good idea to break your rules.

Am I Just the Biggest Person in the House?

When it comes to disciplining your teenager do you ever feel like you are just the biggest person in the house? As young people increase in size, can easily beat you at arm wrestling and develop voices even louder than your own, you may wonder *"Who is in charge?"* Perhaps you should no longer be in charge of the rules? It seems the roles have reversed and your teenage son or daughter has become *your parent*! Perhaps it is time to throw in the towel and retire.

Though the world seems to have opened up for teenagers, they still need limits and boundaries. Your job as a parent is to set those boundaries. Your young expert, *without much expertise*, needs to test your limits to find out what happens. Establishing rules is like setting a speed limit for your teenage son or daughter. As the driver, your teenager, knowing the speed limit, has several choices. He can speed and drive over the limit, he can keep his car within the speed limit or if he wants he can accelerate to mach one and take the chance of crashing. The choice belongs to your son or daughter.

Consequences for your rules are like constructing a brick wall for your teenager. During rebellious times your teenager may go at high speeds coming to a screeching halt just short of the wall of your limits. Another choice is to slow down in just enough time to comfortably stop in front of the wall, respecting your limits. Third, is to try to fool you, take a back route and sneak around your wall (this is the "sneaky" teenager saying what you want to hear and doing something else). And the fourth way, the most defiant, is throwing caution to the wind, carelessly speeding, hitting the wall and crashing and burning.

One of the tough tasks that come along with raising teenagers is figuring out just where to set the speed limits and when to build the brick wall. Be prepared to hear from your young experts that he or she is certainly mature enough to set his or her own limits. Testing the rules is how teenagers learn their limits (and the limits of your patience too!). Your rules and expectations balance much of what your teenager faces in your young person's world.

Teenagers are full of contradictions; though they vie for independence, at the same time they shy away from other responsibilities. Your teenager may demand to be recognized as mature and at the same time act immaturely. Teenagers, with their in-experience and youth, are really just practicing being mature. Maturity, the balance of both wishes for oneself and the responsibility to others, takes many years to develop. Though your teenager may protest, your limits help him or her grow up feeling safe and more secure.

You may also wonder how do other parents set limits and follow through with their adolescents? Most troublesome is that you usually don't have a lot of other parents to talk to about their parenting. The critiques about your parenting come readily from your resident 'expert', your teenager! What you usually hear is "Everybody" is going to this party, "Everybody" gets to stay out late or "Everybody" talks back to their parents. And on top of all that, "Everybody's parents are so cool unlike you!" So there you are, feeling old fashioned and out-dated, thinking you may not know what you are talking about.

Your parenting role can be a tough one when you set limits and ultimately must face adolescent conflict. As outdated as you may feel, your limits are critical to the success of your teenager. Ask yourself: if you do not set any limits with your teenager, who will? Your young person is probably hoping you will believe you are no longer important so they are free to have fun. Teenagers also find delight feeling in charge after convincing parents that they can run their own lives. When parents believe this myth, they loose their opportunity to influence and guide their young person. Contrary to popular opinion, teenagers should *not* be in charge in families, parents should be.

Many parents have good ideas that are right on track for their teenagers. Your expectations are your way of anticipating what is best for your son or daughter. As you tire from battling your teenager over what is appropriate or important, rewards for your efforts come when you see the end result; a respectful, kind, caring, self-reliant young adult. Though you may no longer be the biggest person you are the most mature person in the house and your limits are critical to the success of your young person.

Create a Vision

The best way to begin establishing rules is to have a vision of what you would like your teenager to act and sound like. Don't worry about what other adolescents seem to be doing, think about what you would like to see. Establishing the rules are based on your expectations (not what "Everybody" is doing). It is important for you to think about how you would like your teenager to behave so you will be better able to curb behaviors you don't like. Part of your vision should also include how you would like to be as a parent. Most of us in the face of adolescent antics, want to be calm and collected, still in charge without being too charged up.

It is not unrealistic to expect your teenager to be courteous, kind and show respectful behavior. On the other hand it is unrealistic to think your young person should not be angry or moody. You will need to reassure yourself that in order to do a good job parenting you will have to tell your teenager the 'N' word, "No". Set your expectations high, envision the best.

No Matter Where You Draw the Line

No matter where you draw the line, with your rules and expectations, your teenager is likely to cross it at some point. Some parents, to avoid opposition from their teenager, take the seemingly easy way out by being permissive and not setting many limits. Even with permissive parents, teenagers still find a way to rebel.

Several years ago I became acquainted with some liberal parents and their twelve year-old son, Eric. I wondered if their son would rebel during his adolescence even though he grew up in a liberal home. Eric's father wore long hair, both parents dressed in non-traditional ways, they openly smoked marijuana in front of their son and rarely, if ever, did they set any limits. During their son's teenage years Eric was allowed to swear, smoke, drink alcohol with his friends in their home, have his girlfriend over to spend the night and he could wear anything he liked. He called his parents by their first names and he too, grew his hair long. So as the years passed I watched, wondering if this young man even could rebel with so few limitations. One day, in a most unexpected way, Eric did indeed rebel.

When he was seventeen and a senior Eric cut his hair, put on a three piece suit and tie and joined the most conservative Baptist church in town. His parents came unglued! And to top it off at the age of eighteen, he joined the army. To their further distress, a year after he enlisted, he got married and within the next year, had a baby. Needless to say, his parents wondered how they had gone wrong. He embraced everything his parents were so adamantly against.

Unfortunately there is no way to appease, bribe or convince your teenager not to test you. Testing in adolescence is a given. You won't know when you will get tested, what behavior your teenager might choose or for how long. Gearing up and getting ready for some testing helps so you are not taken too much by surprise.

Too Much Freedom

A number of years ago I worked on an adolescent unit in a private psychiatric hospital. Most of the teenagers, ranging from twelve to eighteen, came from affluent families. The institute had the amenities of a hotel. Life was easy for these teenagers. They did not need to make their beds, had free reign of the grounds, coming and going as they wished. The kitchen served good food and the residents had access to just about anything they wanted. The young residents could visit each other in their rooms, they could smoke cigarettes and say most anything that came to mind to their attentive, supportive adult staff.

One evening disaster struck the unit. Seven of the teenagers had not returned as expected after they left on a walk on the grounds. After launching an extensive search, alerting all other hospital personnel to help, the teenagers were no where to be found.

Shocked by the situation, the staff became distraught. What were they going to do? How could they possibly call the parents of these teenagers and tell them the children in their care were missing and they did not have a clue where they might be?

After phoning the police, alerting parents, extensive interviewing with the few teenagers left behind, some clues were discovered to solve the mystery of the missing teenagers. It turned out the seven had stolen a van from the parking lot, took a joy ride to the nearest city and were attending a rock concert! The staff was shocked.

Once the teenagers were found and returned, safe and somewhat sound, the relieved staff gathered together. The unit psychologist, who lead the meeting, discussed how the limits, rules and expectations for behavior needed to drastically change. Basically, the party was over for this group of young people; no more "Mr. and Ms. Nice Staff Workers" for these kids.

The rules were changed. Now there was no smoking, no swearing, no one was allowed in any one else's room without permission. A dress code was established and the teenagers had to checkout with a staff member to go off the unit. The adolescents had to earn privileges with responsible behavior, like going to the hot fudge sundae machine.

The young residents erupted into full rebellion. They claimed nicotine fits, swearing withdrawal and could not believe what they were told to do. After the initial shock wore off, the young people spent most of their time and energy figuring out how to swear behind a staff member's back and the easiest way to sneak a cigarette. They were so preoccupied with breaking the new rules, the last thing they had time to think about was leaving the premises, stealing a car and speeding to another rock concert.

Your teenager, at some point, is likely to test your limits. Draw the line with your rules and expectations close to what you believe is right and good. If your limits reflect your realistic values and expectations, your rebelling teenager will spend energy challenging these. Being too liberal and permissive means that your adolescent may have to take drastic measures to get a reaction from you. The more freedom you give an immature teenager, the more likely he will be to do the wrong thing and get himself into trouble.

Forgiveness

One of the hardest things a person has to learn is how to forgive. We all make mistakes. It is part of being human, as a parent, as a person and as a family member. Typically, it is easier for most of us to forgive someone we don't know well than a member of our family. For instance, when someone dents your car, initially you might be angry but after the repair shop completes the bodywork you will forget and forgive the mistake. Forgiving someone you love who has hurt you is far more difficult.

Some adults can carry the bitterness of not forgiving someone close to them throughout all the years of their lives. Their bitterness permeates most of their relationships. To forgive takes a great deal of love, understanding and maturity.

Just like you, your teenager is going to make mistakes. Before adolescence there is no way to predict when this will happen or how your young person will err. Teenagers, like all other people, need to be forgiven and given a chance to learn from their mistakes and start again.

Try asking your teenager to forgive you when you yell or threaten them. You will be surprised how forgiving our young people can be. In return, you can tell them too, you forgive them when they make a mistake.

Discipline VS Punishment

Discipline is not a popular word today. Many confuse discipline with punishment. How the two differ is important.

To punish is to inflict harsh physical or emotional pain for some kind of offense. The dominant person intentionally inflicts pain upon another to intimidate them and force them into a submissive position. Through pain, suffering and fear the submissive person is forced to stop what he is doing or to act in some other way. We usually define punishment as spanking, hitting, emotional degrading (like name-calling) and emotional withholding from another person.

We have learned that punishment does not teach positive learning. Force can frighten another person to change behavior. The weapons we use produce *fear and intimidation.* The victims learn helplessness, to fear and come to believe they should be demeaned when pain is used against them. When children who are punished grow up, they repeat the same behaviors with others.

Discipline is different than punishment. A negative behavior is followed with a meaningful consequence that is *not* hurtful or frightening. Examples of negative behavior you may need to tackle include a teenager who swears at you, refuses to come home on time or boycotts the chores or does not go to school. The purpose of discipline is to help teenagers decide negative behavior is not in their best interest. Providing meaningful consequences teaches our teenagers to stop acting out. Through discipline they discover the kind of behavior we prefer.

Schools use discipline to replace the punishing switch. If a teenager skips enough classes, the consequence may be suspension from school. This results in directly involving the parents in their teenager's choice. Parents are more aware of what is happening with their young people and school. This kind of discipline is not degrading to a student. This is one example of discipline through a meaningful consequence.

Our goal with discipline is to make an impact so that negative behavior can be replaced with positive behavior. We know our teenagers need to know what they are doing that is not OK with us and also to know what we want them to do instead.

Why Discipline?

Decisions about discipline start when parents need to respond to negative behavior. If you tell your teenager his curfew is 10:30pm and he walks in at 12:15am, he is testing you. If you respond by saying, "Hey, no big deal, try harder next time" your teenager is likely to continue to ignore the limits you set. This kind of permissiveness is a green light to break your rules and challenge your expectations. When teenagers are allowed to do only what they please, they will not be prepared for adulthood. Instead they will be immature and self-centered.

What kind of discipline is needed so your teenager will not repeat negative behavior again? As you know, lecturing your teenager will not work. Your anger may not have much impact on your adolescent. Getting angry has more consequence for you and your blood pressure than it does for your teenager. You can rant and rave and your young person knows you will love him or her in spite of your angry protests. Your teenager also knows you cannot stay angry forever and eventually you'll get over it. When you are angry or lecturing, you may find your son or daughter tunes you out waiting until you become your calm-self again.

Discipline works well when the result is teenagers learning through experience. When discipline methods work, you will discover you do not need to scream, yell or repeat yourself ten times to be effective. When meaningful consequences work, your teenager is not likely to ignore you. Once you start using these new methods of meaningful consequences your teenager may start begging you to go back to lecturing and yelling. Some teenagers even will plead to have their parents beat them instead of these new methods that work so well.

Discipline with Love

We use discipline to *teach a better way* so that they will learn to make positive decisions. One goal is to *stop* negative behaviors and eliminate poor choices. Another is to *reinforce* positive solutions that will prove beneficial to your teenager. Parents need to *reward* teenagers for making a positive choice instead of choosing a negative one. We know discipline is working when we see our adolescents consistently make positive choices.

When you are disciplining your teenager, you can respond in an angry and hostile way or you can be calm and clear. When you are angry your voice can be cutting and cruel. Good parenting means providing discipline with love, not hostility. Setting limits without yelling or degrading our young people should be our parenting goal.

Truth or Consequences

The results of one's behavior and choices teach the experimental learner. A company I worked for several years ago required all staff members to work with police personnel. To better understand what life was like on their beat each of us went with an officer on a shift. I happened to be eight months pregnant when I joined a police officer on his evening shift or 'cowboy' shift. The officer I went with was assigned to the poor section of downtown where there was a large congregation of street people gathered. Never in my wildest dreams would I venture into this area in the evening.

Some amazing things happened that night. During the evening, we found people breaking the law. Officers took them to the magistrate or to the police station. There were a number of consequences this evening. Some went to jail, others received fines for drunk driving, being intoxicated on the street, burglary, prostitution, theft, loitering and street fighting. It was an evening of *Truth or Consequences.*

Your job of curbing your teenager's negative behavior is similar to a policing role. Like *Truth or Consequences,* good behavior should result in positive consequences. You say "thank you" or share your appreciation with your teenager when you are pleased by what they have done or what they say. With negative behavior, you'll need to develop some kind of meaningful consequence. The consequence teaches your teenager it is not in their best interest to repeat a negative choice or behavior. Unlike grounding, creating a meaningful consequence will capture your teenager's attention.

RULES :
Assumed/Unspoken, Spoken and Written

Before developing consequences, let us examine the three types of rules that exist in families:

- **SPOKEN RULES**

- **ASSUMED or UNSPOKEN RULES**

- **WRITTEN RULES.**

If I asked one of your children if it is acceptable to tell a lie in your family, your child would most likely know the answer. If I asked what was appropriate dress, your teenager could tell me. The rules for younger children are less complex than those for teenagers.

The biggest problem with unspoken or assumed rules with a teenager is that your young person may take advantage of any lack of clarity. With statements like "I didn't know that was a rule. You didn't say I had to be home exactly on time, I thought I could be a half hour late" or "You said I couldn't date but you never said I couldn't meet my boyfriend at the movie." When a teenager plays with assumed rules, he can catch you in technicalities such as, "You said I can't smoke but you never said I can't chew snuff." Tobacco is the issue, not what form is used.

The risk with spoken rules is that, your teenager can choose to use his or her new 'selective hearing', tune you out, acting as if he or she never heard you. If you tell your daughter she is not allowed to go to the mall without asking permission, she could say she didn't hear you say that. Then it is your word against hers. Another problem accompanies 'selective memory' when your teenager admits he or she did hear you but then 'forgot' what you said.

'Selective hearing' and 'selective remembering' are frustrating for any parent to deal with. Written rules work well to solve these kinds of problems with your teenager. It is hard for your young person to buffalo you when the rules are written and posted. The best place for posting rules is the most frequently visited place in your home...on the refrigerator door. Written rules are hard to contest and it helps end 'the great debate' you may be having with your teenager. It is always a good idea to keep some extra copies of the rules because sometimes they just happen to disappear.

The rules you develop should reflect your expectations for your teenager. A helpful guide is to think about what are the rules that guide a good citizen. One first learns how to be a good citizen in his or her family. You can figure out if you have all the necessary guidelines by asking *if* your teenager follows the list of rules would he or she be fulfilling the expectations of your family.

In a family with both teenagers and younger children two sets of rules work well, one for younger children, one set for your teenagers. You can give the little ones the second set when they are about twelve years-old. Here is a suggested *menu of rules:*

- Do what you are told (asked) when you are told (asked) to do it.
- Ask a parent before going anywhere or to activities
- Parents need to know where you are and who you are with
- No fighting, hitting or mean gestures
- No bad words
- Say "please" and "thank you"
- Do your chores
- Be safe and responsible
- Tell the truth
- Do your homework before TV and activities
- Curfew is ____p.m./a.m.
- To bed: Bill 10:00 p.m.; Angie 9:30 p.m.;
  Julie 8:30 p.m.

This first rule, "Do what you are told, when you are told to do it", is a great general rule that covers just about anything you ask your teenager or child to do. Making positively phrased rules will be better accepted by your teenager and are more respectful. Instead of saying, "Don't go anywhere without our permission", you can use, "Parents need to know where you are and who you are with."

Rules like "no bad words" usually do not need explaining but as a word comes up in conversation you may need to say it is considered unacceptable by you. Parents need to think of 'replacement' words for the unacceptable ones. So instead of saying,"This dinner is disgusting", the replacement may be, "I don't like eggplant parmesan."

As you put together your list of rules you and your spouse must not only define what you expect from your kids but also *what to do instead.* You may have said about a thousand times over the years "Don't fight" or "Don't yell". It is important to inform your children what you want them to do instead. When you do not like how your teenager displays anger, you have to come up with new *replacement behavior.* It does not work to say "Don't get angry". Your teenager needs to know how to change his or her expression of anger.

A parent might typically say, "Don't hit your brother... cut it out!" So what is he suppose to do instead when his little brother has irritated him to no end and he is ready to retaliate? Here are some options of *what to do instead.* He can put his hands down and go find a parent. If parents are not home, another option is leave the house and take a ten-minute walk around the block. Possibly your teenager could give his younger brother a warning and then follow it by writing the infraction on paper. When parents return, they can discipline the young siblings, *no questions asked.* Another possibility is to walk away and go to his room and give your teenager permission to lock his door. Another would be to call a parent about little brother's behavior.

When teenagers do replace negative behavior with more positive acts they need to hear praise for being responsible. To forgo punching their little brother takes maturity and self-discipline. We adults need to think of *what to do instead* because our children are not likely to be able to figure it out for themselves.

What Works Instead?

Your involvement is essential in order to teach a better way. Discipline does not occur in your absence. In my work with many families with teenagers, I have seen parents become so frustrated by their teenagers, all they want to do is to drop their kids off at my office and come back later after I have 'fixed' them. One frustrated family I worked with was the Smith family, who brought in their angry son.

I asked his parents to describe their aggressive fifteen year-old son, John's, angry behavior. According to his parents he yells, sometimes shouts profanities in front of other family members and guests, indulges in name-calling and accusations and insists he is right. He postures with clenched fists, an intimidating stance, accompanied with an angry glare. He usually slams doors and stomps to his room. One time he kicked a hole in the wall in his bedroom. After this tirade he usually slams his door and stays in his room with his angry music blaring for an hour or two. Sometimes he'll stay there all evening long. Does this sound like anyone in your house?

These parents did not know how to change their son's behavior. They certainly understood that what they had tried did *not* work. They had yelled, screamed and threatened. Sometimes they tried to ignore his tantrums, which was impossible to do. When they grounded him for weeks at a time, he just repeated the whole angry routine again. His parents did not want to keep grounding him. They were out of possible tools in their toolbox of solutions. Things were not getting better. The Smiths were feeling helpless, hopeless and angry.

I asked Mr. and Mrs. Smith what did they want John to do instead when he gets angry? They both had puzzled looks. After a while they said, "Well, we want him to quit feeling angry so he doesn't act like this anymore;" even though they know angry feelings were not going to go away. Someone can change their expression of their angry feelings but they cannot eliminate how they feel.

Like the Smiths you may not know how a teenager can become angry in a constructive way. It is easy to say, "Don't do that..." It is more difficult to tell your teenager what *to do instead*!

There are a number of better ways of expressing anger than having the typical 'teenage tantrum'. Do you want your teenager to calm down before he may take his anger out on others around him? Do you want your teenager to be able to discuss what makes him angry in a normal tone rather than yell? Do you want him to say, "That makes me mad", rather than call you vulgar names and swear? Do you want him to walk his adrenaline off outdoors rather than leaving his footmarks on the wall or attack a family member?

It is highly unlikely your teenager is going to figure out what he should do by himself. Especially during the heat of battle. You need *to tell* your teenager with an alternative behavior.

Here is a list of possible ways to behave instead of *getting angry*:

- walk away and kick the leaf pile
- walk around the block
- jump rope
- punch a punching bag
- laps around the house
- talk about it ONLY WHEN YOU ARE CALMED DOWN
- leave the room
- shoot basketballs
- ride your bike
- call a parent
- kick the snow
- do push ups
- do sit ups
- hit a ball
- jump on a trampoline
- run
- call a friend

On the Road of Adolescence

On the road of life from the ages of twelve to eighteen I recommend early on you use a fair amount of structure and supervision for your young adolescent. You create rules that represent the speed limit of life. Let them go slowly at first so they can get to become good, conscientious drivers. Put up yield signs and GO-SLOW signs and you monitor them often with your radar. Know where they are and what they are doing. If they get a ticket, make them work hard so they will seriously reconsider when they wish to speed again.

The time you should be most active as a parent is when your teenager is rebelling. As they pass down the road depending on how many detours they take, how fast they speed and how many traffic tickets they acquire, you can increase your confidence in their ability to be responsible, while providing less supervision and structure.

Positive consequences for your teenager can be immediate and specific. And they work best if they are specific to a task or behavior. Saying things like, "I just love how the bathroom looks now that you cleaned it. Thank you." Even if it is at the end of the day we want to look for opportunities to build our teenagers positive sense of self. We want to comment on what they do well. Contrary to this, negative consequences are best if you take your time and are thoughtful about them.

Privileges and Responsibility

Rules and privileges vary as your expectations change for your teenager. Time and responsibilities about bedtime, curfew, chores and homework and responsibilities need to change when the teenager shows more mature behavior.

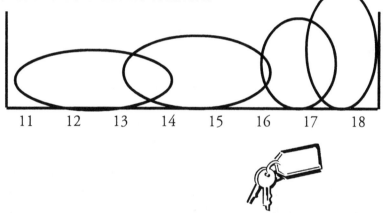

In the first group, during the ages 12 to 14, you should be most strict with your rules and restrictions for your teenager. If your teenager can abide by these rules, they are most likely mature enough to have increased freedom and responsibility.

If your son or daughter rebels and has a tough time following your rules, you know by his or her behavior your young person is not mature enough to handle more responsibility. The limits you have set should remain the same. For instance, if your twelve year old has a 10:00 p.m. curfew and he or she is usually late you may need to change the curfew to a 9:30 p.m. curfew and see if he or she can make that one on time.

Sixth to eighth graders are the most immature and vulnerable. In spite of their immaturity, this is also a time when they many feel like they know the most. What sometimes fools parent is how physically mature your young person can look at this age. Just take a stroll through a junior high or middle school and you will see physically mature teenagers who are immature, insecure and need much adult supervision.

Think of your rules like a hug. When your teenager is the most rebellious and rambunctious, you need to hug them tightly with close supervision. Young adolescents need specific expectations and explanations with *close supervision*. For instance, you may tell your son he can go skateboarding with his friends. When you check on them they have gone to the mall instead. This kind of behavior helps you know your teenager is not mature enough to follow your rules. This is a way your teenager is testing your limits. He or she may say to you, "You don't trust me!" and you can reply, "That is right, honey. Until you can follow our rules we won't be able to rely on your judgement."

Parents who are too permissive and who offer very little supervision, may find their son or daughter out of control. These parents may be relying on the 'buddy-friend' system which usually fails during adolescence.

Sometimes permissive parents change and tighten up the rules only when things get out of control. Such a drastic shift can create even more rebellion and crisis, though teenagers may need this change to feel secure and for parents to be in more in control. This kind of rapid change is difficult for everyone in the family.

If you have a young teenager you can start out being conservative with your rules, allowing your teenager more privileges and liberties over time. Gradual rule changes work better than moving so quickly having to go from friendly to firm.

Until your teenager becomes more mature, you will need to get used to the idea of your teenager blaming you. Being the 'bad guy' by establishing high expectations for your teenager is really being a 'good parent'. Your teenager can blame you for not allowing them to do what is not good for them. This way they can complain, blame parents and save face with their peers.

Jingle the Car Keys

Sixteen is a milestone in adolescence. This is the year young people become much more aware of their preparation for adulthood. For most sixteen year olds, all you need to do is to rattle the car keys and say things like, "What time are you planning on being home tonight?" Their choices are easy. If they do not make their curfew, they lose the use of the car for a week. Then, when their friends ask them for the usual ride, they have to say they lost the car for the next week. This is a tough consequence for a teenager who likes the privilege of driving. With this new motivation your teenager is not as likely to keep disrespecting your rules. We usually see much more responsible behavior once a teenager starts driving. At this age even their friends are invested in them making that curfew as well! There is nothing like positive peer pressure!

As your teenager approaches seventeen or eighteen hopefully most of their rebellious and annoying behavior has subsided and you see the emergence of a mature young adult. You have more trust when your teenager is more predictable.

Changing the Rules

A teenager gets a chance to change the rules by showing good *adult logic* and responsible behavior. This way your teenager has to talk to you and use their best logic to convince you why their rules should change such as curfew being later. If you do not like their logic, do not change the rules. If you do like their logic and they can back it up with responsible behavior, then try relaxing the rules, allowing them more freedom and privileges.

If a teenager has been home on time for the last three months, respectful of the curfew, and he asks for a change I think it is well worth rewarding this responsible behavior. The teenager learns that by following the rules he or she gets more of what they want. Parents in return get a more mature adolescent.

On the contrary, if your teenager is constantly breaking your rules demanding you change them, this is probably not the time to relax the rules. You can say to your teenager, "When we see responsible behavior we will consider changing the rules. For now this is the way it is."

How your teenager responds to the rules is a *test of maturity*. If your teenager is breaking your rules their behavior says they are not mature enough to handle anything more. If you change the rules and your teenager uses the change to break the rules for their advantage they were not ready for more freedom.

A parent asks his teenager why he thinks he is ready for a later curfew. If the teenager answers something like "I don't know", "Everybody has a later one" or "So I can fit in with my friends", you will not want to change the rules. If parents note maturity in their teenager's young adult logic they should consider a change. Remember to take as much time as you need to think about what your young person tells you. If you need a few days to think about a change, take time so you don't feel rushed. Including both parents in the decision to change is very important and that may take a day. It is important to not feel pressured into making a hurried decision.

Check Up

Another way to avoid being coerced into believing what might not be the truth is *to check on your teenager*. For example, if you tell your daughter she can go to a certain movie, go to the theater and check to see where she is. If your teenager is where you expect him or her to be, you don't need to let him or her know you were there. If she is at another movie that you did not approve, walk up quietly, tap her on the shoulder and ask her to step into the lobby with you. Then take your teenager home.

When you catch your teenager breaking the rules, you will make a big impression if you say very little. Your presence says a lot. And they do not have a choice of discussing the issue with you where you found them breaking the rules. Home or a neutral place is the best place. This is family business, not business with their friends.

As additional consequence you might need to escort your teenager to the next few movies he or she attends. This is an example of a logical consequence for a teenager's choice. Checking on your teenager is to make sure he or she is not cheating.

In past years when communities were closer knit, parents had a built-in community support system to help with raising their children. Today few people care if your teenager goes to a movie that you do not approve. Many times if movie theaters can sell a ticket, anyone can see it. If your teenager finds you checking on him and says, "You don't trust me", you can respond, "I care enough to check on you. I appreciate you being where you said you are. It builds our trust in you."

Rebellion Means Supervision

Younger teenagers and young people rebelling need close supervision. You should know where they are, what they are doing, who their friends are, pre-screen the movies they want to see and do lots of follow-up on what they tell you. A rebelling teenager needs much of the same supervision. It helps to keep them close to home during these times of more precarious development periods.

Your teenager's emotional reaction to your limits is a good barometer for maturity. If you tell your teenager, "No, I love you too much to let you do this," and he or she goes into a full blown tantrum then you should know your limits are probably right on track. The tantrum and loss of emotional control is evidence of their immaturity. And if they are this emotional at home, imagine them on their own, out of the house. Discipline during this time requires a close hug from the parents with rules and supervision. Your teenager's tantrum is not a sign of you being a poor parent, that you are failing in your job.

For the moderately acting out teenager you can be more relaxed and looser about the rules. You should still know their friends, where they are going, what their interests are, and the experiences they have. You may wish to give them more privileges and privacy with less following up and checking. But you still need to check up on them, just less often. If they are not doing what they say they are, tighten up their privileges for a month or two.

An example of a response from a mature teenager about the rules might be, "Hey, mom and dad could we get together soon and discuss this thing more?" There is no yelling, screaming, demanding and opposition. When your teenagers show good adult thinking you can feel comfortable giving your young person a good deal of freedom. Sometimes this maturity does not appear until their last year of high school. If they are doing well in school, using good judgements with their friends, acting appropriately and are able to converse with you in a calm manner, they are ready to do more on their own. With occasional checking up you will be comfortable handing them car keys, relying on them to use good judgement in a variety of situations. All of this reinforces and rewards their maturity.

Grounding does Not Work

Grounding is an old parenting strategy. Perhaps even in the days of early man, when a youngster got in trouble, maybe he was relegated to the village with the women and children, only allowed to return when his "time was up". The problem with grounding, especially for longer than two weeks, really doesn't work well.

One of the most common mistakes parents make with teenagers is to use the traditional idea of grounding for disciplining when you are really mad. In a fit of anger, you can threaten to ground your teenager a long time, like a month or a semester or if you are really angry, until they are 21! With the typical grounding, who really gets grounded is the entire family who has to be cooped up with an irate teenager. Grounding can make a bad situation worse for everyone. Many times teenagers have this figured out and they know if they are terrible enough to live with, their grounding time gets shortened because the family needs some relief. The teenager then learns how to successfully manipulate parents.

Creating Consequences

Rules work when consequences work. Meaningful consequences back up your rules, get your teenager's attention, they provide an excellent learning experience. Consequences fall into a couple of different categories; *natural and logical.*

Natural consequences are those responses that occur naturally and are consistent and predictable. An example is the natural consequence of touching your hand on a hot stove. When you do, what naturally occurs is that you get burned. The natural consequence of getting burned teaches you that you got too close to the heat. If your burn is bad enough, another consequence is for you think you never want to cook again and plan to eat out for the next month. As your burn starts to heal you're likely to approach the stove again but with more caution than before. You become more aware of what makes your actions safe and you learn using hot-mitts work as well as not getting too close to the heat. Natural consequences teach us through the outcomes of our choices not to repeat certain behaviors again.

Natural consequences do not occur for many behaviors of teenagers. When their behavior and choices have no naturally occurring consequences, it is up to parents, school or community to create them.

If your teenager speeds in a school zone he or she may or may not get caught. For their safety we cannot allow our teenagers to experience what ever they want to do until certain consequences befall them. If they want to drink and drive, parents can't condone this choice and let them experiment and see what happens. If they want to fail all their classes, it is very hard for parents to say, "Try it and see what happens." Instead we as parents have to create *logical consequences* that teach our teenagers to change negative choices. They also need to learn to do something else to replace the rule-breaking behavior.

Logical consequences are those consequences that occur after a certain behavior. Many times the consequence has a logical connection to the behavior and represents a way of 'undoing' a behavior. An example is a young man who in fits of adolescent rage kicks his door. His parents create a logical consequence for their teenager who leaves holes in the walls and doors. With *logical consequences* to *make amends*, the teenager has a chance to do something positive to make up for the negative behavior. For door kicking a teenager would have to patch the hole, strip and sand the entire door, take off the doorknob, varnish or paint the entire door and replace the doorknob. The teenager must complete the task and *he or she is grounded* from all privileges until the job is completed. This is how grounding does work when the only person who grounds your teenager is your teenager!

Your teenager can take as much time as they like to complete their task and they can be grounded as long as they want to be. You don't have to remind them to do their task or nag them to complete their task. Finishing is up to the teenager. When teenagers complete their work and *do it well*, then grounding ends. By losing privileges during grounding I suggest no TV, radio, computer, walkman, phone, friends over, going in their rooms or special activities until their task is done. If you have an avid reader, no pleasure books. I recommend not taking away sports or special groups or clubs from your teenager. The reason is he or she made a commitment to the team or group and the group should not suffer because your son or daughter cannot attend. During grounding, teenagers go to school, do their chores at home and go on any family activity, like going out to dinner. Your teenager basically get grounded from all the privileges he or she really likes.

The best part of this strategy is you never have *to yell*, or remind your teenager to do their consequence task. Getting off grounding is totally up to your teenager. When you hear your teenager say, "This is so unfair that you have grounded me!" you can reply and say, "Honey, the only person who grounded you is you."

To develop *logical consequences* it is best when the consequence in some way relates to the problem behavior. It helps your teenager if the consequence 'makes sense' in relation to the behavior and the rule that is broken.

Logical Consequences

When teenagers must complete some kind of task to get off grounding as a logical consequence it works several ways to your teenager's benefit. Some kind of task is a way of making amends. Though a consequence they get to experience good hard work and when tasks are done they feel better about themselves and their abilities. Hard work is a great way to build your teenager's self-esteem and at the same time teach them important lessons.

A word of caution, your teenager is probably not going to like this new approach. After experiencing *logical consequences* teenagers usually prefer you yell at them, lecture them and they may even beg you to beat them instead of having tackle some difficult task.

If your teenager chooses to be two hours late for curfew, you want to create a consequence for your young person; an experience that teaches this choice is not a good idea. What follows are a variety of options from which you can choose.

The Swiss Cheese Essay

The Essay is a very basic consequence to use for many infractions, especially the more serious ones.

Essays are assigned and titled by parents and teenagers are off grounding when the essay is written. It should be handwritten (no computer) and run anywhere between 500 and 1000 words, depending on the issue. Examples of titles are "Why I should not lie to my parents" or "How my parents cannot trust me when I break curfew". Don't put an emphasis on grammar or spelling. The 'guts' of the essay is what is important.

Most teenagers do not like to write by hand and may struggle to write down their ideas on a subject related to rule breaking. The essay allows you to understand the thinking and logic that guides your teenager in his or her life. Teenagers can take all the time they want, they are grounded until their essay is completed.

Some teenager's essay attempts can be silly or half hearted, like writing the same sentence over again like "I shouldn't be late for curfew because I get in trouble." If your teenager does this you can say the first sentence is great and if he or she needs help with more ideas you would be happy to repeat one of your lectures. At this point teenagers usually say "no thanks" and go write the essay. If your teenager tells you writing an essay is "stupid", just let it be stupid. Your teenager still has to do it to get off grounding.

Essays help parents look at the *Swiss cheese theory* of adolescent thinking. Parents look for the holes in their teenager's maturity, gaps in moral development and reasoning by reading the *composition*. You begin to see what your teenager does know and what is still left for you to teach him or her. When their logic is good and they present some very valid points, you can see how they are maturing. An added benefit; your son or daughter's handwriting may improve too!

Chore Cards and the Spotless Home

The chore card concept consists of assigning a chore for infractions. You will like this strategy because you no longer will need to yell, threaten or plead. First, give your teenager a warning to stop or start doing something. Let him or her know, "If you don't do _____, I will give you a *chore card*." Then, wait a few minutes and see what happens. Your teenager must decide whether to test you.

If your teenager decides to refuse to do what you have asked, for instance he swears again at his brother, or refuses to do his dishes, you give him a chore card. These 3x5 cards, contain a designated chore on it, the date and the name of the person who breaks a rule. Then the parent that assigned the chore card puts it up, usually on the refrigerator.

Parents need to always pick the chore and *not* let the teenager decide. If teenagers complains about the chore, they must do it and not be allowed to swap for one they like better. Someday you may need two baskets of laundry folded, the leaves in the backyard raked, the bathrooms cleaned or the living room vacuumed. When you need a meaningful consequence you can give a chore card for the chores your teenager likes the least.

Chore cards are effective when your young person is then grounded until the task is completed. When your teenager can't watch TV, listen to music, use the computer, play Nintendo, talk on the phone and friends can't come over, he or she will know how serious you are about not breaking the rules.

Your teenager can take as much time as he or she likes before completing the chore. This creates an experience whereby you do not need to coax or nag them to do their chore. When a friend calls on the phone you can say something like, "Jim is not able to come to the phone, I'll check to see when he can." Then ask Jim when he might be ready to return the call. He might huff and puff and say about a half an hour. The tasks help your teenager learn he has grounded himself. He will begin to take you more seriously the next time you want him to stop swearing at you or hitting his brother.

The card is taken down by a parent and grounding ends when the job is done and done well.

A parent may have to check on a chore several times until it is completed to your satisfaction. The chores you assign are best if they are different from the usual weekly chores. If you give your young person a chore card for the dishes, he or she may choose to watch them pile up for a week or two, just to teach you a lesson. Think of chores that you have a hard time getting to or are ones that take too much time.

When you need to check a chore, it is easy for you to respond negatively when your teenager does a job poorly. One of two things is usually going on: either the teenager does not know how to do the job or he or she thinks the job is finished. In the first case an adult needs to show him how or the teenager may be discouraged or bored. I think it is best to always praise the effort of starting a task even though the task has yet to be completed.

If your teenager thinks he or she has completed the chore but you think he or she can do a better job, always say something positive first before pointing out the negative. Lets say your teenager has to sweep out the garage for swearing at his brother and he thinks he has finished the job. When you check he has only swept the middle of the floor. You might say, "Hey John, the middle looks great. (pause) I'll come back when you have finished the corners." Return when he says he has finished.

Please thank your teenager when the job is finished even if it has taken them a week or two to get around to completing it. Then remove the chore card, amends have been made and your teenager gets a fresh start again. No lecture is needed. The task will teach.

One creative father thought of using different colored chore cards, one color for outdoor chores and another color was for indoor chores. You don't need to make cards up ahead of time. You can make up cards when you need to give one out. At that time you can think about jobs that you would like to have done. A side benefit of chore cards is that you get the unattended chores done, have a spotless home, all at the same time!

The Big Meany, the Little Pest

It is 4:00 p.m. when Jordan, an eighth grader, is just entering the front door. Before his mom can say "hello" Jordan is grabbing little brother Matt by the neck. Matt screams that Jordan won't let go of him. Their mother Amy tries to break up the fight, begging Jordan to stop. Jordan says, "He's bugging me, the little punk," and eight year-old Matt screams "I am not!," jumps on Jordan and starts hitting him. Amy is *so* frustrated, she doesn't know how to get them to stop. Unfortunately, this scenario happens often. She hears Jordan is mean to Matt or Matt is harassing Jordan. Amy's yelling is not much of a deterrent to the boys.

What would work better for Amy is to give the boys one warning to stop saying, "If you both do not stop there will be a consequence." She waits a minute and notes Jordan persists in the fight. She then tells Jordan he has to hug his brother and say he is sorry and he is grounded until he does. A consequence for both not stopping is for the two to hug each other and apologize. Jordan says he would rather die. Or the sibling who started the fight can make the other sibling's bed for a week, all seven days, do his or her dishes or chores for the next week, in addition to their own.

Make Me!!

Jenny is in a foul mood today. She enters the kitchen and yells at her sister. Her mother asks her nicely to take her things out of the den and she yells, "No." Her mother insists she pick up her things and Jenny gives her *the look* and says, "Make me!!" Under her breath she swears at her mother. Jenny's mom cannot believe her daughter would ever say this to her. Jenny's mom tells her she is grounded for life.

What would work better would be for Jenny's mom is to give her daughter a more meaningful consequence. She could ground

Jenny until she has written her a fifteen word note of apology to her. In addition, another consequence would be for Jenny's mother to select Jenny's clothes for the next week. With this consequence, Jenny could protest, detesting the idea of her mom picking out what she would wear to school. How could her mother ever do such a thing? For the next week Jenny would probably gripe to her friends how she is humiliated having to wear her "oldest, ugliest clothes" *and* how she has to write that stupid note to her mother.

It Takes Two to Tandem

A couple, both school teachers, shared a meaningful conse-quence they used with their two teenagers. Every summer they traveled by car state to state for their summer holiday. They hooked a tandem bike to the back of their recreational vehicle. When the kids started to argue they would get one warning to stop. If they chose not to stop their parents would pull off to the side of the road where they would park the kids and the tandem bike. They would get back in the car and drive down the road within visibility of their teenagers. The two would not only have to work out their dispute, but needed to cooperate enough so they could pedal the bike together to get back to their parents.

The Swearing Tree

If your young person wishes to swear at you or other family members a good consequence is to take him or her out to the nearest tree and tell your young person he or she can swear at the tree. Swearing won't hurt the tree's feelings, so there is no emotional damage done.

Another consequence includes fining your teenager 25 cents a word. You can take this out of their future allowance and keep a tally on the refrigerator or they can put the money in the 'swear jar'. This money can become a donation to your church or to a local charity.

You can also have your teenager write what she could say instead of her new swear word and then read the paper to you. Your teenager can also write a fifteen-word apology note, he is grounded until it is delivered. For persistent swearing you may need to use a chore card or remove a privilege.

No Homework?

Frank is a single father of three teenagers. He is insistent his children do well in school. Last year he kept getting the same answer when he asked about homework. His middle school daughter and his two sons in high school would say they did not have homework after school. After conversing with teachers he realized in order for his children to do well in their classes it was reasonable for them to have something to study and work on every weekday. So when he asked if they had homework and his young people said "no", he would assign them an extra chore so they would have to work to do. When Frank introduced this consequence an amazing thing happened: his teenagers no longer had days without homework!

Feeding Spotty

The responsibility of caring for pets is great practice for being a parent. Cats, dogs, puppies, bird and fish are dependent on the humans for their daily needs like food, water, walking, training, attention and love.

Jeff is a sixteen year-old sophomore with a busy baseball schedule. He has had the responsibility to feed his little dog, Spotty for four years. He comes home from practice and is distracted from all kinds of things he is supposed to do. One day before dinner his mom, Sara, asked if he fed Spotty. He answered, "Yeah." Sara went to Spotty's dish and found it empty and saw his water was at least a day old. She called the family to dinner. Jeff was there first, announcing he was starving. There was no food on the table as usual. When everyone was seated, Sara told Jeff that he would *not* eat until his little dog was fed first and in the future she expected him to be honest about feeding his dog. She told him it was not fair to his dog to shirk his responsibility.

Taxi Fare

If your teenager is a night owl and getting up in the morning is a real chore, you may have to deal with her tardiness to school because of her late night habits. The first consequence would be for parents to not sign for the tardy slip sent from school, to be excused, rather let your teenager suffer the consequences. After you have offered plenty of reasonable solutions to getting up on time, then let your teenager experiment in getting him or herself up (they may request an alarm clock that drags them out of bed). Another consequence if they are late, is to have to walk to school or ride a bike, if it is safe. Another option, if you must drive them, is to learn what the taxi fare would be from your home to school and then charge them the same fare every morning they are late. Your teenager must pay before you start the engine. The first time you may wish to call a cab and have your teenager pay for the service.

Verbal and Written Apologies

Verbal and written apologies are logical consequences that help increase ownership of behavior. You need to hear apologies to know they have been completed. Written apologies are best when they consist of at least ten words. Without specifying the number of words your teenager may just write, "I'm sorry." Or if you don't check it they may write, "I'm sorry you are such a jerk."

Once these notes are written, your teenager needs to deliver it to the person receiving it. Apologies may be for teachers, peers, siblings, relatives, either parent or both, principals, neighbors, coaches, store owners and anyone else. The teenager has a chance to make amends with the person to whom they have been disrespectful.

When in Doubt Take Away TV for a Week

If you are not sure what kind of logical consequence may match an infraction, you can always take away TV and movies for a week. This is a sure way to get your teenager's attention. This consequence can have some positive side effects. The break from TV can help your son or daughter find other interesting things to do, like a hobby, art, reading or even doing a better job with his or her homework.

If your teenager sneaks off and watches TV during the week when grounded, you may have to turn the television off for everyone else in the family, except parents. Once you do this the other children will make sure the person grounded does not watch TV so they will not get grounded from television again.

Sarcastic Statements

You may object to your teenager's tone and sarcasm. You first must reach a consensus with your young person about what *exactly* you want your teenager to change. Many times it is not what they say but *how* they say it. If you say, "Don't talk like that," your teenager is likely to respond, "Like what? I'm not doing anything!" To clarify what you mean, you may want to say your teenager sounds huffy, smart, snide, ridiculing, loud, mean or demanding or sassy, etc.

Once the behavior is pointed out you can present to your teenager how and what you would like him to say *instead.* A logical consequence for tone of voice is for your son or daughter *repeat* what he or she wants to say in the right tone at least three times. This helps the teenager undo what he or she has said that isn't working.

Here is an example of a new script. Let's say a teenager says, "This dinner is nasty," and what he has to say instead is, "I don't care for quiche." This rehearsal prevents your teenager saying; "I don't know what you mean." When your teenager has the *experience* of how to say things in a courteous tone, he or she will take you more seriously. You need to listen patiently as your teenager attempts to change what they have had to say. If it is embarrassing to them, others can leave the room. When your teenager has finished you can thank him.

Some parents may have gotten so accustomed to sarcastic or derogatory talk that it is hard for them to hear it anymore. If this has happened to you, start listening to your teenager's statements. Many negative and rude statements start with the word "You". When your teenager starts with the word "You" it is usually critical and is a way to begin a fight with another person. If your teenager says something like, "You are so old fashioned." Change this way of talking by asking your teenager to begin his or her sentences with the word "I" instead of "You". Beginning a statement with the word "I" makes it much more difficult to sound bossy, derogatory or demeaning. Here are a few scripts for your teenager:

- " I want you to listen to me" rather than "You never listen to me"
- "I don't like your limits" rather than "You are the worst mother.."
- "I wish you wouldn't drive in front of the school" rather than "You always embarrass me in the car"
- " I don't like all this health food" rather than "You are a real granola cruncher. Your food is sick"

You can also use these scripts to change how you talk to your teenager as well. It makes for far more civilized conversations.

The Ball, the Window & the Estimate

Logical repair means if your teenager breaks it, he or she needs to fix it. Now even though the family may not be able to reuse the 'fixed' item it is still the 'repair' part that is the issue.

One day, a sixteen year-old named Andy got so angry at his dad he picked up the toaster and threw it across the kitchen. He become angrier when his parents told him he was grounded until he took the toaster apart and put it back together. Andy thought it was not fair because the toaster was broken, his father bought a new toaster, and he was still grounded. His father explained to him the point was not whether the toaster worked but rather the task of 'undoing' what he had done. After many hours of labor the toaster came apart and then Andy put it back together. At that point he was no longer grounded. He was right, the toaster never worked again but since that time he has never thrown anything in the house again.

Another 'fix it' job happened when thirteen year-old Mitch threw his baseball too many times in the living room. When his last toss shattered the front pane he knew he was in *big trouble*. For a consequence his parents had him call four window repair service companies, meet each contractor and take the bids. Then when his parents selected the contractor, Mitch had to call him, set the date for the repair and be there to assist. He also had to give up the next three months allowance toward the cost of the window. Mitch learned a lot, about contractors, repairing a window but most of all the risks of throwing a ball in the house.

Logical repair may mean taking on a task that is foreign to your teenager, like repairing a dented bumper or gluing a vase. It is fine for a parent to show young people what needs to be done, check on them, encourage them and even work at their sides. The bottom line is that the teenager must do the majority of the work. It is best for the parent to be patient and not get too frustrated before grounding is ended.

Curfew: Beat the Clock

One of my favorite stories comes from a very bright teenager, named Jill, who told me about her father and his curfew. The curfew procedure in her house was established by her father, who was a very strict disciplinarian. On weekend nights he would set an alarm clock for the first of this three teenagers, strategically placed in the bathroom next to his bedroom. It was Jill's 'job' to get home in enough time to 'beat the clock', turning off the alarm before it rang at her curfew hour. If that alarm were to go off and she was not at home by her designated curfew, father would be awakened and that meant *BIG TROUBLE*. There was also a warning if a brother or sister turned off the alarm for the missing sibling, their consequence would be doubled. In all her years at home, neither she or her siblings ever failed to 'beat the clock'. The clock was a great reminder of the importance of being home on time.

Jingle the Car Keys

If your teenager is driving, losing the privilege for a week can be a very meaningful consequence. It is best to put vehicle registration in both parents name so you can easily withdraw the car. If your teenager has a permit, you can post it on the refrigerator until his or her week is up.

Jingling the car keys is a good reminder of having your teenager to be responsible about following the rules. You can hold the keys and say, "What time are you planning on being home this evening?".

Get a Phone , get a Permit

Why is it a good idea to get a young teenager a phone by 9th grade (not their own phone line) and their learners permit? First of all, both of these things are privileges you can take away and that gives you some leverage with your son or daughter about testing the rules.

It is usually a good idea to allow your teenager to get his or her driving permit as early as possible. When a teenager sits in the driver seat, they attain an adult status, driving with other adults. This encourages responsibility and maturity. Having a permit is handy when you need a meaningful consequence for rule breaking. Your teenager loses his or her privilege to practice driving for a week or two when they break the rules.

It is also helpful to get them their own phone, which is a privilege. Your teenager then gets to show you if he or she can follow your expectations for time on and off the phone. Then when they fail to do so, you take away their phone for a week. By the way, the best place to put phones and other things you take away because of negative behavior is the trunk of your car. When you leave so does your young person's phone.

Sixteen year-old Jenny loved being on the phone. Her favorite person to talk to was her boyfriend. If she was late from curfew or got rude with her parents, they took the phone away for two or three days. When they did, she almost went through withdrawal. Your teenager may also have some privilege that means a lot to them. A consequence for one teenager may be a piece of cake and yet poison for another.

"If You're Going To Yell..."

When Chelsea's father called her to come into the den., she screamed at him from the kitchen, "I don't want to!!" Chelsea's mother said to her, "If you are going to yell at your father, say 'please'." Asking your teenager to be polite while they sound demanding can take the 'edge' out of their message. Your teenager must say, "Dad, would you *please* stop teasing me?" which sounds very different than the commanding, "Dad, stop it." When your daughter yells, "*Please*, get out of my room, mom," it is much easier on your ears than, "Get out of my room!"

Mousse and the Hairdryer

Another major consequence for a *major* infraction for daughters is taking away mousse or the hairdryer for a week. These items may seem like essentials for the right kind of look for your daughter and not having them can be a major trauma. One daughter did lose her mousse and hairdryer, so she got up early and hurried to the bus stop where friends helped her with her new hairstyle. After her week was up, she never swore at her father again.

The Bedroom Door

For *major* infractions like sneaking out in the middle of the night, drinking and driving you will need to think of major consequences. Taking away the bedroom door for a week can mean your teenager loses his or her privacy and it is a reminder they did something wrong when they are in their room. Parents just pull the hinges and remove the door until the week is up. This is a big consequence appropriate for a major breaking of a rule.

Garbage In, Garbage Out

A hardship for parents occurs when the school calls you to notify you your teenager has misbehaved in school. One upset father, Neal, came up with meaningful consequences for his son, his son's girlfriend and another friend who were caught putting rude and obscene jokes on the school computer. The parents got together to discuss what the teenagers had done. Neal came up with the ideas of the three of teenagers, with the supervision of adults, collecting 50 bags of trash found along the city streets, in addition to letters of apology for the principal and entire teaching staff. Dad's motto was, "Garbage in, garbage out".

The Car Fender

Oops, your teenager dented the car fender! While you're calming down, you might think about consequences like how your teenager can use certain tools to pull out the fender. This can be done by your teenager before you take it into the body shop. And your teenager can also collect three estimates on repair and drop off and pick up the car. No driving until the car is repaired and "driving repair taxes" are collected.

Borrowers Beware

When your teenager borrows from others in the family without asking that other person's permission you can start by having your son or daughter return the item. Then the child or person who has had something taken can go into the teenager's room and take *what ever* he or she wants to borrow for a week or two. This includes radios, stereos, computers, TV, jewelry and clothes. Make a card with the borrower's name, the item 'borrowed' and the date items need to be returned.

No Nag Theory

If you have trouble getting your teenager to do his or her chores, try negotiating with your teenager the time he or she will complete the chore. Find a time that the two of you can agree on. Then you make a deal and agree *not* to nag your adolescent unless he or she fails to complete by the hour agreed. If your young person chooses not to make your deadline you will get to nag your teenager to your heart's content. So save up all your lectures and all your complaints until he or she is late .

To be fair, once the chore is done then you will have to refrain from nagging and complaining.

Chores and More Chores

So your teenager won't do his or her chores? You can give them a warning and wait about twenty minutes. If they have chosen not to respond, then you can give them a chore card for another chore. Obviously, you have failed as a parent teaching your son or daughter to work hard. Some of the reasoning here is that if your son or daughter is having a hard time doing one chore perhaps they need more chores so they can learn how to be a harder worker.

Feed the Poor Without Diplomas

If your teenager is expelled or suspended from school I recommend never leaving him (or her) home alone. Instead your young person should spend his day in a productive way. He can spend his day doing community service at your local food distribution center for the poor and homeless. It is likely you will need to escort him and provide supervision. You can also find a senior that will help supervise if you are not able to do so. I also think your teenager should make up his missed work and do some extra credit on the next weekend. A note of apology to teacher and principal may also be in order.

This logical consequence helps your teenager take a closer look at what can happen when people do not finish high school and cannot find work.

Skip School, Skip the Fun

When you are dealing with skipping school, several consequences will work well. Start with a 500 word essay on <u>Why I Should Not Skip School</u>. Several chore cards involving some good labor would also be appropriate, such as washing and vacuuming the family cars. The final consequence is that parents do not excuse the absence.

No Sympathy, No Shopping

Recently following an accident, Laura, mother of three, was told she needed immediate surgery. Her doctor scheduled her to go into the hospital the following day for the procedure. When she called home, her teenage daughter, Angie, answered. When she heard the news about her mother, she got angry and yelled at her mom because she had promised to take Angie shopping the next day. When her father heard about Angie's response to her mother, he told her she was grounded from shopping for the next month, in spite of school starting soon, and owed her mom a note of apology. Angie could not go to any mall; she was even banned from the grocery store.

No More Dandelions

Logical and creative consequences can happen in our schools as well at our homes. A principal at an elementary school was proud of her lawn, there were no dandelions in sight. The reason for this had to do with disciplining the children. Whenever a student came in her office for an infraction, she would hand them a bucket and a weeding tool. The student was not allowed to return to the classroom until the weed bucket was full. The kids were able to make amends. Some of the students I am sure even grew fond of gardening.

Telling Off the Teacher

A number of parents have gotten accustomed to their young child telling them what they should do and eventually become immune to disrespectful behavior. When young people are allowed to feel like an equal, they become empowered and think they can do whatever they please. In the classroom these students may readily tell a teacher what to do or be demanding, in a very disrespectful way.

The school may provide consequences for this kind of behavior, like a visit to the disciplinarian's office, visiting the principal or spending time in suspension from the classroom in a detention classroom.

A logical consequence for this behavior, in addition to what happens at school, is an apology note of 30 words given to both the teacher and the administration, including what the student should have said or done instead. In addition to the note, another consequence for the teenager is to bake the teacher cookies. This way of making amends can help a teenager realize respecting others promotes harmony rather than creating conflict.

Phone as a Hobby

In her fifteenth year, Crystal discovered the phone. She has found she can spend long periods of time catching up on the latest gossip. She can even do her homework on the phone too. Actually, she can stay on the phone for hours, just hanging out, sometimes just breathing. Unfortunately, her new hobby does not make her parents happy. They actually expect her to stay on the phone for a mere 30 minutes and then get off (and of course be totally bored) for the next 30 minutes before she can get back on.

An excellent experience for a young person to learn about respecting others and moderating the things they love, is asking for time off the phone. If your teenager has a difficult time following your rules, the logical consequence is to take the phone away for a week. If your son or daughter is very attached, like Crystal, a week could be far too traumatic. Another option is to reduce their time from 30 minutes on/ 30 minutes off to 20 minutes on/ 20 minutes off, for the next week. If your teenager can handle being respectful of this limit, they can return to 30 minutes on/ 30 minutes off. The problem with getting your teenager his or her own phone line is that you may have trouble controlling how much time they spend calling friends. If they are paying for their own line they may tell you it is not your line and you can't take it away. Just think, your son or daughter may be your tele-marketer of the future!

He Never Reads

One consequence for a break in your rules is to assign a book to your teenager and he or she is grounded until it is read and a book report is written. Teenagers who are not avid readers do not like this kind of consequence and may barter to get you to change your mind. Reading a book you select and your teenager likes may ignite a spark of interest in reading.

Give a Warning and Wait 5 Minutes

When possible always give your teenager a warning to stop a behavior before giving them a consequence and then give them time to think about it. You can say, "Nick, please stop throwing the ball in the house. If you don't you'll get a chore card." Then *wait 1 to 5 minutes.* To your surprise when you walk away and wait, many times your teenager will have stopped.

When parents get into a big debate with their teenager, telling them to do something *"right now"*, this kind of pressure is likely to start a fight. Waiting *5 minutes* is respectful of our teenagers having different priorities and interests than we do. Most of them don't really care about a neat room, swept floors or clean dishes. They have other priorities, like the meaning of life and whom they like the most this week.

Take Your Time and Timing

Take your time when deciding on consequences. Be thoughtful. Remember the *Time Delay.* We get trained when our children were younger to respond to situations as soon as they occur, for example, running into the street after a ball. Unlike little people, with teenagers, it is best to take your time to think through each situation presented to you.

Take your time means to get together with your spouse or a friend to discuss the situation. With a *Time Delay*, you can take an hour or an evening. While you are deciding let your teenager wonder and ponder what will happen to them. This is good for them. It promotes adolescent *thinking.*

To present the *Time Delay* initially you can say to your teenager, "There will be a consequence for this..." If your teenager asks, "What is it?" you can answer you need some time to think about it, meet with mom or dad and you'll get back to him or her. Until you decide, your teenager is to stay at home, grounded. This *Time Delay* keeps you under good control and you are not as likely to over-react in the heat of your anger or disappointment.

Sometimes it may be hard for you to wait. Your timing can be critical in helping your teenager learn an important lesson. An example is when a couple's fifteen-year-old son called his parents from the police station, and said, "I am at the police station and I need you to come get me out of here right away!" He explained he had been at *the party* he was not allowed to attend, where others were drinking and using drugs.

As hard as this may sound, instead of racing down to assist their son, his parents just listened. They told him they were sorry he had used such poor judgment and he must be pretty scared. Then, they told him they would call him back! What a shock to this young man. Together his parents discussed the situation presented to them. They then called the police officer to follow up on their son's story, found out it was safe to stay there a little while and asked the officer to please impress upon their son the seriousness of his action.

Five hours later they arrived to pick him up. He could not believe his parents did not immediately respond. He spent five hours *thinking* about what he had done and *experiencing* what happens because of his choice to go to a party his parents forbid. He also was thinking he never wants to do this again and wondering why his parents were not rescuing him?

Sometimes our teenagers get themselves in situations that create a significant consequence that can provide an excellent opportunity for them to learn an important lesson, if parents do not come with assistance too fast. This does not work if a teenager's choice puts him or her in an unsafe or dangerous situation.

You want to be very thoughtful and to take your time when dealing with your adolescent. If you aren't sure they should go to the party "everybody" is going to tell them you'll respond to their request in a few days. This gives you enough time to check with "everybody's" parents.

Reward the Truth

The truth is sometimes very difficult to tell. It takes courage to own up to one's mistakes. Asking for truthfulness takes special consideration by any parent. If you value the truth, at times during adolescence you may have to buckle your emotional seat belt in order to prepare for some things that may be hard to hear. When the truth means you are at fault, it takes courage to face up to your own mistakes. Imagine how difficult it is for a young driver to say,"I hate to tell you this, but I dented the car."

To get your teenager to tell you the truth, you must reward the truth. When your teenager has the courage to be truthful, in spite of what your teenager may tell you, it is important to respond positively. This means if your teenager tells you he is flunking a class, *instead* of immediately getting angry it is best to take a deep breath and say, "Thank you for telling me, I am sure that was not easy to do." Then, if you feel a need to scream, go for a ten-minute walk, settle down and come back and talk about it.

Many choices our teenagers make are a mix of both poor choices and good choices. Your teenager may choose to go to a party you said "no" to attend but call you before the police arrive and ask you to take her home. In order to reinforce telling the truth you must *initially* accept whatever your teenager tells you, no matter how intense you feel about the situation. Teenagers still need consequences for their negative behavior and poor choices but these are best dealt with *later*, after you have *first* rewarded the truth.

Later you can deal with the problem or issue presented by your teenager. If you get just as angry or upset when either your teenager tells you the truth or when he or she lies to you, what is the advantage for your teenager to be truthful? If you know you're going to get a hit on the head, why would you want to get hit sooner rather than later? Most young people will take their chances and wait to see what might happen, hoping they might be lucky and maybe get away with their mistake.

If you value and *reward* the truth, even if it proves painful, you will be well informed about your teenager. To not know what is happening puts you in the dark and distances you from your young person. For example when your teenager calls you from the house he or she did not have permission to be at, it is best to go fetch your young person, say thanks for being honest and take him or her home. You can say, "we will discuss this in the morning." Let your teenager know he made a good choice by calling you. And he also made a poor choice going to the house which was off limits. Let him or her know the consequence for going to the friend's house will be milder than if he or she had lied or had not told you.

During my adolescence a friend of mine gave his mother a pair of "roach clip" earrings. She really liked the long silver earrings and wore them often. One day some fellow noticed them and commented, "Hey, lady nice earrings." She thanked him and he commented about them being "roach clips". She said, "What do you mean?" He told her that roach clips were clips used for holding marijuana cigarettes. She was not aware she was wearing roach clips, compliments of her son. She went right home to have a few words with him about this embarrassing situation! She was angry her son allowed her to wear them, not telling her what they were. He had lied by allowing her to assume there was nothing unusual about them. She asked her son, "I understand these are roach clip earrings. Please explain this to me."

Deciding how to give consequences and reward the truth may takes some practice. For example, if your teenage daughter would call and tell you she went out at night when she was not allowed to. Let's say her ride home never shows up and she calls you to come get her. When you pick her up, tell her you are proud of her because she was brave enough to tell you the truth about what she did that was wrong. And tell her you will discuss her choice to go out without permission in the morning. Rewarding the truth does not mean you need to accept her behavior.

Now several consequences have already occurred. She called and you responded by offering her a way out. That was a good decision to call on parents to assist rather than risk more trouble. She found out that a consequence of acceptance occurred when she said what she did, that it is OK to tell you when she made a mistake. Her other consequence is your *timing*. She might stay up much of the night wondering what her negative consequences will be for her choice to go out when she was not allowed to.

Most teenagers prefer you get angry, fly off the handle and say what you don't mean, like, "You're grounded for a year." When you take your time this is not as likely to happen. Waiting means she had to *sweat* her behavior and *think about what she did*. That is exactly the experience we want to create for our teenagers. We want to encourage them to continue what they did that was *right* and discontinue what they did that was *wrong*.

A Lie is a Lie

Not hearing the truth from your teenager can make any parent feel disappointed. It can prove very embarrassing when you find the truth out later from *someone else*. Lying is a way many teenagers rebel. Some lie to avoid consequences of getting in trouble. Others do it for privacy and some teenagers do it for sport.

While grabbing the clothes for the wash one day, Barb picked up Becky's jeans and a pack of cigarettes fell out. Shocked, she confronted her fourteen year-old daughter immediately saying, "I can't believe you are smoking!"

Becky responded: "I am not."

Barb responded: "You are too; here is proof!"

Becky protested: "They aren't mine someone put them in my pocket."

Not believing her, Barb angrily demanded: "Who?"

Becky said: "I'm not going to tell you!"

What a dilemma for Barb. Maybe someone did give them to

Becky, it would be great if that was true because then Becky wouldn't be smoking. On the other hand, what if she is smoking and lying about it to cover it up? Barb needs to find a way to uncover the truth.

When you suspect your teenager is lying it is best to catch them in their lie. One way that works well is to predict when your teenager might engage in some problem behavior. Now for Barb's situation. With her Polaroid camera in hand, she could sneak up on her teenager, when she least expects it and shoot a picture with her daughter smoking a cigarette. Then she could ask her daughter to please come home. Even without cameras, just showing up will provide all the evidence you may need. Things you may have to catch your teenager doing might be swearing on the phone to friends, not being where he is she is expected to be, taking your clothes without asking or drinking.

One of the best consequences for lying is a handwritten essay, usually 500 words. The essay could be entitled <u>Why I should not lie to my parents</u> or <u>What is the truth about my smoking</u>. If you have repeated lying, it's good to add a chore card.

Choose Your Battles

If you pick the battles that are really important, you will win the war with adolescent rule breaking. You will need to let some of the little stuff go. The consequences should fit the behavior. It is a good idea to ask yourself before reacting to you teenager, "Is this a big deal or a little deal?" If your teenager is sporting a new hair color like chartreuse green you need to *stop* and think about it. Ask yourself, is this major rule breaking for you? You do not want to give out your biggest consequences for little annoyances. You need to wait to see if you'll need them for big annoyances.

Sometimes you have to reconcile that what your teenager does about his or her personal appearance may not be as big a deal as other things that are, such as breaking curfew, swearing at family members, lying, refusing to attend school, smoking, drinking, being late for school or being with unacceptable friends. Hairstyle or dress may be individual expression and an experiment in a new way to look. A smaller logical consequence for the green hair or an odd haircut or dress might be telling your daughter she cannot go out in public with the family until her hair is a more acceptable color or dress, etc. It is helpful to remember, if you find yourself overreacting to hairstyle or dress to just imagine that your teenager is in costume. When clothing is unacceptable, obscene or derogatory to others, it is reasonable for your teenager to change it.

If your teenager is getting your attention through annoying or teasing it is not appropriate to give him or her *big* consequences. Your teenager may never do anything that even requires a *big* consequence. The more serious the rule break the more serious the consequence. For instance, some of the *big* consequences would be going out into the community and doing tasks for others as well as a major labor job at home. When you are deciding if the problem is big or small, be sure not to do so when you are really angry or upset. You may dish out a consequence that is far too harsh for the infraction.

Deciding on Consequences

Consequences should not be the type that last too long. If your teenager applies himself he should be able to finish the task in 2 to 3 hours. On the other hand, consequences should not be too easy. If a chore card takes fifteen minutes it won't make much of an impression on your teenager. I see a number of teenagers that have no idea what it means to work hard. These kids complain that school is too hard, teachers are too tough and they cannot be expected to do much. This kind of laziness can be 'worked out' of a teenager with meaningful consequences.

When you give consequences, do so by being respectful to your teenager. With consequences you will no longer need to yell to express your anger or put your teenager down. Your respectfulness will help your teenager follow through. Allow the consequences to teach. When your teenager makes a mistake it is important to forgive them and allow them to make amends and be given a chance to try to do better in the future.

You might like the results of having your teenagers work hard. So much can be gained by hard work besides having a way to make amends. Doing hard work allows an opportunity for your teenager to do something positive. It is in the hard work that our teenagers learn not to do something again. They begin to recognize the only person that got them into this predicament was themselves. Taking on challenging tasks and a job well done are corner stones to high self-esteem. Work builds a sense of capability, independence and productivity. Teenagers are very capable. Anything most adults do for house and yard work, a teenager can do as well. Your teenager can vacuum and wax cars, wash windows, vacuum rooms, do dishes, paint, clean, sweep, build and rebuild. You and the family benefit as well by your young person sharing the household tasks.

THE MAJOR LEAGUE

The Big Rule Break

This story is about a serious situation that requires a serious intervention from parents. Fifteen-year-old Abby is having two of her friends over to spend the night. Mom and dad don't know these new friends very well. After a late night her parents go to sleep aware the girls are still up talking. In the wee hours of the morning, Abby and friends sneak out her bedroom window. When her mother gets up to check on the girls, she notices suspicious lumps in the bed and in the sleeping bags on the floor. When she checks closer, she finds the girls gone. It is 2:00 a.m.

As they planned, Abby and her party meet up with several guy friends around the block. When Abby returns at 4:00 a.m., as she tries to open her window, to her shock, her parents are waiting in her room to meet her.

The first thing her parents say is, "We are glad you are finally home. We have been worried sick. You know better than this." Abby hears her parents call the police to report the three teenagers are back home. Then her friends are told they have five minutes to call their parents (who have already been notified). If her friends decide not to call, Abby's parents will call even if her friends beg them not to tell their parents. Her friends nervously decide to phone their parents who come over to take them home.

The next morning Abby and her parents have a meeting. Abby is offered a chance to tell her story and given these consequences:

1. The Essay. 500 words. Title: Why it is not safe or wise to sneak out of the house in the night.

2. The Friends. Abby is not allowed to socialize with these two girls for the next three months. (Though she will see them in school, she is not allowed to go out with them outside school).

3. Chore Consequences: Clean the gutters. Wash the windows inside and out, if she sneaks out the window, she can wash them. (Major labor can take 12 to 20 hours).

4. Community Service. Mow the family lawn *and* choose a neighbor and mow their lawn two times, *without pay*.

5. Abby cannot come home after school alone for the next month. She must go to a friends home and help take care of the after school children, without pay.

6. A consequence she doesn't know about is that her parents have installed a window lock just in case this would ever happen again.

Abby is grounded until her essay and chores are done. She has to arrange to do the neighbors lawns. If she is done with her other tasks before the month is up she still will have the neighbor' s lawns.

Do you think if this was your teenager he or she would want to leave the house again without your permission? I think it would be highly unlikely. This meaningful 'experience', created by parents, may counter balance the teenager's initial experience. In a sense, you do not have to get mad, you have to get creative. You certainly do not need to tell your teenager ahead of time about the possible consequences. You can develop them from the chore menu at the time of the rule infraction. This way you can fit the consequences to the situation, their age, attitude of your teenager, even the weather. You can decide what is good, hard labor for the situation. If your teenager knows ahead of time what the consequences will be, they think it is worth the risk getting caught. Not knowing can be a deterrent, making them wonder what could happen to them.

Here are some more examples of possible consequences. You can mix and match according to what you think is best for your teenager from the menu below. When you find the right meaningful consequence you will definitely get your teenager's attention. The last section are major consequences that should only be used for major rule breaking.

MENU OF CONSEQUENCES

- Essay 500 - 1000 words
- Written and verbal apologies
- Repairing any broken item and restoring it

- Earning money for damages and paying it back
- Chore cards
- Reading a book on : alcoholism, drug addiction, fiction, non-fiction, etc.
- Time out
- Loss of phone for 1 day, 2 day, week, etc.
- Loss of TV time
- Repetition of the right thing to say
- Dishwashing
- Doing the wash
- Folding clothes (# of baskets of laundry)
- Losing 15 minutes of bedtime
- Vacuuming: living room, house, car
- Raking leaves
- Mowing lawn
- Pulling weeds
- Dog do removal
- Trimming the hedge
- Washing/ sweeping off the drive way
- No Television for one to two weeks
- Washing windows, outdoor or inside
- Dusting
- Loss of item they will not share
- Cleaning the refrigerator
- Cleaning the oven or stove
- Polishing the silver
- Brushing the dog
- Washing the dog
- Sweeping the garage, walkways, floor, etc.
- Making a family member's bed
- Cleaning any room
- Making meals

- Washing and waxing the car
- Cleaning cupboards
- Washing family bikes
- Mop floors
- Watering plants
- Watering the lawn
- Washing a floor
- Cleaning a bathroom, all bathrooms
- Hauling trash
- Dusting shelves
- Washing glassware
- Painting
- Sanding
- Building something
- Mending
- Assigned math, English, geography
- Making 3 to 5 meals for the family
- Cleaning the garage can
- Verbal apologies

MAJOR CONSEQUENCES

- Picking up bags of trash from the community
- Community service 10 - 20 hours of volunteer work, no payment at all
- Homeless shelters, Head Start, women's shelters, Low income family projects, elementary school, junior high schools, food   programs, senior centers, literacy programs, etc.
- Group Meeting with other teenagers involved with their parents
- Street/ sidewalk sweeping
- Helping neighbors with tasks (raking, yard work) with

out pay
- Losing mousse and hairdryer
- Losing favorite clothing for a month
- Losing driving permit, one month
- Losing the use of the car, one month
- Losing activities, sport, hobbies
- Letters of apology (25 words +)
- Building something for someone outside the family
- Painting for someone outside the family (like an elderly person's home)
- Mowing neighbors' lawns (without pay)
- Shoveling neighbor's snow (driveway and walks)

Catch Your Teenager Doing it Right

The best consequences are the positive ones. It is important to notice when your teenager is doing things the right way instead of just paying attention to when he or she is breaking the rules. When you catch your teenager doing things well say "great job!"

When you start creating meaningful consequences for your teenager it can really throw your young person for a loop. They may start begging you to just get mad and yell at them. They may plead with you to just hit them or ground them, anything instead of hard work they do not like!

When you are clear about your expectations with the rules and follow through with consequences you may find yourself much more in charge and less charged up.

CHAPTER FOUR

Help... My Teenager is Rebelling!

Rebellion is a time of turmoil. It is different than ordinary testing, more challenging than an ugly mood. Teenage rebellion is more extreme, with defiance that creates distance and separation from the family. The most precarious and rapid changes in your young person's personality development usually occur at the time of adolescent rebellion. A teenager's emotional instability shows most vividly during the time when a young person 'loosens' his or her personality at the same time he or she demands disconnection and independence. During this time sometimes loosening the personality can look like losing one's mind.

This time correlates with the 'terrible twos'. When your toddler becomes antagonistic, you know what you are dealing with requires more active parenting, establishing more limits and paying more attention. The difference with adolescent defiance is that the reaction is louder and bigger. It can also occur at any time in the six or seven adolescent years, sometimes more than once.

This is a time when dealing with your teenager is probably the most trying. 'The Rules' for teenagers in full rebellion:

1. Be invested in making sure you do not get along with your parents
2. DO NOT cooperate under any circumstances
3. Defeat any parental attempt to make you behave
4. Be as annoying as possible
5. Last (but not least); do whatever you want to do, when you want to do it.

The stormiest time between a parent and a teenager occurs when an adolescent is rebellious. Conflict comes with the anger, animosity and distance that is typical when a teenager defies his parents. As unpredictable as teenagers are, when a young person rebels, the extent of their defiance can range from mild confrontation to bold and blatant behavior.

Teenage rebellion is confusing for both teenagers and their parents. Many times whatever parents want, teenagers will do the opposite. As parents wish for peace, a teenager greets life with unsettled abandon and chaotic demands. Adolescents seem to delight in new oppositional behavior. Sometimes the behavior can be extreme, adamantly breaking your rules, testing all the limits, traumatizing you and others.

Usually a rebellious teenager decides on something that will shock you. Now that your son or daughter has figured out how to push your buttons, during this rebellion, your young person can find ways to light up your whole panel. In the unpredictable course of adolescence, how and when your teenager might rebel is an unknown.

Some teenagers rebel quietly. They are passively aggressive by non-compliance with your wishes or expectations. They simply do not do what you ask them to do. They may seem pleasant and accommodating but they passively avoid what is expected of them. When confronted they deny any aggressiveness or non-compliance.

Some teenagers are the sneaky type. They are savvy to what parents want to see and hear. So they 'appear' to be the perfect teenagers. Behind the scenes they are breaking their parents rules.

Other teenagers are more blatant in their rebellion. They are openly aggressiveness, clearly hostile and angry, saying hurtful things or deliberately acting out. They are usually direct in their confrontation and purposeful in their obnoxiousness.

How to calm the storm of teenage rebellion is a perplexing task for many parents. Sometimes everything you may have tried may seem like it is not working. Parents can try being nice and kind, or firm and businesslike. However, no matter what you do your teenager remains hostile.

It is difficult for parents to not take their teenager's rebellion personally. Many parents blame themselves and think that what is happening is "all my fault". Thinking if they had been better parents, this rebelliousness would not have occurred. It is not happening because you are the parent. Your teenager reacts to you because you are close to him or her and your young person trusts you. Rebellion is a test about growing up.

The unsettling confusion about self is at the heart of teenage rebellion. Rebellion is an adolescent's expression of confusion and becomes a way to create distance from family. The experience is more painful for parents than for teenagers. Rebellion is a time when a teenager is most impulsive and confused. The adolescent can be very irrational and naive about both him or herself and others.

To leave one's family is a painful process. There will be times your son or daughter finds it frightening to be alone. This fear propels the adolescent to migrate to his or her peer group. This association with other adolescents supports their need to individuate from one's family. This group too reinforces and encourages rebellion and distance from one's family. One girl complaining about how awful her mother is will find good company with girlfriends who feel the same way. It is here, within the peer group, a teenager strives to establish a new identity and develop support.

The period when an adolescent rebels may not coincide with the level of their maturity necessary to be independent of their parent's guidance. The dilemma for parents is to decide when their teenager is finally ready to distance himself (herself) from the family and is prepared to take on the responsibility for himself. A thirteen year-old may not be even close to being emotionally prepared to take on the responsibility of his or her own life and decisions, even though he or she will protest.

Is there something parents can know ahead of time in order to prevent this from happening? Unfortunately, because of the precariousness of the process of adolescent development there is no sure way to prevent rebellion from happening. There are, though, many things you can do to respond to the rebellious behavior of your son or daughter that can ease this time of transition.

Clueless

Teenagers are annoying to others when they are rebellious, particularly targeting their parents. Most are not aware of just how upsetting they can be to others. Adolescents can be so self absorbed they have a difficult time thinking about anyone else's feelings or concerns. You will notice that they can seem clueless when you tell them they have hurt other's feelings or they have done something annoying.

So when mom says to her daughter, "Jody, what you said to your father was rude. I can't believe you said it!" And she replies, "It was not! What are you talking about?" She seems unaware her snide remark and aggressive tone bothered anyone else. Focused on her needs, her mood and her opinion, Jody seems indifferent to how others feel. It doesn't really seem to matter right now.

Being clueless doesn't mean your teenager is blameless. Your young person has to be responsible for his or her behavior, even if what happened occurred because of his or her impulsiveness. So don't be too surprised when your teenager seem oblivious to how others are reacting to his or her antics.

Why do Teenagers Rebel?

In Search of Separateness

In order to be different, the immature young teenager just chooses the opposite of what you care about. If you are against drug use, he or she may give you a lecture about becoming a big supporter of legalizing marijuana and cocaine. Then your teenager seems satisfied with the response: a big reaction from you. When this happens, your teenager feels different and separate from you. By feeling separate, your young person has taken the first step toward becoming an independent young adult..

Creating Independence

Curious about their ability to take care of themselves, a teenager will feel a need to be distant and independent from their family, especially their parents. This distance is based on a lot of testing. A teenager tests while they feel secure. This is a test about being capable of making decisions for themselves. When your teenager is away from you does he or she have confidence in their own ability to be responsible for themselves? To create this new independence, anger and rebelliousness is part of this kind of testing.

In rebellion there is ambivalence, especially with the young teenager. Wishing for independence can be an emotional mix of feeling afraid of being alone on one's own and at the same time accompanied by the welcome challenge of deciding for oneself.

This distance from the family is not typically a permanent separation. A number of teenagers, ending their rebellion, settle down when they are more comfortable with themselves. Then they rejoin their parents and family.

Confusion

"So, what is the meaning of life? What is it all about? Who am I? What should I do?" ponders the teenager. An adolescent faces his or her fear with a mix of uncertainty and blind confidence. The world is confusing and yet at the same time, it is an intriguing place. The key to adolescent confusion is that most teenagers don't know they are confused. This kind of circular thinking is part of their confusion. To help mask the confusion when a young person is in the company of friends, having the same perplexing experience with life, seems quite normal. Other immature peers can provide both security and validation.

When a young person is confused he or she needs gentle guidance toward making good choices.

Curiosity

"What is it like to be on my own?" questions each teenager. Curiosity about the many intriguing things that lie ahead leads young people to venture away from the protectiveness and guidance of their parents. On their own they begin to explore experiences that test their abilities and take risks so they can experiment with new things or ideas. Some teenagers, less brave and bold, only explore by association with others, who are less cautious. Vicarious learning comes from observing other teenagers experimenting with things they are not willing to do. Greater risk takers will satisfy their curiosity by direct experimentation. It is like the case of the monkey and scientist. The scientist is not the monkey but learns about being a monkey by observing and interacting with him. This curiosity is part of what drives a teenager in search of self toward adulthood.

Testing the Rules and Limits

In order for a teenager to accept their family's values they need to ponder and experiment with the basic values and ideas they have learned. Many do so through direct experimentation. Many times the test is to try the exact opposite of what they have learned, questioning if it is right or valuable.

For example, your teenager may decide to test a family value, truthfulness. In your family, he or she may have learned that lying is wrong. If you lie, your life situation can get worse. The lie may come back to haunt you. People cannot trust you if you lie.

So the teenager decides to test this out, by lying. And for a while, if the teenager is not caught, he or she may rethink that what they learned about truthfulness is wrong. They got away with it and it is not big deal. Lying may create a feeling of autonomy and separateness.

Now when they are caught they find themselves in deep trouble. Their consequences may be losing the privilege to go out with friends on the weekend because they have the chore of painting the back fence. They have to really ponder the issue of lying in their fifty-word essay entitled, "Why I can't be trusted if I lie." Through these experiences the teenager learns something else; the consequences may not be worth the lie. They may also learn they felt guilty when they were caught in the lie, especially when one lie led to another to cover the first fib. In time, with experimentation, the teenager may decide that lying is not the best choice for them.

Testing family rules and limits does not mean something is wrong with the family rules or values. They test to experience limits, even when the rules are liberal. No matter where parents draw the line, a teenager's choice and challenge during rebellion is to step over that line.

To what extent your young adult will test rules is a great unknown. Your response to their choices about testing can create limits on how much they do actually test and rebel.

In Search of Yourself

Part of the rebellious experience, creating distance, is a teenager saying I am different from my family members. Sometimes radically different. The teenager thinks, "I cannot be like anyone else. I must be 'me'." So rebellion is an attempt to separate from everyone in the family. The goal is to somehow be so unusual or different that they become recognized for their individuality, even if it is negative.

Be assured, however, by the time your young person matures as an adult he or she will typically espouse many of the values important to you.

Expression of Anger

Being angry is a way to break away and distance oneself from others. For some teenagers they are very clear about what they are angry about. It may be how they perceive they are treated. Or how much respect they experience with their parents. Another complaint is how little their parents trust them. Sometimes the anger is about how they hate rules or expectations. Others get mad because they want to be in charge.

The combination of hormones, being impulsive and strong encouragement from peers can really fuel irrational and generalized anger in a teenager. This anger occurs when your young person does not know why he or she is angry. There seems to be no reason as a basis for their angry and sometimes aggressive responses. Being angry is just an overwhelming feeling.

Adolescent anger can sometimes be contagious. One teenager's hostility seems to trigger an angry response in another sympathetic teenage friend. It can rub off on you and you too may find yourself defensive and irritated by the seemingly unnecessary conflict. And it is understandable to be puzzled how to calm the storm of rebelliousness. When you are mad at your teenager, he or she feels more independent of you and the family.

The longer issues go unresolved the more intense the anger

and power struggle can become. The support of a peer group encouraging your teenager to stay angry may encourage a teenager's rebellion. It also strengthens their common bond of being angry together.

Negative Attention

Sometimes negative attention can be habit forming. A teenager initially may think others don't like him, a teacher, group of kids or a parent. Then he acts badly because his feelings are hurt. Others respond to his behavior in a negative way to make his belief become a self-fulfilling prophecy.

If a teenager does not feel validated, significant and productive they can try to get some negative recognition by becoming a rule breaker. Even though the reaction from others is negative, at least others pay attention to them. It is better than not being recognized at all.

With defiant behavior at school, a teenager may find they have created labels for themselves with teachers and administrators. Other teenagers' primary aim with their rule breaking is getting attention from their parents. Some teenagers go as far as getting the attention from non-family members by confronting teachers, administrators, police officers or store security guards. Some end up in juvenile confinement if their rebellious behavior becomes chronic.

Some teenagers seek negative reactions which give them a sense of power and autonomy, especially with their parents.

In Search of Love

Adolescents who believe they have found a true love can muster all kinds of feelings of independence. They will, on occasion, distance when they have someone new to love them and take care of them. This experience can lead them to believe they no longer need their parents or family.

This kind of separation usually lasts about as long as the relationship. If being in love does not last they then usually calm down and want to return to the warmth of the family.

Everybody is Doing it

Well, if everybody is needing to rebel this week, why not join in? This may be part of the adolescent's logic about rebellious behavior. Your teenager may not want to miss this experience.

Getting caught up with the crowd and being more of a follower than a leader can create rebelliousness through association.

Driven by curiosity some young teenagers just want to be a part of what everybody is doing. Many teenagers believe they have to follow the fearless leaders. This is especially true of the young teenager who impulsively jumps right in and test things out, only to think about the consequences when they happen.

Alcohol and Drugs

A symbol of adulthood for many young people is to drink or smoke. A way to rebel and feel like an adult is to use alcohol and drugs. Though some young people are attracted to these symbols of adulthood and independence, smoking and drinking can be detrimental to their emotional and physical health.

Sometimes when a teenager becomes caught in the trap of using alcohol or drugs it creates a false sense of security for himself. To continue the habit he may feel he has to distance from parents and family in order to maintain their use. While he associates with other people that are into alcohol and drugs, he also becomes an isolate .

Use of alcohol and drugs can create serious problems for adolescents. Chapter 9 covers what you can do if your teenager is using alcohol or drugs.

What to Expect

Expect the opposite. If you treasure quiet, you may hear blaring music and loud shrieks. If you love healthy food, get ready for demands for junk food or a boycott against anything green. If manners are important be prepared for belching, slurping, passing gas and swearing. When the truth is important your teenager may experiment with lying or leaving out part of the truth. Conservative parents may see creative dress or hairstyles that test your taste. If your family values peace and harmony be prepared for demands, debates and arguing.

Rebellion against what parents stand for does not mean you need to change your values. The opposite opinion or value is sometimes the easiest thing for a rebellious teenager to express.

Hate is a common presentation. You may hear your teenager say he or she passionately hates you, the family, all his teachers, everybody and everything. This hate is sometimes noted just by a look in their eyes or the way they might posture. You might see clenched fists, a stiff body posture and a spitfire look that seems to say, "I am in charge, no one can control me."

Do no take this behavior personally. Usually what the teenager does hate are the limits, expectations and your concern about their welfare. Not you. Your teenager needs you to love him or her. Adolescents rebel against convention and the loving connection with their family as a way of becoming independent. If you get too upset with the words, "I hate you," it allows your teenager to overpower you with their immature words. Accept their anger. Don't bank on their words.

Ignoring you and the family is another common characteristic. It is easy for the teenager who strives to be distant and separate to appear to disregard membership in his family. A feeling of independence comes from distancing from the family, refusing to participate with traditions or go on outings.

Fighting is quite common. Arguing can surface about seemingly ridiculous, insignificant things that your headstrong teenager seems to invite. These clashes can seem like small emotional explosions that occur out of the blue. In the commotion the two of you may be faced with a struggle for power. The underlying question; "Who is going to be in charge of the teenager?" A power struggle with you can be exciting for your teenager and be a big headache for you. Your teenager now thinks he or she is ready to be in charge. You may be not convinced they have enough maturity to be in this position.

Outbursts can occur at any time, usually when you least expect it. Some adolescents are verbally abusive, yelling, screaming or demeaning with their demands. Enraged with the pressures of rebellion, a teenager's physical acting out can range from stair stomping and fist clenching to breaking something. Some like to kick a door or wall. On a more serious side, if a teenager is outraged enough he or she may physically threaten or abuse others in the family. Such behaviors require professional help.

You may notice that your teenager seems much more comfortable with the commotion he creates than you are.

Rule breaking can take all forms. Refusal to comply can happen with family, school and community. Breaking rules at school may result in suspension or failing grades. Disobeying family rules by becomes an opportunity to get your attention. And your teenager is likely to try to get away with breaking a rule. They are not likely to tell you about it.

When you are confronted with the rule breaking of your teenager you need to respond with some kind of consequence. If you choose to let it go and not respond, your teenager is likely to break more rules to get your attention. When a teenager is confronted with consequences for what they have done, they begin to receive the message they should stop.

Rebellion: When and How

Children in the same family rebel at different times and in different ways. Some rebel at home and others wait until they leave home. If they rebel at home, you will have to confront their behavior. Knowing this could happen, you will not be surprised if your teenager rebels several different times during adolescence. Teenagers who rebel against parents do so, in part, because they feel safe and secure enough to express their defiance.

What can Parents Do ?

There is nothing you can do to prevent your teenager from rebelling. Rebellion is a normal part of adolescence. There are a number of ways you can respond to your teenager's rebellious behavior.

It Takes Two to Fight

If your teenager can elicit an equally angry response from you so that you engage in a fight with your adolescent, he may feel empowered. If you in turn scream at your teenagers they have managed to bring you down to "their level". If this occurs they seems to smile as if to say "Gottcha".

If you don't want to fight, just listen. Sounds easy but it is hard to do. When you let your rebellious teenager talk, you may learn more about what is troubling him. You should insist as the ground rule that your young person cannot swear or yell. Another strategy is to walk away. You will leave your teenager yelling at the refrigerator.

If your young person is getting too angry, too irrational or aggressive you need to use a time delay to wait until he or she cools down. You can use solutions to reduce that angry response such as getting them to walk with you or delay the time when your young person can respond.

Some parents think that by listening to absurd ideas from

their teenager it means that they may change their limits or expectations. Instead, it means you will listen and take your teenager seriously. In fact, just by listening, you may find that your teenager is not very serious about his or her position.

You may find your teenager is presenting a valid point. Then you may be able to find some solutions that resolve the angry issues. Sometimes giving your young person a chance to do something, with the promise of good choices and behavior can prove a great challenge to your adolescent.

If you do not hear mature, rational and realistic requests from you teenager, you will need to accept that you teenager is just angry with you for setting limits. You must set limits and establish rules you believe are in the best interests of your son or daughter. And at times you may have to say it is OK your young person is unhappy.

Rebellious teenagers may never be happy with any limits. They may become angry because of homework or chores. The car you drive is irritating. They even get upset because they have to go to school. Simple things like spaghetti for dinner can set them off. This kind of anger may not seem logical to you. Even though, at the moment, it makes perfect sense to your teenager, at least for the hour. Within the next hour, things may change.

Don't Fuel the Fire

Any teenager that is angry has to feel discouraged in some way. They may want their way and do not know how to get it. They may feel their parents do not give them enough attention, trust, confidence, love or even like them.

Sometimes teenagers become discouraged because they are not all grown up and cannot pass the hassles of adolescence. They feel they are stuck still being a kid. They may feel they have the only parents in town who set limits for their teenagers.

Your teenager's perception is paramount to your understanding of what is going on. His or her view may not seem logical or rational to you in any way. What does not work, especially with a rebelling teenager, is a debate about perceptions. This is what usually fuels the fire of anger. This typically occurs when a parent tells his young person that his or her opinion is wrong. With statements like, "What you are saying is not true." Such comments can create an explosion of anger that is fueled by the debate about your teenager being wrong.

Being calm is critical. You can show your teenagers by your presence and example, what you want from them. Listen and try to hear their feelings and understand their new ideas. And listen without a need to change anything. Just let the feelings and ideas be.

Remember how your teenager learns is through experience not lecture. Just set limits and give consequences until some kind of change in rebellious behavior occurs.

What to do When Your Teenager is "Mean"

When a teenager, or anyone for that matter, spouts off to others with mean, cruel or vulgar comments, he or she is out of line. No person deserves to be treated this way. You can allow your young person to have his (or her) feelings and still limit his offensive language. You can use this statement: "You can say you are angry but you cannot be mean." Some suggestions for things you can say to your teenager:

• "You may say you don't like my dinner but you cannot use that name you called me."

• "You may say you're mad at your teacher but you cannot call him vulgar names."

• "It is OK to be mad at your brother but you cannot hurt him with your words or your fists."

• "I understand you are angry. Say what you are angry about but you cannot be mean to me. I do not appreciate hearing you hate me. I do love you and I (we) will do what I think is best for you."

The goal here is to tackle the behavior, not the anger and rebellion. The rebellion is a process that needs to run its course. Anger is a normal reaction based on feelings and perceptions.

Big or Little Deal

MINOR RULE BREAK   **MAJOR RULE BREAK**

(let some stuff go)   (Big consequences)

* school   * drug/alcohol

* peers	* sexual promiscuity
* friends	* breaking the law
* dress	* chronic rebellion
* language	* school suspension or expulsion
* "self"	* suicidal gestures
* silly gags	* cruel or violent behavior

Knowing the difference between a big deal and a little deal can prove helpful, especially during a period of rebellion. You can overlook little things, like green hair, hideous clothing or hostile attitudes. If your teenager persistently annoys you with too much of the annoying little stuff, it is time for you to respond and set some limits. Just letting your teenager know you are unhappy with their choice is sometimes enough to satisfy their need to rebel.

Look around at other teenagers and decide if what they are doing is a big deal or little deal to you.

During adolescent rebellion sometimes things never seem to really settle down. One emotional eruption follows closely after another. And sometimes the smoke never seems to clear. It may not be just one small thing but many small complaints and criticisms that accumulate to create a general annoyance. Many times the rebelling teenager is going to be unhappy with whatever you do, so be true to yourself and your values.

So you will have to set minimal consequences with the little stuff. This lets them know they have crossed a line of your approval. Doing these small things to annoy you can satisfy them in their attempts to rebel. When enough little things get your attention or some medium things occur and you react, sometimes you can head off the possibilities of the big things happening.

Big deals require *BIG CONSEQUENCES*. Serious behaviors include violence, breaking the law or sneaking out. This is when you have to step in and give them an eye opening experience to help them learn you are serious about your limits. These issues present serious safety concerns for your teenager.

Rebellion Styles

There are four basic rebellion styles. Your teenager may use all of them.

The first type, the most obvious rebelliousness, is the **Bla-**

tant- **Angry Teenager**. These young people are usually 'hot tempered'. They get mad easily and immediately become verbal about being angry. They don't keep their issues or feelings hidden in any way. These young people may be generally mad at everyone and everything. Even the family dog may be cautious about being in the same room with your young person. Parents may have difficulty calming down these teenagers because they tend to react emotionally and can easily misinterpret what is going on.

Frank is the kind of boy all the ninth graders have pegged as hostile. When he was angry at a teacher, especially with Mrs. Allen, instead of keeping it to himself, he blows up in class, calls her names like "Stupid" and then is suspended from class for a day or two. Right now a lot of classmates steer clear of him. He wears black and usually has negative things to say about everything. He talks about stealing a car and moving away on his own. At home he is verbally abusive to his parents, swears in front of the family as well as relatives and visitors. When his parents ask him to stop, he says, "No one can make me do anything." He says he doesn't care what anybody thinks; "If they don't like me they can. . . "

The second type is the **Direct Teenager**. These teenagers are not as hot tempered as the Blatant-Angry Teenager but they are vocal about what they like and don't like and what they want their parents to do. They will directly defy parents, openly doing the opposite of what is asked or expected. They tend to be very honest and open about what they are doing. You may hear a statement like, "I am going to do_____ and you can't stop me" or "Make me." They demand independence and autonomy even though they may not be old enough or mature enough.

Sheri is fifteen and hangs out with a mix of kids at school. A number of them are well known for using drugs and all are smoking. Though she is not allowed to smoke by her parents, she smokes off school grounds. Her grades have been slipping and she is doing very little homework. She has changed her hair color to dark purple and now wears strange dark clothing. She thinks school is a waste of time. With her friends, her main complaint is about her mother who she refers to with swear words.

At home she spends most of her time in her room on the phone. She announces frequently she hates being with her family. Usually when her mother tries to talk to her, she yells at her and tells her to get out of her life. When asked to join in family activities, she refuses and threatens to run away. Her biggest complaint is that her mother won't let her go to her friend's houses for the weekend.

The third type is the **Sneaky Teenager**, who appears to be saying and doing all the right things but who is breaking your rules behind your back. Adept at covert behavior, these teenagers are able to cover their rule breaking behavior well by lying or avoiding talking about it. The sneaky teenager is able to convince parents he or she is a 'perfect teenager' and behind the parent's back he or she will swear, steal, drink, use drugs, go places he is not allowed to visit and may even sneak out. Usually avoidance, lying or manipulating is part of his deception. Parents are typically shocked when they find out what their teenager has been doing behind their backs.

Daniel, sixteen, a member of a high school student council told me about his sneaky, rebellious behavior. He was clean cut, wearing his letter jacket and looked like a handsome 'All American' fellow. One year he was involved in assisting in a schoolwide Drug Free week of programs. He thought he was doing a cool thing by getting high and then talking on the intercom about not using drugs! As part of his 'fun' he spent the majority of that week smoking marijuana.

The fourth type is the **Passive-Aggressive Teenager**. This teenager tends to be quiet and reserved around the family. Friends at school may know what this young person is angry about but parents usually are not aware. At home this teenager passively avoids tasks to antagonize his or her parents. These teenagers won't answer questions, stall doing homework or chores. They appear to be cooperative but basically don't follow through or leave things in such a manner as to anger his parents. They tend to be reclusive and parents do not know their friends or some of their activities.

At school Katie's teachers are frustrated with her. She used to do well in seventh grade but in eighth she is failing several of her classes. She won't turn in work, seems to do little or nothing in class, doesn't appear to study for tests. When asked by her teachers, she shrugs and won't answer their questions. At home her parents cannot get her to do her work or if she does it, she only occasionally will turn it in. Her parents cannot get her to talk. She does not seem very interested in doing much besides watching TV and gabbing with a few friends on the phone. When they ask her to do something, she will agree but she won't follow through. When her parents become angry she seems passive and able to ignore them.

Pick Your Speed Limit

If a driver has a hard time keeping the car at the posted 60 mph and continues to get speeding tickets, do you think the driver is ready to drive 80 mph? Think about your teenager the same way. If your thirteen year-old cannot make it home at 10:30 p.m., is she ready for midnight? You want to see if you can post a reasonable speed limit and your young driver can respect your limit. When your teenager is able to do so you will see consistent and responsible behavior. Your teenager will actually go where she says she will.

Hand out speeding tickets when you catch your teenager speeding, not when there is a rumor they are driving 90 mph. So you'll have to set up speed traps and use your radar. Then you can hand out consequences and confiscate licenses.

Allow for Radical Opinions, not Behaviors

Once you've been informed that certain views are lame, stupid, bad and dumb (old words that now have new meanings), it is critical you allow your young person to express radical opinions. Teenagers who persist in extreme or radical ideas may become more convinced they need to act on their notions. If they do you now have a problem. When negative ideas persist too long, without change, in many cases, unacceptable radical behavior will follow. Applying consequences helps your teenager understand, that you will *not* allow radical behaviors.

Jeanie is fifteen, small, quiet and a little over weight. She seems determined to wear 'grunge' attire to school, big worn T-shirts with death symbols, baggy old jeans that trail on the ground. Her hair looks snarled and appears like it has not been washed or combed for days. Her make-up is dark, to match her mood. Last week, without permission, she dyed her hair black. For the last few months she has become increasingly more hostile toward her parents. She is very secretive, refuses to introduce her friends to her mother and father and sneaks out in the evening without permission. The school counselor has called several times, worried about the possibility that Jeanie could be getting involved with gang activities.

These parents became so worried they found professional counseling so that they could help their daughter untangled herself from the gang members from whom she was getting attention. Finally to break the grip hold the gang had on her Jeanie left the state to live with her grandparents.

What Teenagers Need

Rebels at Home

It is important to allow your teenager to feel independent and autonomous. If you can stand back and provide responses to their choices from a loving distance, your young person will be able to enjoy solo experiences and also know you care. If you stay at a distance your teenager feels free to learn and also to make mistakes.

After tasting her cherry pie Aaron told his mother the only way to make good pie is to start from scratch. Margaret took offense and started to lecture Aaron why pre-made crusts produced good pies. Aaron started to argue. Then Margaret stopped, "OK, Aaron, why don't you show me?" Her thirteen year-old son, who rarely cooks, gladly agreed. He told her he could do it himself if she would leave him alone. Over the next hour she occasionally peeked into the kitchen to see a huge mess of flour, pots and pans as her determined son was cooking away. She asked how it was going and he said 'great'.

Two hours later when Margaret entered the kitchen to her surprise Aaron was just getting his 'pie' out of the oven. It was a creative jumble of crust pieces and pink goo. The kitchen smelled like smoke from the pie juice that caught on fire in the oven. Aaron thought his pie experiment was a failure. When Margaret tasted it, she raved. It was delicious. Aaron smiled and was proud of his independent experience and he learned a new lesson not all things are 'as easy as pie'.

So when your teenager critiques how the wash is not done correctly, your dinners are lousy or you take too long to get ready, put your young person to the challenge to prove you wrong. Let him discover 'pink' white clothes from the washer and the challenge of making a tasty dinner or have a race with a timer to complete a list of things he must do before leaving for school. These are examples of great learning experiences.

You can tackle their rebellious behavior with consequences that teach. Not all lessons apply for experiential learning. If your teenager thinks using drugs is OK, it would not be a wise to allow him to experiment with illegal drugs. When it is safe, let them learn from their own mistakes.

Managing Anger

When you are faced with an upset porcupine it is wise to step back and keep your distance. The same rules apply to hostile, rebellious teenagers. The best thing to do is to give them plenty of space and time to settle down. Some need to have time for those hormone levels to lower, to get enough sleep or to refuel with food. Look for opportunities when your teenager is calmer to engage in conversation.

Though it doesn't feel good, remember your teenager may need to aim his or her anger at someone. And your young person needs a target usually you. If your limits allow your teenager to grow up more slowly than others, they will feel safe and more secure, even though they continue to be angry.

Let Consequences Teach

Remember it is OK to take your time deciding about consequences. Your teenager should be able to do them on his own and should not require much, if any effort on your part. For example, you may not want your teenager to paint the front door. It could become an imposition to those who need to use it. Such chores only complicate matters. Consequences will depend on your son or daughter's age and ability.

Negotiating a consequence because your teenager doesn't like it and he or she want to trade it for something dilutes your parenting decision. Other things are open for negotiation, not consequences for infractions.

During the time your teenager is grounded as a result of choices he or she has made, you need to let the impact of your decisions have a chance to settle. When your teenager blames you for his or her consequences, a few words will suffice, such as, "I did not make the choice about going to the party you did." If your teenager thinks you gave the 'wrong' consequences or ones that are 'not fair', it is worth considering his or her view. If you think your young person is protesting because the consequences are effective and appropriate, it is best not to change your ruling and let the lesson be learned. You can always modify the kind of consequences you give next time.

Who's Problem is This?

Adolescents can be very inconsistent. On one hand they insist on complete responsibility for themselves and yet when faced with a messy problem run to you for help. Pause and ask yourself before you rescue your teenager, "Who's problem is this?" Part of growing up well is to take on all the problems that belong to you, not just the ones you prefer to deal with. So if your teenager has upset a friend of yours, is it your problem and do you need to apologize? If your teenager is failing in school, who's grades are they? When your teenager insults a friend, who owns the problem? These problems belong to your teenager. Your young person may choose to break one rule after another. You may find your teenager has started to smoke, skip school and swear. To top it off, they erupt like a little volcano and blow their stack whenever you are around. When you see a pretty big change from what you are used to it means it is time to keep your teenager at home. What usually happens is they keep getting more consequences and in the end ground themselves for a long period of time. This may be your teenager's way of showing you he needs a break from the peer group that might be influencing him.

Give Them Some Rope... Make a Lasso

When your teenager has graduated from grounding and returned to the everyday routine, it is important to give her another chance to show you she is more responsible. Your young person must be give the opportunity to return your trust. During rebellious times it is easy for parents to feel hopeless, thinking you will never be able to trust your teenager to be responsible again. When you give them another chance by giving them some rope, your teenager may break the rules again, only if she has yet to become mature. Then you lasso your teen back in and wait a bit longer. Your teenager will eventually realize things are better when he or she follows the rules and more of a hassle when your son or daughter does not. They will then be more serious about doing a good job following parent's rules and to your delight, you will see more mature behavior.

More Love, More Distance, More Patience

It is not uncommon to hear from parents their teenagers may ask for more than they seem to be able to give. Tired parents, under the siege of adolescent rebellion, may find it difficult to muster more love when your teenager is being so difficult. It is down right baffling to discover just how your teenager needs you to be distant and yet close when they really need you. In the midst of broken rules it is hard not to lose one's patience. In spite of these impossible requests, it is similar to the vows, "for better for worse, for richer for poorer, in sickness and in health." The real test of your love as a parent occurs when times are toughest. In this confusing time, your teenager is likely to feel lost and when this happens he or she will need you.

Your silent love can be your teenager's main support. He or she is secure knowing parent's love and respect remain intact. With confidence, you stand and wait for your young person to come around.

WHAT PARENTS NEED

Pick your Battles

When your teenager taunts you, be sure to take your time and think about what is happening. If it is the fourth time this morning you have gotten a sarcastic answer and your young person seems to be begging for a fight, decide if you are ready to take on this battle. Some days you will feel exhausted from the kind of demands and antagonism spilling from your young person. This may be the best time to take a walk, head out the door to the grocery for ice cream or spend some time alone in your garden.

You can't avoid all the battles. Just pick the ones you are sure are significant problems. The rest of the time ignore the smaller annoyances.

Team Up

It can be very helpful to an exhausted parent to have another parent help make decisions and respond to rebellious behavior. In a number of families, fathers don't take as active a parenting role as mothers. During adolescence a young person needs both parents to be involved. This is a time when fathers should realize the important role they play in parenting.

Even for the single parent, there may be an opportunity to find another adult to assist with ideas and support. Some parents find support in a group of parents. Just having a phone buddy can really help a single parent slow things down and give that parent a chance to talk about options and consequences with someone supportive. A team is much harder to manipulate than one overwhelmed and frustrated parent.

You Will not be Popular

Not feeling popular can really seem like an understatement when your teenager lashes out in fury. It is good to remember this kind of behavior is not going to be permanent. Many teenagers eventually say they are sorry for their poor behavior. Actually by not engaging with them when they are so rebellious and angry, allows them to begin to hear how mean and hostile they actually sound. When you do engage in fighting, your young person will just hear you yelling, and calling names, no longer hearing themselves. The teenager usually believes they are simply following your example.

To balance feeling so unpopular, seek out your spouse, friends or family who really like you. Spend time with them so you can get rejuvenated. Look forward to the day you hope your young person will end his or her rebellious time and move on to positive things.

Be Steady, Steadfast and Resilient

Does this sound like we're talking about a workout at the gym or on a steel beam? If you are steady when your teenager waivers, then only one of you is wavering: your teenager. It is less chaotic and confusing when parents are steadfast and stay firm about their beliefs and values. If you make too many changes in response to your rebelling teenager, then you too become unpredictable. Your maturity and steadfast concerns help with the kind of responses that can settle a chaotic teenager. Being resilient means your teenager can test you and you will stick with your beliefs. There is comfort for them to know their anger is not going to wear you down and force you to change.

Getting Professional Help

Some teenagers make immature choices that get them into deep trouble. For some young people the choices they make can put their life and safety at risk. Drugs and alcohol addiction means a teenager will miss a good deal of growing up and put their emotional and physical health at risk. Others get mad and think running away is a solution. Just look on your milk carton and you'll know the dangers of that choice. Some young people allow other people to take advantage of their vulnerabilities. Be alert to these kind of possible situations. It usually takes a hunch on the part of a parent to detect these kind of problems early. When serious problems surface, you may need to get professional help to get your teenager back on track.

Light at the End of the Tunnel

Rebellion will someday end. When it subsides, don't be totally convinced it is over for it may resurface again at a later date. But there will come a day when it really is over. Your teenager will seem to be resettled as an mature adult version of the child you used to know. And you may find yourself very happy and proud of your young adult.

Throughout your teenager's adolescence compliment them when they are doing well. More positives than negatives are always a helpful balance. And when you do not see any positives, offer your love and concern. Even if you are ignored, your concern can melt a seemingly cold and angry heart.

There is light at the end of the teenage tunnel. Look beyond yourself. Find others that have passed the test. Even in the most difficult times there is much joy to be found and great strength to be gained.

CHAPTER FIVE

HOW DO I TAP MY TEENAGER'S POTENTIAL?

TALENTED TEENAGERS...
Tap their energy
Tap their excitement
Tap their insight
Tap their interest
Tap their creativity
Tap their efforts
Tap their work
Tap their youth
Tap their humor
Tap their excellence
Tap their beauty
Tap their talent
Tap their caring
Tap their kindness
And tap their love!

Parents have the greatest capacity to offer the gifts of optimism and strong self-esteem to their children. Your words can give your teenagers great confidence in themselves. You have their hearts in your hands. Treat them kindly and gently. Guide them to understand they should be proud of who they are, not only for what they do or what they achieve. Encourage the potential that lies within.

Being optimistic may be the most critical factor in determining how successful and happy we are in life. Optimism is a belief about being valuable, respected, accepted, being liked and loved. Optimists believe they do indeed make a difference in the world.

One of the most important responsibilities you have as a parent is to help your adolescent develop positive attitudes about him or herself for a foundation of self-esteem that can last them a lifetime. Self-esteem changes as we do. We develop it through feedback from others, the world around us and from our efforts and behaviors. Young people need both verbal and non-verbal affirmations renewed daily to be emotionally healthy.

Self-concept is the identity each person forms about himself or herself. It is based in your beliefs about yourself, your abilities, characteristics, traits, appearance and personality. Adolescents are in the process of developing their adult self-concept. Self-esteem is how one feels about their self-concept. Self-esteem influences self-confidence. Optimism is a positive look at self, problems are temporary, self-worth is permanent.

A great deal of human potential is underutilized, ignored, discounted and wasted every day. There is so much more each of us has the potential to produce and become. Many people have spent their lives doing things that they never critically evaluated. They don't ask questions like, "Am I using my talents and potential?" "Am I doing what is important and meaningful?" Looking back at their lives many adults come to the realization that they spent so little time on the things that really mattered. They do not have a sense of accomplishment or success. What they have done in life was not enough, not important enough, or they have talents that were underutilized or never used.

At the end of one's life how sad it is to have regrets about what you did with your life, wishing to have accomplished more, loved more, spent more time with loved ones. We do not want these regrets; not for us, for our children or for the people we love. Really, not for anyone.

There are a number of people that have bought into the notion that they were meant to be failures. They have come to believe they are not as good or as capable as others around them. They see themselves as second-class citizens. A negative notion, often repeated or reinforced, becomes a belief. That belief in turn becomes part of a person's personality. On that belief the person then produces a reality of being emotionally and potentially stifled.

Since developing self-esteem and optimism in your teenager begins with you, I would like to start by offering you a rocking chair. Imagine right now you are 83 years old. There you are, looking good for 83, on your porch, somewhere in America. Look around you , listen to the sounds, smell the air and see the sights. As you get comfortable, rocking back and forth, swaying in the breeze, take a deep breath and begin to look back at your life. What stands out about your accomplishments? What were the

highlights that brings a smile to your face? What were your relationships like with the people you love? What is most important?

Now, still in your rocking chair, see yourself today. Looking
back, here you are, this day, in plain view. As you rock in that
chair, let's say you feel peaceful and have few regrets about your
life. You are happy and content. What must you accomplish this
very day so that at 83 you have no hesitation to say you had a
great life and you are pleased at all you accomplished?

Most of us look at life for the moment. We live day to day. Or
we spend a lot of time looking back and wishing we were younger
or lamenting we could have done more. Few of us project far into
our futures, getting a view of the big picture of our lives, like this
rocking chair exercise. If you do this kind of projecting into your
future often enough, I think you'll do more important and better
things in your lifetime. To have few regrets means for most of us
we need to do our personal best every day we live. What a world
we could live in if everyone was doing their personal best, with
their children, with their families, with their belief in God, in
their personal relationships and their jobs, everyday.

This parental rocking chair exercise has an equivalent for your
teenager. We want our children and teenagers to look ahead to
the chair in order to be prepared for their future years, knowing
the choices and decisions they are making today will have an
impact on their futures. So as we encourage our teenagers to look
farther ahead into their future, we say things like, "You've got to
think about college or how this will affect getting a job." This
look ahead can also work for us parents as well. For a teenager,
the idea of thinking of college while they are in high school, takes
courage. Looking ahead can be a scary proposition. When your
teenager is in junior high or middle school, thinking ahead to
high school may seem monumental. When we look ahead on the
road of our lives, we face ourselves, our potential and our fears.

Young people, who are courageous and confident, find success by projecting themselves into their futures. Doing so makes
daily decisions easier and they are more confident about their
direction in life. Just as you might be fearful of facing your own
rocking chair at eighty three, your teenager is also likely to be
fearful of all the possibilities that lie ahead. Facing these fears
and concerns together can be helpful to a teenager. If you cannot
be introspective yourself, your teenager is not likely to do it for
him or herself. This projection does much for a person seeking to

find excellence in living.

Everyone is a potential winner. Most of us are given the chance to live a life of excellence. It can be hard for parents to see past their teenager's attitude or behavior and recognize these young winners. Sometimes parents are just too worried about their offspring to see their young person's potential.

Adolescence is one of the most welcome times to tap your young person's potential. Teenagers are open and impressionable as they move toward adulthood. Sometimes your young person is in pain, sometimes in costume, at times the most delightful and entertaining person you have ever known him to be. Teenagers can almost always use a boost in their self-esteem (parents can use boosts too). Your encouragement and the inspiration you provide for your young person is the key that unlocks their personal potential and success.

All of this encouragement your adolescent needs takes real love. Really loving a person is not based on what someone does or does not do. It is rooted in loving your child for their basic essence and being, no matter what or how he or she chooses to be for today. Your love for the person does not change or waiver. What your teenager chooses may or may not be compatible with your expectations or wishes. In spite of their choices and behavior, real loving and liking them does not change. Love never gives up or caves in. Love endures. This kind of parental love and concern is basic to building self-esteem in children and teenagers.

It is basic to your young person's self-esteem to not give up on the notion your son or daughter will be successful. Teenagers need someone to inspire their dreams. They need your courage and confidence to begin to try. And to keep persisting when they want to quit. People who accomplish the most are those that dream the most. It takes a dream or a vision to start anything. To give your teenager a chance at success you must inspire their dreams, entice them to try and invite them to become all they aspire to.

Expect the Best

What you expect of your teenager, over time, is usually what you will eventually get. If you believe your son or daughter has talent and the potential to be successful, your child has a very good chance of attaining their goals. If you question the abilities of your teenager, lose faith that he or she will be successful, your son or daughter is likely to doubt their own abilities and strive for less than their best. Many parents of teenagers want to stay confident about their teenager's ability but are not always sure how to do so.

Self-esteem

Self-esteem is based on how we feel about ourselves. If a person has high self-esteem they have a belief about themselves that they are capable, confident, valuable and are content with who they are as a person. When someone feels good about themselves they usually behave in ways and make choices that continue to enhance their positive feelings about themselves. All of this has a lot to do with our efforts to be successful.

Low self-esteem is depicted by negative, angry or complaining comments. These people seem dissatisfied with others, themselves and the world around them. They approach situations with little confidence, fears, worries and have a self-defeating belief they are not important, valuable or capable. A person with low self-esteem has a poor opinion of himself and lacks confidence to change that perception. These people are pessimistic about themselves as well as life. Those with low self-esteem can get caught in a series of poor choices so negative feelings about themselves are validated by their mediocre outcomes.

Self-esteem in teenagers, like their development, is usually in flux. How a teenager feels about him or herself is a lot like a roller coaster. Some teenagers can fluctuate so much in how they perceive themselves that they can move from the heights of enthusiasm about their character and then, within hours, plunge into depths of despair.

No doubt this is a perplexing picture for any parent to try to figure out. These changing moods indicate teenagers are in process of developing their own identities. Teenager's self-esteem is tied to several things. One is the person they believe they are. Another is the person they believe they have the potential to become. As our teenager vacillates between these two, parents can guide our teenagers toward success. In the adolescent process, teenagers are open to change and to new ideas. They are intrigued with and question the world around them. And most importantly, they can be influenced about who they are and whom they are becoming with ideas and encouragement about their capabilities.

Even the most self-assured children, during adolescence, seem to struggle with their self-confidence. Most have to wrestle internally with how to feel good about themselves. As their bodies change, their ideas about their identity must go through developmental changes as well. The teenager is in a process of asking "Who am I?" "Who will I become?" "Where and how will I find a place for myself in the adult world?" "Will I be happy?" "Will someone love me?" "Will I be successful?" These are just a few of the questions a teenager can ponder in a day about who they are and what lies ahead. Young people are searching for what is unknown and hidden.

Your teenager is usually susceptible to what their peers lead him to believe about himself. If others like them, teenagers feel validated and decide they are OK as a person. Acceptance by peers can be short-lived as their friends change and migrate away from them. If they experience rejection from their peers, without parental support, they can begin to reject themselves.

When you feel bad about yourself, you can't really distance the feeling. So a teenager will not feel good about himself when others don't like him. This easily leads the vulnerable teenager to believe he is not likeable. Without a parent helping with this scenario, the teenager develops low self-esteem and locks into a negative self-image. To gain some kind of acceptance he may start seeking negative attention rather than fail at obtaining positive attention.

Many teenagers involved in being negative get a lot of attention from their peers. Let's say you have a hungry little boy who comes to you for some food and all you have is a soggy sandwich that someone sat on. The choice for the little boy is to accept the peanut butter mess or have nothing. What do you think the child would choose? He or she would probably choose the soggy sandwich. Why? It is better than nothing. If a teenager perceives he gets nothing from his parent or his peers, he might decide to become 'soggy' to get the attention he needs. Why? Because negative attention is better than no attention at all. He may seek the company of others who have chosen the same soggy life style too. This way he is not alone.

Always Happy

In our society, you may be encouraged to believe that your teenager should always be happy in order to have high self esteem. You may think something is wrong if your teenager isn't happy; that somehow you have failed as a parent.

It may seem like there are more periods of time when your teenager is generally miserable. Always being happy is not the typical nature of a teenager. The happy-go-lucky, always content, teenager rarely exists. If she or he does, that teenager is pretty unique. We usually see drastic mood swings as a teenager faces the challenges of growing up. Mood swings can shift hour to hour or day to day. Dramatic mood changes are common among young people.

A more realistic goal for your teenager is that he or she is generally happy, usually is productive, confident and makes attempts to try to succeed. These young people are usually talkative, open and strive to do their personal best most of the time in school and other activities. They can share both their successes and failures and are open to others, particularly their parents. There is a pride in who they are and they are optimistic about 'who' they are becoming.

When optimistic teenagers become depressed or feel sad they are able to discuss or work through these feelings with some kind of positive resolution. Their days tend to be more positive in mood. These teenagers possess high self-esteem and are confident in themselves. Typically behind each of these teenagers you will find a parent who is confident in the young person's ability to be successful, happy and capable.

The teenager with high self-esteem has a feeling of being significant. They feel important to their parents, their family, their schools, peer group or friends and in their communities. This respect and acceptance needs to be initially conveyed to the teenager, primarily from a parent, before the teenager finds it believable that they are significant and worthwhile.

Giving 100%

There is a theory about numbers that applies to teenagers. Years ago, in a small town, two young men were working in menial jobs in the same factory. The first young man was disheartened about the poor work conditions and pay. He gave only fifty percent of his effort. The young man came in late, or sat down often at his job and frequently complained and blamed others. The boss would threaten him, warning him he would lose his job because his work was so poor. This young man believed he was mediocre at best. His world, his boss and co-workers, clearly told him he was right. He learned to believe that he was a 50% kind of guy.

The second young man, facing the same work conditions, was far more optimistic about his abilities. He gave one hundred percent of himself. He worked hard, was on time and was neat and clean in his appearance. He was cheerful with his boss and readily accepted more responsibility without more pay. His boss praised his work efforts and spoke highly of him. This young man's reality told him he was worth a lot. The feedback from his boss gave him further encouragement. In a year's time he was promoted. Years later he became part owner. The first young man still toiled at his menial job, feeling dejected and hopeless.

Your role with your teenager is much like this boss. The important difference here is that you have a much greater investment in your son or daughter than a factory boss. And you can ignore your teenager's feeble attempts at trying. You can be so convinced that your teenager can give 100% of his or her efforts that you persist in your belief that your teenager will be very successful. Over time, your young person will get tired of trying to prove you are wrong. You and others around him will recognize his efforts. Just one shot at 100% can give a teenager the hope and encouragement to be successful. And then he or she can do it again and again. This is how you begin to instill the building blocks for developing high self-esteem.

If you give the world 50% of your efforts the world will reinforce that 50% as a reality feedback. When you decide to give the world 100% the world usually gives back 100% as a reality feedback. So if you decide that as a parent you are going to give the effort of raising your teenager 100%, no matter how poor the working conditions or wages, in time, you will see the fruits of your persistent effort, your 100%. And you will see it with yourself. And most importantly, you will see this kind of success in your teenager. In this ripple effect, not only will you feel accomplished but your actions will teach your teenager as well.

Meaningful Roles

Today, unlike past generations, our teenagers must search for meaningful roles rather then just falling into needed family and community roles. Youngsters today don't get a chance to help plow a field or assist on a farm. Instead, our teenagers seek to find meaning in passing an algebra exam. The responsibility of watching yourself pales in importance to watching four or five siblings and meeting all their basic needs of the farm family. Our kids need more than just the job of going to school and doing a few chores around the house to build a strong character and sense of competency.

It is out of hard work that many of us derive a sense of self-worth and self-esteem. In your own life, think back to years ago when you had to work very hard for something. It might have been a project, a sport, having a baby, building something, helping someone else, getting an education or your work. Your effort, though frustrating, gave you something very valuable. Looking back you may not readily remember the times you felt like giving up. Usually, you bask in the end result. The things we work hard for usually have much more value than something that comes to us easily. The catch is that we don't enjoy difficult tasks. We do want the end result, the feeling of accomplishment with the end result. We know we cannot get the satisfaction we desire without the effort of hard work.

As families prosper and can offer more to their children, affluent children and teenagers can begin to lose something important. They may get so much of what they need and want without any hard work or effort on their part. They are given games, toys, TVs, computers, sports cars, gas and credit cards. They do not have family chores, like making beds, laundry and yard work. Or they are over paid for what few chores they do.

A number of our young people lack meaningful roles. Many do not have something they can work hard at and see they make a difference because of their effort. They don't have the satisfaction of something tangible and created with their hands. Our communities have a large numbers of teenagers who are in limbo, searching and struggling to find something important to do. Our communities do not offer many opportunities for our teenagers to feel important and worthwhile while involved in meaningful roles.

The teenager who has little to do becomes quite miserable,

even depressed. Group boredom, coupled with immaturity, impulsiveness and curiosity about the adult world, can result in disaster, participating in the use of drugs, alcohol or sex. Left with peers raising peers, without adult guidance, coupled with boredom, puts these teenagers at risk. Many of these teenagers seek the thrill of getting in trouble to relieve the boredom. Having everything you want without working for it can leave one feeling empty and unfulfilled.

Busy teenagers present a very different picture. One adult joining a group of teenagers can guide and inspire the young people, tapping their talent and energy. Ideas will emerge, like a group of teenagers may start mowing neighbors lawns, planting flowers and gardens, sharing the profits. Another group might start recycling paper, bottles and plastic from their neighborhoods. Some could decide to rebuild a junked car or a group of young people could sit around with mom and see who could tell the best joke. With practice teenagers could become experts at ping pong or at pool. The list goes on about how productive our young people can be. Being busy and productive adds the substance and experience our teenager needs to get feedback from the world as to whether he or she is important. In addition, what young people accomplish helps others and is meaningful.

The Guy with the Brand New Sports Car

One day I overheard the young guy named Mike talking with the checker while he was bagging my groceries. He commented about the fellow that had just walked into the store. Rolling his eyes, he said the guy made him sick. His father had just given this guy a brand new red sports car for his sixteenth birthday. He said he did not think this fellow would ever amount to anything. In his view, this young man's fellow student was spoiled and self-centered. On the way to my car I asked him if he had a car. He said no, but he planned on getting one. I asked if his dad was going to give him a car. He replied, "No way would my dad give me a car." Proudly, Mike told me he was going to work to earn the money for his own car and buy it by himself. He told me he would be more successful than the guy that got things handed to him. What a capable and confident young man! I would not be surprised that he owns a car with the money he earned. The pride and determination this young man possessed was impressive. I thanked him and wished him good luck.

Some teenagers really miss out by not having the opportunity to become involved in community service. They may miss out on the experience of giving gifts and food to the poor families in their communities at Christmas. They may never know what it is like to work hard at a school dance or homecoming. Many do not have the experience of taking care of grandparents, providing the attention these aging parents may need. Without contact with elders our young people miss sharing in the wisdom of their life stories. Avoiding involvement with others will make them self centered. This helps explain the emerging 'Me generation'. If a situation does not seem to have immediate benefit for them, many teenagers become apathetic and refuse to get involved. With the encouragement of a more mature person, usually an adult, teenagers flourish. They will participate in service activities, sports, music or groups like scouting which they are not likely to initiate on their own.

If you take a bored, self-centered young person and get him or her involved in helping others we see an increase in his self-esteem and an increased level of self-satisfaction. Initially, your teenager may protest. Once he gets started, his protests diminish and he begins to join in activities showing little or no resistance. Encouraging teenagers helps them to feel included and therefore worthwhile and significant.

In many communities, high school and middle schools are over-crowded, classes are large, so it may be difficult for a teacher to reach out to every student. Typically, teachers have time to recognize three groups of students: students excelling academically, the most social teenagers and the kids failing or breaking the rules and testing limits. The student that pulls C's, sits quietly in class, or isn't involved in extracurricular activities, may not get much recognition or attention. These 'middle of the road' teenagers may have very little interaction with teachers in any classes. In crowded or highly competitive school situations, some teenagers may choose 'soggy' friends like themselves to get some negative attention; it is better than nothing.

One creative solution to our over-crowded schools can begin with bringing more adults into our school systems, especially middle and high schools. When we see more adults in classrooms, in the office and in the halls interacting with students, we begin to see more success stories with our young people. More adults working with teenagers ease the pressure on one teacher who has to attend to over thirty students in one hour. This is the real meaning of the PTSA: Parent Teacher Student Association.

You can do anything.
You can be anybody you want to be

That was the message my mother and father gave me as they encouraged me to dream of having a meaningful and happy life. What a great gift they gave me. Even when I wasn't convinced myself that I would be successful, my parent's confidence in me never wavered.

Teenagers are more open or interested in change than any other time in their lives. Most are receptive to and intrigued by the positive and negative influences around them. A teenager's main job is to change and grow in an effort to modify much of his or her childhood identity. If we channel our teenagers in positive directions, helping to use their talents, interests and energy we have a promising future generation. It begins with you finding ways to involve your teenager in productive and meaningful roles. This may present a real challenge for you as it does for many parents.

In addition to telling your son or daughter they can do anything, you can also say, "The world is open to you. You can go anywhere and pursue your dreams, whatever they may be." This is a significant motivator for teenagers. Sometimes a young person will light up like a bulb when I give him or her this message. Teenagers are so receptive to encouragement from others.

An adolescent is freer than any other time in life to explore the many roads to success. Let's say you have a teenager in a wheelchair and she wants to be a ballerina. Now, she may have to be very creative in how she could accomplish this goal. But in the Special Olympics may be a place for her. We should never be critical of our young people's dreams and plans. We adults can help our young people look to the future with hope. If you have a teenager who has a talent riding bicycles, you may not believe he could be the best bike racer in the United States. I would encourage you not to stop him from racing, if that is what he loves to do. I think it is vital to not take away your kid's dreams. The world may do that for you. If the teenager decides his attempt at bike racing is not working out for him then he can decide to change his own dream. Teenagers don't need to hear, "You won't make it."

My idea of success has little to do with winning. It has everything to do with playing and participating. It does not matter if the team wins or loses, what is important is that everyone suits up and gets out on the field and tries. There is so much to learn by just trying. This is what real success is all about. On the flip side, your children should not feel obligated to live out your dreams instead of living their own.

Talent Search

So many people have so much talent and potential that is never given an opportunity to blossom. Many people would be very successful if they would just try. A lot of people get discouraged and never make the first steps toward what they really want to do. They give up easily when trying something new. Change can feel risky, you never know if what you're trading will be better or worse than what you already have. We know a person cannot win, if they do not try. That is a given. Even if you were discouraged when you were young, give your teenager a chance at his or her dreams.

My father told me and my four siblings we should love what we do. Maybe one of us would grow up and become a garbage man, he would say (that was not a negative profession). Or a politician or a physician. Our job in life was to love what we do. Each one of us was responsible for our own personal happiness and liking what we chose to do in adulthood was a priority. So as I grew up and I made choices about my work I would ask myself, "Is this work what I really love to do ?" or "Is this going to make me happy tomorrow?" And I would pursue a new job in search of finding something I would be happy at.

Throughout my job history, starting at age 16, I left a number of jobs because my interests changed and I thought there was something else I would like better. Sometimes I left because I had an opportunity to learn something new. In the pursuit of being professionally content, my goal was to help others and as I learned more I gained more education. It was a great way to grow up thinking about striving for personal happiness in work. How I look at success is it is not the house you live in, the car you drive or the money in the bank. If you are happy with your work, you feel good about what you do and live according to your beliefs, I think you will find a great deal of meaning in your life.

All kids, deep down inside, want to be winners. If a person does his or her personal best, that person is a winner. Many people, young and old, do not know how to start. Some do not even know how to dream. Others do not know how to believe in their dreams. The road to success begins with the courage to start trying something new and in this process, finding something you love to do. From here you then begin trying hard at what you love to do. Success will follow in time as long as you don't give up on the pursuit of your dreams.

One day I was golfing with a man who worked as a top executive in a large Fortune 500 company. Talking about his love for the game of golf, he said what he really yearned to do was quit his job and drive a lawn mower on a golf course. His dream was to leave the corporate world in which he was enmeshed and spend his days doing something simple like cutting grass. One job may seem more important or meaningful than another but if each person contributes positively to the lives of others, they are both important. Each person needs to decide the importance of their work for him or herself. Wouldn't it be a great world if every person could love what they did for a living. There would be no 'work'!

It takes a lot of courage and self-discipline to pursue your dreams. We need to instill persistence in our young people. If our children don't learn to follow through with tasks we find as adults they'll be less likely to learn to do so later in life.

How do you get a teenager to persist? Begin by being at their side. Listen and look straight into their eyes. Make sure you are giving them 100% of your attention. Encourage them every step of the way, even if their steps are small, even if they get scared and want to give up. Never give up on the notion they can be successful. When they have finished a step, praise them sincerely. Provide more of the same attention and encouragement when they proceed to the next step. You have become their cheerleader and coach. Your persistence to be there will help them persist in their task.

Encourage your teenager to go for it... find a way to be happy, discovering what he or she loves to do. And strive for his or her personal best. Most teenagers eat this stuff up. It feels great when someone is enthusiastic about your ideas. And if your young person persists in his or her belief, backed by you, it is hard to fail.

MEANINGFUL ROLES FOR TEENAGERS

- Kids cleaning up their school grounds
- Helping teacher at old elementary school
- Serve food at a homeless shelter
- Gift giving for a needy family at holidays
- Neighbor to Neighbor program
- Paint the town (painting elderly person's home)
- After school care for children
- Habitat for Humanity
- Adopting a needy family
- Peer counseling
- Take a foster child into the family
- Take a foreign exchange student
- Senior citizen assistance program
- Literacy program volunteer
- Tutoring
- Reading program -middle school students in elementary
- Work in an after school program for elementary students
- Apprenticeship (electrical, mechanical, body shop)
- Work groups of teenagers (recycle, small business, etc.)
- Picking up highway trash
- Painting school trash cans
- Recycling
- Sports Referee
- Wall murals
- Assistant coaching
- Senior Girl Scouts/ Boy Scouts
- Volunteer camp counselor
- Volunteer at a retirement home
- Community service groups acting with teenagers.
- Spring clean-up
- Daycare for welfare mothers
- Work a day with professional of your choice
- Start a band
- High School Seniors talk to eighth graders about what to do, what not to do in high school.
- Horse manure, cart and horse business
- Start your own business (Espresso drive-up)
- Restaurant food recovery for the needy
- Teach religion class or help in nursery

- Pick a new sport (Karate, golf, tennis, etc.)
- Raising money in car wash for a charity
- Local county fair young people's exhibits
- Kids in Business program
- Head Start volunteer
- Special Olympics volunteer
- Babysitting volunteer for single mothers

The Only Failure There is

"The only failure there is, is the failure to try," our dear Nana would say. If you try and fail, you know you gave yourself a chance. If you are never brave enough to try, you can count on always wondering 'what if'?

Ted does not believe his son, Josh, will ever be very good at playing soccer. He is even reluctant to let Josh try. He loves his son and does not want him to be disappointed. His mother, Kate, thinks Josh deserves a chance. When this young thirteen year-old suits up and goes on the field, it doesn't matter to him if his team wins or loses. It doesn't matter if he is the slowest guy on the team. Like Josh says, someone has to be the slowest. He feels great when he walks onto the soccer field, in the background his mother is rooting for him and cheering him on. His mom tells him she is so proud of him. In spite of making the team, Ted still doesn't think Josh should play.

After many invitations, Ted finally decides to come watch Josh's play. As he approaches the field, tears fill his eyes as he spots his Josh, nimbly lifting his artificial leg, hustling after the ball, with a huge grin on his face. This day his dad learned an important lesson, one Josh and his mom already knew: win or lose, trying is what matters. Trying for one's personal best is the key to success, happiness and contentment in life. With this kind of experience this young man can strive to be successful again and again.

The Spark

Failure comes from never beginning. Not putting your name on the paper. Leaving the paper blank. Not opening the book to study or not going out for the team. If your teenager makes an attempt at his English assignment, that is a start.

Think of success in steps. The first step begins with a spark of encouragement from an adult who cares and believes in the teenager. With even a little encouragement a youngster can strive for great things. Then once they are encouraged they then take the first step. Simply by starting your teenager completed the toughest part of the success challenge. Next comes practice to improve, exploring a young person's interest and talent. After continued effort and persistence he or she will reach a level of achievement. And as time passes your teenager will be able to excel with their efforts.

An insecure or fearful teenager may require a good deal of encouragement with each step of the way. An adult's concern can motivate him or her to the steps toward success. Once your teenager has participated he or she will have the beginning of the foundation that confidence is built on.

If You Don't Have Anything Nice to Say

Sometimes developing confidence begins with not saying what you think at a time you are worried or frustrated with your teenager so you don't rob them of their belief in themselves. So if you think that your opinion may disappoint your teenager or stop him or her from trying, it is best to keep your opinion to yourself.

Parents are mature enough to really think through what they have to say and evaluate the kind of message they may send to their children. This is like having a fire side chat with yourself. When in doubt, count to 10 in a thoughtful pause and you will do a better job parenting your teenager.

What Do You Want out of Life?

Each of us measures success in different ways. How you define success may not necessarily be how society defines success. Our ideas about happiness and success change as we get older and we learn more about the world and ourselves. For some it has to do with the people and the relationships in their lives, how much they contribute to other's lives, for other's money and possessions. Others find their health takes precedent. Many, especially close to death, measure success by their relationship to God.

Another thing most of us want is to be loved. To be loved is an essential factor in the make-up of a person's personal happiness, especially for children. Being loved can get you through the toughest of times. Not feeling loved can make you feel as hopeless as a human being possibly can.

Perhaps not as important to adults, but very important to teenagers, is the wish to be liked. Feeling liked is different than feeling loved. There are people in your life that you may love but may not like them as much as you love them. You can love someone in your family and find you clash with their ideas, ideals or personalities. You may not like them. When someone likes you and you like them it is the basis of friendship. There is genuine interest and endearment when someone likes you; you can see it in his or her eyes and in their responses to you. Liking someone is genuine, sincere feeling and cannot be manufactured. It just happens.

Teenagers are exploring happiness. What makes them successful? Who loves them? Who likes them? As part of the challenge to be different from parents and others, their search can take them to ideas and choices that are in opposition to your values as they go on expeditions in their social world around them. You have much to contribute by helping your teenager find what makes him or her happy. You might be wondering how you might do just that.

Before you look at how you really feel about your teenager, it is important to look at any roadblocks you might have in the way of your feelings. You can be very angry at someone you really like and love. Your anger about what they have done or are doing can create a block so you recognize the anger, not the positive feelings. It is important to look at all the feelings you experience. To decide if you really love or like your teenager you have to remove all the encumbrances. This is a tough task for many parents of young people. For most this means forgiving and accepting the other person as they choose to be.

Imagine you learn your teenager was in a serious car accident. As you rush to the hospital, guess what you might be feeling. Do you imagine you are angry because you wanted your teenager to be more careful? Are you terrified of what might happen to your child? Panicked if your son or daughter will live or die? What are you most worried about? (Thinking of all the possibilities of what could or might happen.) All these feelings are paramount in most people's reaction to a trauma.

Now imagine you are at the hospital and you see your child. What do you think you might be feeling looking at your son or daughter in a critical care unit? Most of the negative feelings melt away and what you feel is very deep and emotional. You may feel overwhelmed with feelings of love and care, like a huge wave just hit you. Engulfed with powerful feelings of love, in traumatic situations where time together is precious, the blocks to those loving feelings can disappear. Tough as it may be, times of difficulty help us get down to basics; feelings of love and care for your child.

It is understandably difficult to get in touch with your basic feelings when the things your teenager does make you angry. If you really think about it, we like and love our children, not based on what they do but because of who they are. To help your teenager it is important to come to grips with your basic feelings about your child, beyond anger, frustration or disappointment.

Occasionally a parent loves his or her child but does not like the child much. This usually occurs because the youngster's personality is just the opposite of theirs or sometimes their personalities are so similar the two are in frequent conflict. These parents do well seeking some professional help so the child' feelings are not hurt by the parent's honest feelings. The goal of therapy would probably be to find a healthy way to interact without harming the child. Usually we help the parent find others who do like their child and help them participate in raising that young person. That may be the other parent, a relative or a friend.

Most parents feel lucky to have their young people. If you look beyond the teenage mood, attitude, odd hairstyles and strange outfits, you see the one thing that does not change, their eyes. When you look closely, teenagers have the eyes of children. Eyes that are open, interested, watching, taking in the world around them. The eyes of these very young adults, sometimes shy, are curious and hopeful for the future.

HOUSE OF MENTAL HEALTH

When we look at the mental health of a teenager we can begin to see how strong and sturdy their house is. Like any house the foundation is critical. The foundation of a teenager's mental health consists of their self-esteem, which effects both who we are and how we act. The teenager's self-esteem colors and reflects how that young person acts and responds to the people and situations around them. If a teenager feels bad about himself/herself and has low self-esteem he or she is likely to act out in negative ways. So when we see cracks in the foundation of our

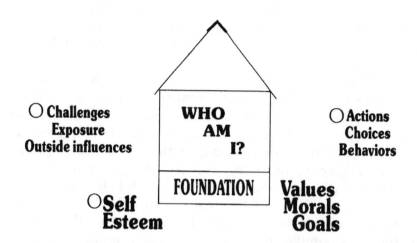

○ **Challenges**
Exposure
Outside influences

WHO AM I?

○ **Actions**
Choices
Behaviors

FOUNDATION

○**Self Esteem**

Values Morals Goals

young people we need to begin to look at how to repair those faults and make the house more secure.

Our teenagers get feedback that will help them determine how they will build their houses of mental health. Information comes from the world of their peers, from parents and family, teachers and their school. The scope of their self-esteem comes from their efforts and accomplishments and the recognition that follows. All this information helps build the foundation. Working hard at things and getting a lot of positive feedback builds a strong and sturdy foundation. These positive and strong foundations can last your son or daughter a lifetime.

Teenagers are vulnerable and fragile in their view of themselves because their "self" is a work in progress. As they begin to put together their house of adulthood they can be greatly effected by the weather conditions that surrounds them. So with stormy weather of peer pressure and a strong wind of challenges in their worlds, we hope our teenager's foundations will be strong and sturdy and they will make good decisions for themselves. In the event of storms and cold we hope their homes (their 'selves') stay intact and remain sturdy and strong.

Like a pyramid, your teenager's self-esteem starts with parents at the top. It is always easier to evaluate others than it is to take a critical look at yourself. How a parent feels about himself has much to do with how a teenager can feel about himself or herself. Your feelings about yourself and your life filter down to your son or daughter. To help you take a look at yourself here is the parent check. It will help you assess how you are doing in your own life which is important for the success for your teenager.

Parenting is a Privilege

When I had my first child I leaned from my children's Nana what a privilege it is to be a parent. Not all parents see their parenting as a wonderful opportunity. Especially during adolescence, weary parents can feel this way. Ask yourself is there any more important role than raising your children? Though it will be full of challenges, I think our children are wonderful gifts. Life, like parenting, is not supposed to be easy, without risks or challenges. Your child's passage to adulthood will make your life richer and fuller. Being a parent can give you great meaning and purpose in your life. It may indeed be the most important role you ever have in your lifetime.

If you do not think your job of parenting is very important, look around you and discover the origin's of that point of view. Does it come from your spouse? From your workplace? From your friends? From society at large? If it originated from others, you can help yourself by reaffirming your own values. Your boss may not think the task of raising your child is as important as your job at work. Or your spouse does not agree with you. You, alone, can evaluate the idea of parenting as a privilege. What you think is what is important. You decide for yourself.

Our Children Move Through Us

Our children are in process from the day they are born to move through us. They are not part of us. We do not own our children, they own themselves. We can guide them, protect and love them. We can cherish them but there is no ownership with children. Though we may always have a relationship with our children, when they leave, you will never have the same parent-child relationship again. Your time as a parent will pass. When your young adult child says their final goodbye, leaving you, I hope you will feel successful as a parent.

Are You Happy?

There are three important questions to ask about your own personal happiness. Are you happy as a person? Are you happy as a spouse? Are you happy as a parent?

Are You Happy as a Person ?

As the person you are, are you content with what you are doing with your life? With what you are doing and how you perceive yourself? Are you healthy enough? Are you finding meaning in your everyday living? Is your spiritual life rich? If you are unhappy it is unlikely that your children can be happy as you struggle with your own satisfaction. They learn more from what you do and how you feel than from what you say. If a parent is having a difficult time striving for their own happiness and questioning their own self-worth, it may prove extremely difficult for that person's child to have a sense of personal happiness and strong self-worth. Like the pyramid, what is at the top effects all that is below. You have to deal first with yourself and be OK before you can help and care for others around you. Self care is not an option.

What can you do to improve your own personal happiness? In this chapter you will find a menu of ideas and solutions for your own happiness. There is a list of many things adults do to find their own personal happiness. Those ideas are there for you to think about and to incorporate into your life.

******MENU FOR PERSONAL HAPPINESS******

- Get in shape
- Eat healthy foods
- Visit your friends regularly
- Attend church/ bible study
- Find a sport
- Join a health club
- Lower you cholesterol
- Lose weight
- Volunteer to help others

- Help the elderly
- Join a parent's group
- Join a therapy group
- Start counseling
- Walk an hour a day
- Fix a bodily defect that bothers you (warts, bunions, etc.)
- Take a vacation with your spouse
- Take a vacation by yourself
- Go on a retreat
- Go to a spa
- Redo your hair style
- Change your style, wardrobe, look
- Start an exercise program
- Find a rewarding job that fits your values
- Spend time with your parents
- Spend time with your brothers and sisters
- Meet your spouse for lunch once a week
- Do something fun (see fun menu)
- Take a bubble bath once a week
- Plant a garden
- Think of your favorite place and go there as often as you can
- Teach Sunday school
- Go on a date with your spouse once a week
- Watch old movies
- Listen to your favorite music everyday
- Take time to play with your pets
- Spend time alone with each child once a week
- Spend time in your child's school
- Sit in the sun several times a week
- Hike into the hills and find a peaceful spot once a month

- Join a hobby group
- Join a service organization
- Find a job you love to do
- Be comfortable in your home, fix what is not comfortable
- Laugh at a good joke once a week (ask your teen ager)

***************** **FUN MENU*******************

- Take a bubble bath
- Have a water fight
- Do some prank jokes (macaroni in shoes, etc.)
- Play softball
- Go to a sporting event
- Bowling
- Swimming
- Skiing
- Play with cornstarch and water
- Have a pillow fight
- Play musical pillows on the floor
- Play cards
- Play board games
- Hike a mountain
- Have a picnic
- Swing
- Put up the tent in the yard or living room
- Have a spelling Bee
- Have a candle lit dinner on Wednesday night
- Eat dinner with your hands (Moroccan)
- Have a tacky party
- Have a holiday party

- Carve pumpkins and have a contest (everyone wins a category)
- Dye eggs and have a contest
- Play leap frog
- Play volleyball, badmitten, basketball, tennis
- Sleep in a hammock
- Play crochet
- Play killer scrabble, with the use of a dictionary
- Have a scavenger hunt
- Play hide and go seek in the dark
- Visit a comedy club and laugh
- Attend concert, play or opera

Are You Happy as Husband, Wife or Partner?

Are you happy as a husband, wife or partner? Are you alone and a single parent? How do you feel about your situation? Are you content in your role? Does it work for you? If it is not going the way you want, you may need to pause to take time to sort through your personal relationship issues to reach a level of contentment with this aspect of your life. For many parents, they are in "middle marriage" which is one of the toughest phases of marriage to be in when they have to deal with their adolescent. Marriage needs time and attention. The high divorce rate is due in some measure to a spouse leaving the relationship when things get tough for a couple.

Problems that you may be struggling with will erupt in your family. It reminds me of the bumper sticker that says, "If mama's not happy, ain't nobody's happy." I think this goes for fathers too. So when, "dad's not happy, ain't nobody's happy."

Are You Happy as a Mother or Father?

How do you feel about your role as a parent to your children? Are you doing the job you think you should? Are there some things you need to change or modify?

Do you sometimes feel so frustrated you feel like giving up? Pinpointing the problems is the first step. The second step is finding ways to solve the problems you encounter as a parent. It is important to resolve conflicts, no matter how long it takes or how difficult they may seem.

How is Your Marriage?

How long have you been married or together? What have been the best years, the best times? What has been difficult? What is currently difficult? How are you feeling about your partner? Here is a tough question: What do you think it is like for your spouse to live with you?

Marriage is the nucleus of a family. The health of the nucleus is what determines the viability of a cell. If the nucleus is unhealthy or not functioning well it makes the cell weak. It may not endure very well. Kids are like barometers with the relationship of your marriage. They watch closely and listen intently to what happens between you and their other parent. They can tell when the pressure is up and may act out when they feel the marriage is unsteady. Your children are invested in your relationship. They like it when their mom and dad stay together and are happy.

When parents are in crisis, in conflict, fighting or thinking about divorce or separation, children and teenagers become desperate and emotionally traumatized. They stop being kids and become absorbed in the darkness of their parents lives. Usually feeling helpless, confused and lost they ponder what they could possibly do to help their parents love each other again and their family return to happier times. They begin to give up on their needs and become absorbed in the conflict in their family. Until the crisis is resolved they usually remain in an unstable and vulnerable emotional state.

If you need some work on your marriage, it is helpful to begin to make a plan on what you can do to improve your relationship. This is not an easy task. My definition of marriage is rather short: Marriage is hard work. Marriage requires work from the day you are first married until the day when you are no longer alive (or you are no longer married). If more people actually worked on their marriages we would probably have a much lower divorce rate. We would have fewer children who suffer as the casualties of divorce.

Twice as Much Time with Your Spouse

Many parents struggle with how to spend their time and energy. Do you expend yourself as a father and a provider and then have little time left over for your wife? Do you spend all your time at home with the kids being a super mom and then balance work, other activities and then only on rare occasions spend time alone with your husband? In terms of time if you spend more time on your marriage than your children, your family has a great chance at being successful. The time balance here is for every hour you spend with your children, spend two with your spouse. It is good to spend a good number of those hours out of your house. Many parents tell me they have never taken a vacation or had a weekend away from their children.

Once you make a commitment to work on your marriage, you may be surprised to find what many couples find once the kids leave home. They do enjoy each other's company and it is nice to have each other to talk to. The work of spending time on your marriage provides great dividends of happiness.

If you and your spouse are taking good care of each other, your children will be happy. They will have a great feeling of security in their family.

When you cannot solve your difficulties alone there is plenty of professional help to help you with the work of your marriage. There are a number of resources available to you. For starters, books, couple counseling, marriage enrichment weekends, couples groups and classes.

How Much Water do You Have in Your Bucket ?

Beyond the needs of your marriage, meeting the needs of your family presents a challenge. You may have to set priorities of who gets your attention and care in your family first. Not to say all your children need the same thing from you. When you set those priorities look at who is needing the biggest boost in their self-esteem. Which child seems to be in need of the most attention to feel good about him or herself? It may be the child who is at the most difficult stage growing up. It might very well be your teenager. You should spend most of your parental time and attention with the child that needs the most.

If you are not really sure where to start or what you need, you might want to look over the menu to find your own personal happiness. If what you need is to get away, you may have to be creative and committed to take a vacation as soon as you can. That may mean taking a weekend away by yourself by going to a nearby cabin or lodge. If you need to date your husband or wife, find a way make to that happen. You may need to improve your spiritual growth to find more meaning in your life. If you need to change your profession or take some college classes, do it. Sometimes, what you really need is to just to take a few naps in a week. Meeting your own basic needs may be the start. No one is as capable as you are to assess the things you need to do to find a balance in your life. By accomplishing this goal, you will have enough time and energy for yourself, your children, your spouse and your family.

Giving, Getting Back Two-Fold

There is usually reciprocity in giving. Many parents feel their giving is returned when they give love, attention and kindness to their young children. You smile and your children smile back. Your younger children readily return your hugs and kisses. They greet you with open arms and open minds. The same holds true for most adults. So you get something back which makes you feel good. The only exception to this kind of reciprocity occurs during adolescence.

Not hearing "thank you" from a teenager can be discouraging. Even though you give a lot to your teenager you may feel like other parents who do not get much back from them. Just because teenagers don't openly express positive feelings for you does not mean they don't feel deep love and are committed to you.

Eventually your teenager will give back all the good you have given to them... in time. And that might not happen until they are in their early twenties. It is not realistic to expect your teenager to say, "Hey, mom and dad, you were right on track not letting me go to that party... Good job parenting!" Waiting for this feedback requires a lot of patience on your part. And a lot of love. To survive your adolescent, you need to look other places for recognition and appreciation.

These checks are also dynamic. The answers change over time, as you change and grow as a parent. Things change as your life and family grows and reaches new stages. So answering these questions is not a one time event. Your work on your own personal happiness is a lifelong task. And happiness and finding meaning in your life is not an entity that is static or definite. It is a process, felt in degrees, and changing over time. It is not a black and white issue of whether you are happy or not. But a matter of how happy and content you are for today. We each need to strive for degrees of being 'generally happy' and content in our lives.

The House of Self

Now that we have completed the parent check, you can check your teenager. Again we look at the adolescent question,'"Who am I?" This question is focused on the here and now. Most teenagers question themselves about their budding identity in some way almost on a daily basis. Asking, "Who am I today?" is the ultimate adolescent question. Since your teenager is in the process of finding him or herself, this question is dynamic and changes over time.

How you as a parent begin to assess 'who' your teenager is and how they are doing starts with evaluating their actions, beliefs, behaviors and choices. Wondering about your teenager's current identity you can look at their behavior, their mood and their statements. You can also examine their choices, what interests or intrigues them, what they choose to wear, who they select as friends and the activities in which they participate. You can also use grades, a willingness to help others or involvement in family activities as other ways to assess your teenager. You can make some evaluation by the messiness of their rooms. Do they tend to be more responsible than irresponsible? Is your teenager a hard worker? What do they consider as moral, ethical and doing the right thing?

A teenager, developing his/her self-esteem, reacts by soaking up either positive or negative feedback directed to them, especially from a parent, someone to whom they are most attached. So if you are having a hard time being sincere about something positive, sometimes you have to really search to find a positive response rather than continue your negative remarks.

Giving positive feedback for children and teenagers is not a one time event. If you say, "I love you" or "You did a great job" your child will register that you acknowledge them. These statements help build their confidence in themselves and feed their self-esteem.

Here are many ways to say, "Good job." Each statement can be said according to your own personal style. How a dad may say something can be very different from how a mother might respond. You may find you say the same thing very differently to each of your children. The important thing is to keep saying positive things.

50 WAYS TO SAY 'GOOD JOB'

good work	wonderful	fantastic job
great!	nice work	I like it
good boy/girl	that is awesome	cool
terrific	that is neat	good start
I love it	You're neat	clever!
you are smart	Wow!	You did well
You are so creative	nice start	Excellent
alright	You did great	keep it up
You can do it	You can do it again	Fine
I am impressed	I am proud of you	You did it!
You are on your way	Fine job	Your best work
You're doing it	You are funny	I like you
Way to go	You are OK	You're brave
I believe in you	You are special	That is it!
This is great	You got it	You can do anything
What an idea	out of sight	
Great performance	I am happy for you	I knew you could do it

Learned Labels

People cannot be fairly defined by a single title or one specific label. A person may be a president, another an inmate, another illiterate. A mother may be a computer technician, a wife, a foster mother, a choir member at church, a daughter, a sister, a cousin, a sports fan, a good friend and a brownie leader. And her roles go on, as well as change over time.

Your teenager is far more than just a single label. He may be a drummer, a joker, a son, a brother, a best friend and a cousin, just to name a few. It is easy to put labels on our teenagers, depicting what we would most like to change about them. You may want to label him 'sullen', 'irresponsible', 'aloof' or 'selfish'. Or we label her 'stubborn', 'angry', 'difficult' or 'lazy'.

With enough repetition, the teenager then makes the negative label a reality, rather than be motivated to change. Positive labels work much better than negative ones. You can give your teenager not just one positive label but many like; 'productive', 'capable', 'independent', 'courageous', 'brilliant', 'kind', 'talented', 'sweet', 'loving', 'artistic', 'creative', 'powerful', 'funny', 'sincere', 'perceptive', 'honest' and 'important'. These are the labels of life our young people need so that they can have a great start in life!

Sharing the Characteristics

In your family you may notice if one child is succeeding in one area the other child may be reluctant to try the same thing. Your older child may do well in academics and the younger child may not try as hard with his or her studies. Some children may be more interested in being successful in the social world around them. The oldest child may think he or she is not as adept at making friends. Encourage all your children to try at everything they do, like academics, sports, hobbies and making friends. It also helps to encourage your children to try doing many things in addition to their interests.

If all of you in your family sat at a table and everyone drew a vase of flowers, would all of you end up with the same picture? I think each picture would be different. Each person would draw in their own style and way, capturing something unique and individual. When we encourage our children to try many things, we can reassure them that even by doing something another brother or sister does, how they accomplish a task will be unique. Invite them to share any of the characteristics that they admire in a sibling or parent. That characteristic, like being funny or intense, will manifest itself very uniquely in the person exploring it, just like a drawing. No two people express themselves in exactly the same way. Each has an original and individual expression.

Your Confidence is Priceless

In numerous studies, a significant reoccurring factor is the role played by a parent as a primary motivator for a talented young person. This is true whether the teenager becomes a tennis star, a pianist, math scholar, gymnast or excels in sports, music or academics.

The adult has to believe the child will be successful. The adult never loses his or her confidence that the young person has talent. Even if the teenager puts down her tennis racquet and says she doesn't think she can win, that adult never gives up the notion she will be successful.

Your young person, like other teenagers, cannot make it alone. He or she needs you. Your teenager needs at least one adult who believes in him or her. As a parent you do not need a special talent to lead your child down the road of success. It does mean you must believe and can not give up.

As your teenager's interests change you too can add new beliefs about how they can be successful in other areas too. Even though your teenager no longer plays a clarinet you continue to believe if he puts an effort into playing he would be very successful. This does not mean you make them play the clarinet. Your teenager may need a break, try something different and then come back later. Or you may suggest he might try another to learn another instrument.

Immature young people do not have the confidence they need to make their lives successful. If they feel no one believes in them, they will eventually give up. Young people have immature egos. They can only gain strength in self-confidence from more mature people who believe in them. Adults possess a maturity and wisdom about life young people are just beginning to discover. To foster success, you must be persistent in your belief in your son or daughter.

Talented Teenagers or Wasted Talent

I remember the mother who told me her fourteen year-old son had no talent for school and she did not like his friends. In her eyes there was nothing this boy did that was positive. I asked how her son spent his time. He would work on his snow machine in the garage, an activity she thought was a waste of time. On the weekends he would join other youngsters and fix their snow machines. He also liked to go riding with his friends. She thought he should do well in school, like his brother. Do you think this young man has a talent? He might very well be a budding mechanic. He might also be inclined toward snow machine racing. His mother could not see her son's talent because it was not what she expected him to do. Her son did not live up to her expectation of what he ought to be.

When your teenager begins to explore his or her talent, you may have to put aside some of your own notions and expectations of success. There are many things that interest and motivate our teenagers that are hard for a parent to accept. Here are a few more examples.

A fifteen year-old young man came into treatment because he was failing at school. He preferred to be outdoors rather than indoors. He was fearless. He would get hurt jumping off the roof, racing on his bike and cliff climbing. He found school very boring. His parents wanted him to finish high school and to join the military or go to college. I told his mother this young man does have talent and has great potential to become a stunt man. He liked this idea so much he decided to start working in school so that he could attend stunt school. Someday I expect to see this young man in the movies.

In a family session a fourteen year-old girl on the honor roll said she wanted to be an architect but found architect's work generally boring. Her mother interrupted her and told her how her goals were unrealistic because she would just have to get used to doing the boring stuff if she wanted to be an architect. After talking to her, it was clear her interests were not in traditional architecture. She did not want to draw floor plans of buildings or houses. After exploring what did interest her, I discovered she loved the architecture she saw in the movies, especially in animated films. Guess what we came up with? She is now planning to pursue a career as an architectural animator. She dreams of drawing the houses, buildings and landscapes in cartoons and animated films.

Consider the interests of your child when he or she was young. What made your child laugh? What intrigued your youngster when they were five, six and seven? Besides TV, what captured your child's interest for hours on end? TV doesn't really count because it calls for mindless attention. If your child would leave the TV set and then set up a pretend recording studio or start directing her friends in a play then media like television becomes a valid, creative interest.

Now what does your teenager like to do today? What takes up a good deal of his or her time? Many parents tell me they think their son or daughter would like to become telephone operators because of all the hours they spend on the phone! Put aside your first impressions and search for 'raw' talent. You are seeking early interests that will develop into something as your young person reaches adulthood. If you feel your teenager lacks experience in areas of his or her budding interest provide them with the opportunity to experiment. Your goal is to have your teenager become excited and interested in something they think they would eventually love to do.

For example, a daughter who seems determined to argue about everything might be a budding attorney. A young man who hangs around the kitchen may have interests in becoming a chef. Do you have an avid shopper? This young woman may be interested in becoming a buyer or do well in retail. A teenager that loves to play could do well working for a toy manufacturer, creating new toys.

MENU OF TALENTS
- Academics
- Art
- Acting
- Arguing
- Architecture
- Archery
- Drawing
- Inventing
- Shopping
- Entrepreneur
- Being sensitive
- Skateboarding
- Skiing
- Being thoughtful
- Surfing
- Caring for animals
- Automotive
- Making friends
- Being funny

- Helping friends
- Outdoor Activities
- Automobiles
- Shooting/hunting
- Medicine
- Parties
- Automotive maintenance
- Good listener
- Communicating
- Sharing
- Flight
- Politics
- Debate
- Computers
- Games
- Sports
- Leadership
- Animals
- Religion
- Directing
- Clothing
- Hair styling, cutting
- Philosophical thinking
- Writing
- Music: listening, singing, playing, writing
- Radio
- Resolving conflict
- Mentoring
- Phone
- Flying
- Eating
- Politics

- Rescuing needy friends
- Cartooning
- Shopping
- Cooking
- Critic
- Sensitive to others
- Being an expert
- Art
- Aircraft
- Making things with their hands
- Reading
- Creative rule breaker
- Being unique
- Thinker
- Selling things
- Saving money
- Driving
- Teaching
- Romantics
- Dreamer
- Speaking out
- Making acquaintance with people of all groups
- Singing

Try Five Times

A woman in therapy shared her fear of flying with me. She told me she had been terrified of flying since she was a youngster. Her husband was a pilot and wanted her to go places with him in their small plane, which frightened her the most. So with all her courage, a pounding heart and a sick stomach, she timidly boarded the small plane. To her amazement she did not faint or get airsick on her 'white knuckle' flight.

She was still frightened and had feelings of panic when she boarded the plane for the second time. Each time she flew with her husband she feared she would die. By the fifth time something happened; her fear subsided. She now flies frequently with her husband. Recently she started taking flying lessons!

Her experience with other things has been similar. By the fifth time she has found herself more adept at the task or more comfortable with what she is doing. So if you offer an activity to your teenager tell them they need to try it five times before they decide if they like it or not. It might be five times to the soccer field to play, five times to karate class or learning to baking bread or five lessons on the tuba.

Opportunities to explore their talents and creative abilities brings meaning to your young person's view of him or herself. If there is something they can do and feel successful at, they build positive self-esteem and develop confidence in their abilities. Usually a teenager with an encouraging parent behind him will experiment with something new which might enhance his interests and help reveal hidden talents.

Try giving your teenager a list of after school activities from which he or she can choose. Your teenagers can add their own ideas if they don't like the ones on your list. Then once they choose, they can participate for a semester. If they don't seem to want to participate in this decision, after a few days you can choose for them. Then they must go to five sessions before deciding if they like what you picked. The next time you may find they are more willing to choose for themselves. No matter what their mood or attitude may be, the only thing that is important is that they try.

Lisa at fifteen couldn't have looked much darker. She was dressed in black, had cinder black hair with lips and nails to match. She was sullen, depressed and silent when her parents brought her to me for family therapy. We decided she needed to be busy instead of doing nothing and being so bored. Her parents offered her a choice of things in which she could participate. After a week she refused to choose so her parents picked soccer, her old sport, which she used to like. So her mother, Alison, braced herself all the way to the soccer field with a daughter spitting fire, saying she refused to play and there was no way she would cooperate. When they arrived at the field, her mother opened the door, waited for Lisa to emerge with a huge chip on her shoulder. As soon as she was out , without a word, Alison drove off. An hour and a half later, Alison returned. On the field, wearing black, was her sweet Lisa, chasing the ball like she used to do.

The idea is to promote the use of one's talents and abilities. Many adults become wrapped up in the idea of seeing end results. The most successful way to work toward end results is to emphasize first steps for the start. Then once they have started encouraging them to continue creates opportunities for success.

If you have a 'TV kid' who doesn't show much interest in anything but television the first step is to turn off the TV for a month. This may mean no one in the house can watch TV. You might have to lock the set in the closet or store it at a friend's home. It usually takes a minimum of a month to have your teenager go through withdrawal (other family members too!) and to become motivated to do other things. After a month you may decide more objectively how to bring TV viewing back.

Approval versus Acceptance

There is a big difference between approval and acceptance of our children. When we approve of something our teenagers do our teens may feel like we are approving of them. What we usually approve of or disapprove of is our children's behavior and choices. We might not like their dress, their hair, their language or their how they treat their brother or sister, or their behavior.

Acceptance of a person is different than approval. Acceptance is recognition and respect for the person, young or old, for whom they choose to be. True acceptance means accepting them without expectations of how they should change or be different. It is to love them for who they are. No strings attached. No expectations of how they ought to be. You cannot change who your teenager chooses to be. It is up to your teenager to decide that for him or herself. We may not like the behavior. But it is so important to like the person.

To begin to separate approval and acceptance for your teenager is an important step. A message to your teenager can be, "I do not like the choice you made and your behavior but I do like you." Acceptance does not change how you feel about the person because of the choices they make. Acceptance is not based on their behavior. So if your job as a parent is to accept and love your teenager, you do not have to like or approve of their behavior. Teenagers need to hear the difference. Your teenager needs to know you do not like their choice to drink alcohol or skip school but you do respect and love them. And you are angry because of their choice not because of who they are. You are upset because you love them and know they can make much better choices for themselves. You are angry because you care and don't want them to hurt themselves. What does not change is your belief and caring for your teenager; your acceptance of them.

Conditional versus Unconditional Love

Conditional love is a love based on what you do. If you are loved conditionally that would mean if you do certain things or achieve specific things like status, grades or accomplishments then what you get is love and recognition. With conditional love if you do not achieve status or accomplishments then you will not be loved. Or if over time, you loose your status or do not continue to behave in ways you always have you will also lose feeling loved.

Every human being has a need for love and recognition. It is basic to the mental health and the spirit of any individual. Children growing up with little love and recognition are emotionally handicapped. Its importance ranks just after food, water and shelter needs are satisfied like in Maslow's hierarchy of needs.[2]

Unconditional love is a love that is given without terms or expectations of what you do. This love is based on who you are and with this kind of love you can't ever lose. This love is what a mother feels towards her helpless infant. This love is given without any expectation or condition of something in return. It is a mature love in that the person giving the love and recognition does not put any expectations on the person they love. Their love is forgiving and accepting. The love for the person is based on that person being just who he or she is. It does not change if the person does something wrong or acts in unacceptable ways. Unconditional love does not fade away over time. There are no conditions on which this love is based.

When you are given unconditional love from someone else, this love is based on who you are, not what you do. When you are loved unconditionally you can never lose, no matter what. The love from another is always with you. You always feel the caring and concern. This love is respectful of the individual, their needs and concerns. This mature love is not selfish or demanding.

Animals, especially dogs, are a great example of showing unconditional love. If a dog is mistreated or ignored that dog will continue to approach the owner, tail wagging, giving his or her owner another chance. If they are mistreated enough they may be fearful, their tail tucked under them, but the dog will usually still approach the owner. Dogs are unconditionally attached to their owners. Unconditional attention and commitment is not based on the owner's behavior but is generously given.

Children are not the only people who need unconditional love. Adults do too. If a child grows up feeling she is loved because of who she is, they will grow up to become a stable, confident person. Growing up with conditional love creates instability because there is an underlying anxiety that if your status or achievement changes, you risk losing the love you need.

The greatest gift you can give your child is to love them unconditionally. That love is a given for their lifetime. It is an honest love, a love that respects their individual ideas and interests. Loving them encourages their individuality. With such love you and your young person can never lose.

Helping and Helplessness

Do not do for your children what they can do for themselves. If your teenager can do his or her own wash, and if you never let them do that chore, he or she will struggle with everyday living in early adulthood. If you think of the things teenagers need to learn to take care of themselves, giving them a chance to work at these tasks will develop confidence. One of the big risks of giving your teenager preparatory experiences is you may have to face the possibility of shrunken clothes, meals burnt or a big dent in the car.

To be a thoughtful parent requires that you ponder what is best for your child. What does he or she need to learn to grow up confident, independent, hard working and capable of taking care of him or herself? It is easier to do things for them rather than to take the time to teach a young person a task or chore and then following up on their work. A teenager needs to know they can do the basic chores of living to be confident as they enter adulthood.

There is value in hard work and a job well done. If you let your teenager settle for a half-baked cake, a poorly swept floor or incomplete homework assignments, then they learn that a poor job is acceptable. Do not let your son or daughter settle for less than their personal best. To discourage a lazy effort ask your teenager if what he or she is doing is his or her personal best. If it is not, you can check the task later on. You can offer instruction after they explain their understanding of what needs to be done and they seem to misunderstand something. You can show them how to do something and then let them take over. You can say, "I am confident you can finish this and do it well." If your teenager does not learn to work hard as a young person, they may never learn to be a hard worker.

Imagine one day you are walking out of a store carrying a bags of groceries. As you head toward your car, you notice a boy scout running up to you. He insists on carrying your grocery bags for you. So, probably a little surprised, you let him carry your bags, thanking him when you get to your car. He makes sure you get inside and waits on the sidewalk until you drive off. The next time you leave the store, you find the boy scout there again. Instead of helping others around you, he wants to help you. So again he escorts you to the car. You offer to pay him for his help and he refuses any money. You might start wondering why is this guy helping you, rather than others around you? What is his motive? A third trip to the grocery makes you a little leery as you venture from the store with your bags. Sure enough there is that boy scout, heading towards you, passing by people much older than you. And he insists on helping you again.

Why does this young man think you need so much help? Does he think there is something wrong with you? Has he mistaken you for someone else who might be really weak or sick or something? This experience would make you really question how your own abilities are perceived by this young man. Why doesn't he think you are capable to carry your own groceries?

This is the experience of being helped and cared for by someone else when you can take care of yourself. If you do everything for your child through adolescence, your young person may not grow up confident in their own ability to care for themselves. So if you re-make their bed, re-clean their room, cook their meals, wash their clothes, make their appointments, what message are you sending? All your help can start out as innocent caring. If it goes on for too long, you are sending a message of incompetence.

If you wait to help only when your teenager asks he or she will become self-reliant. So if you don't nag about homework, your teenager will eventually take on the responsibility. When your teenager requests your help, try to allow your young person to figure it out for themselves by leading them with your questions.

Taking on the challenges of daily tasks builds a confident, independent young person with high self-esteem. Being able to care for your own basic needs is the basis for self-esteem. Through experience your teenager learns to be a hard worker and builds confidence he or she can to do a good job meeting basic needs.

Chocolate Chip Cookie Story

Years ago when I was a young adult, I met a new guy at a friend's house. He was very quiet and obviously pretty shy. While we were there, everyone was getting hungry and someone suggested making cookies. So this fellow said he would make some. When we got into the kitchen I stood around watching him prepare chocolate chip cookies. To my surprise, he put the eggs in the bowl, followed by the sugar, butter and then he heaped on the flour. Then in went the chocolate chips, nuts, vanilla and last salt, all without stirring a thing. Only when he had put all the ingredients into the bowl did he take a spoon and start to stir. The cold butter made the stirring slow. Now I had been cooking for my family of seven since I was twelve and I was pretty good at making cookies. I wanted to help this fellow, but I didn't want to hurt his feelings.

After he stirred and stirred the cookie concoction, it had turned brown. I remained quiet and he put the big piles of cookies on the sheet. As I watched this cookie experiment, we talked about other things. When they came out of the oven this young man said to me, "These don't look right. Do you know why?". Only then, did I say that if you follow the recipe it says to cream the sugar with butter and eggs, then add the dry ingredients, then they turn out more like the recipe.

Today this man has become a great cook. He is well known for his seven course gourmet meals. I think interfering too early could have embarrassed him and he may have given up trying to cook again.

Experiments in Confidence

Your encouragement can assist your teenager to choose for him or herself. You will need to be cautious about your own 'expertise' and the urge to tell your teenager what to do. It is better for your teenager to experiment. So if your young person thinks he can go weeks without doing his homework and still get an A, let him try. If she thinks she can skip showering and still look and smell fine three days later, let her try too. Some teenagers insist they are not tired and can stay up late. Let them stay up as late as they would like for a period of a week. (You will have to monitor late night activities like TV.) Then by Thursday, they can see how hard it is to keep those eye lids open in class. Then when you talk about being tired from too little sleep your teenager understands what you mean.

Teenagers need to become confident in making their own decisions and learning about consequences, even if the results are sometimes painful. If they were convinced their tanned legs will keep them warm in the middle of winter, you may need to let them stand at the bus stop and get cold. If the weather forecast brings the risk of frostbite, this would be too dangerous a lesson. If it is not freezing and your teenager would get the shivers, this may be a helpful lesson. The debate about wearing long pants would probably end for the remainder of the year after they got cold. So if the choice they make is safe, it is best to let your children make their own decisions to learn about their capabilities.

It will boost your teenager's confidence to comment on their new style that you have not seen before. In the clothing store let them try on the clothing you know you will disagree with. Let your daughter try to bend over in the dress too short or your guy try to keep his pants on when he jumps with his hands in the air. The dressing room can be an entertaining experience to prove your point. You may not always like a new hair style but you allow the experiment because you like the person.

The Battery Theory

You might be wondering what a battery has to do with raising a teenager but it is actually very important. When teenagers need to be corrected I like to think about car batteries. A battery has a two poles, one positive and one negative. Giving a criticism is almost always registered by the teenager as negative. Most teenagers when they hear something negative immediately get angry and tune you out. They don't want to hear negatives so they avoid the issue any way they can.

With the battery theory, the idea is to always connect with the positive side before you deal with anything negative. When you tell your teenager something positive first, they are much more apt to be able to listen to something constructive that follows.

For example, if your son or daughter has completed half a chore, like sweeping out the garage, and thinks it is done. You do not say, "You are not finished." Instead, what you could say is, "The middle of the garage looks great. Why don't I come check it when you have finished the corners?" Another positive approach is to have your teenager do his or her own critique after you say something positive. So you could say, "The middle of the garage is swept well. What do you think about the rest?" When you praise the half of the task your teenager has done well he or she is much more willing to hear about the rest of the chore at hand.

Once you have commented on the part they have done well, teenagers often will begin to offer their own critique; you won't even have to mention the negative or the constructive part.

This car battery theory works well with others too. Most people like to hear something positive first, like spouses and little kids. It could even work with your mother-in-law.

Frustration and Confidence

When we see our young people struggling, the 'super parent' in us jumps out and we rush into help. So when your young guy has decided to use chocolate chips and toothpicks to make his molecular model, you might want to tell him he is doing it all wrong. Instead I would recommend you take a seat next to him, put your hands in your pockets and just watch. As he puts the toothpicks into the small chips, they begin to melt and his model falls apart. Then when he gets frustrated, restrain yourself from helping. Just ask him some questions like, "What do you think would work better?" Maybe then he will try dry elbow macaroni and realize that doesn't work either. Keep asking questions. Allow frustration and let him figure something else all on his own. Eventually he will come up with something like marshmallows or gumdrops, without your help.

When a teenager can learn to tackle frustrations and overcome them they feel a sense of accomplishment. This life lesson of overcoming frustration is invaluable. Too many of us think frustration is bad for our children and our teenagers and we want to rescue them from distress when in the long run we are actually hindering their passage to be independent and confident.

Overcoming frustration is the reward for building confidence. It is not always the end product that is most important. A teenager is likely to remember the hard work of achieving the goal as a memorable experience. When your teenager gets tired and starts to lose patience, your investment in their activities will pull your teenager through.

If your teenager wants to quit or give up when they start comparing themselves to peers around them, he or she needs your help. Your teenager may be afraid to test his or her limits. He or she may not know what their personal best is. When teenagers know their family believes in them, it doesn't matter as much what the other kids are doing. The essential ingredient in the formula for a successful teenager is a parent saying, "I think you are terrific. Just do your best. I think you are doing fine."

If you give in when your teenager faces difficulties and challenges along the way of what they choose to do, your teenager may give up on himself or herself. Your persistence and belief in your son or daughter is the key to his or her success.

Compliments are like Raindrops

As often as you tell your teenager something positive about themselves do you notice how they may persist in telling you that you are wrong about them? Sometimes teenagers are really critical of themselves. Or if you told them last month that you love them when they are upset at you, they will insist that you do not love them. Sometimes they say no one loves them.

It can be a confusing picture to a parent who feels she is telling her teenager positive things. Compliments are a lot like raindrops. Over time they evaporate in the minds and hearts of our teenagers and children. So even if you rain compliments, soon they will dry up and things won't grow as well. So you have to keep repeating all those positive reassurances of your love, caring and concern for them because these messages evaporate with time. It is best to err on the side of giving too much reassurance and too many compliments than not giving them often enough.

Be Sincere and Honest

No matter your personal style as a parent, it is important to be sincere with your teenager. To make up things you do not believe in will prove phony to you and to your teenager. If you honestly believe something about your teenager and that belief will encourage your teenager, share your feelings with your young person. How you do so needs to match your own personal style. If you are a quiet person, you may find you are most comfortable saying something in a quiet way and using brief sentences. It is perfectly OK to match your own style of communication with the positive feedback your give your son or daughter. You do not need to sound like anyone else. What really counts is that you sincerely mean the compliment or statement.

Teenagers want the truth, not something that is false. Part of being honest is to evaluate what you have to say to your teenager. If what you honestly have to say calls for an expression of anger and truthfulness that could really devastate your teenager, it is best to pause. Consider what this information will accomplish for your teenager. Will this degrade or belittle your young person? If so, I think it is best to wait and really consider what you have to say.

At times your teenager may ask you questions you will find you are reluctant to answer honestly. You again may have to pause and ask yourself why your teenager is curious and what meaning it has to your teen. What if your teenager asks you if you used drugs when you were a teenager and your answer is yes? You may wonder how do you present this information to your teenager. You do not want to encourage your teenager to use drugs. I think it is best to be honest about your past and to add what you learned from your experiences. What is it you wished you did differently? What makes your experience different from the situation your teenager faces today?

Saying what you really believe about your teenager is best given in the best light possible. If your teenager asks you if you think he is acting like a loser, because of his poor choices, you may need to dig deep to find what little encouragement you have for him that is honest. You might say you think he can learn something from his poor decisions and can put his life back together in a better way next time. Or that you are confident he will not repeat this choice again because it turned out so bad for him. And of course you can always say you love him and care for him.

If you want your teenager and children to be truthful with you, you must be honest with them. They learn directly from your behavior. Most teenagers get very angry when a parent lies to them and leads them to believe things that are not the truth. Part of being a teenager is to seek the truth about themselves, the people around them and their worlds.

The Five T'S

Here are five things that begin with 'T' that will be easy for you to remember to give your teenager.

T#1 Offer Your Time

Number one is giving your time. Like any endeavor, to do a good job, you need to spend enough time at something to help it prosper. Finding time for your teenager to say nice things and pay attention to them is very critical to helping them build positive views of themselves. Many parents have to look past the mood and attitude and still offer their time in the face of great resistance.

Your teenager knows that you spend your time on what is most important to you. When you have a busy schedule you either have to look for windows of opportunities or actually schedule in family time. Few parents would dispute that a two year-old needs a good deal of a parent's time to raise them and give them a good start in life. I think teenagers need more of your time and attention than when they were little people.

T#2 Offer Your Trust

Your teenager needs you to have confidence in his or her ability to do what is right. So when they get an opportunity to test out their decision, you can encourage them with your trust that they will do the right thing. When they fail in their attempts to do what is the right thing, encourage them again to make good choices. This requires a lot of forgiveness on the part of the parent. You may trust them sometimes when they are having difficulty trusting themselves.

Part of building self-esteem is to believe they know what to do without being told. Or if given enough time, they can finish the task that they begin. A big step for a number of parents is to trust them to do their homework and maintain their grades in school. This kind of trust builds self-confidence and encourages mature decision-making.

T#3 Offer Your Touch

Touching your teenager can be a difficult proposition when they tell you they no longer want you to hug and kiss them, like you used to do when they were younger. I think one of the best ways to touch your teenager is with your eyes. To look at them while you are listening to them or just smile at their eyes can be a warm reassurance of your love for them and you will touch their hearts.

Other safe ways is to touch their arms, their heads (if you aren't messing up a hair style) and a pat on the shoulder. Sometimes when you offer a hug, you'll get a side or a partial hug. Just accept what your teenager is comfortable with. A number of teenagers do have difficulty accepting hugs and kisses because they are exploring their sexual feelings and interests. A touch from a parent can be uncomfortable and awkward for them.

Some teenagers will accept some touching from you when they are alone at home or going to bed at night.

T#4   Offer to Talk

Talking to a teenager has a lot to do with listening to your son or daughter. It also means genuinely asking questions to understand your teenager's point of view. And the No Lecture Method of talking to a teenager opens up communication by helping you ask questions instead of lecturing. Most teenagers long for a forum to talk about their thoughts and ideas with their parents. And they love it when you take them seriously.

T#5   Allow Teasing

Not being able to communicate with your teenager or not resolving your differences can be a serious problem. If you have observed groups of teenagers you'll notice they love to be with friends, to laugh and talk. Your teenager can be a lot of fun. They usually do not tolerate being the focus of a joke but most of them love to make jokes. It is helpful to have some fun with your teenager. And they can have fun with their families as well as their friends. Using humor with them can lighten a serious mood and avoid an argument.

Strategies for Building Self-esteem

No Buts About it

When you use the word 'but' in a statement it is like using a big eraser and you take away whatever you said that was positive. If you say, "You did a really great job your homework, but it took you three days to do it." The teenager thinks at first you are praising him and then when he hears the word 'but' he thinks you are critical rather than encouraging.

So, instead of saying, "Thanks for cleaning the kitchen but you forgot the pans on the stove." Try this; "Thanks for cleaning the kitchen." Then breathe, take a deep breath, pause. Then ask, "Were you planning on doing the pans on the stove?" Your compliment takes hold as your young person ponders how well the job was done.

Critical Review

Too much criticism will teach your teenager to condemn him or herself and to find fault with others. Vulnerable and confused about their own identity they are very sensitive to criticism, especially from a parent. The world of their peers is not always forgiving and kind. Teenagers can be very cruel to each other.

Once a teenager begins to condemn him or herself it takes a lot of repair work to rebuild positive feelings. For a number of people negative information is easier to believe than positive. Have you noticed when someone compliments you, you may not always believe them. If someone says to a woman, "Your hair looks good." She might readily say, "Oh, I was just going to get it cut." Or, " I think it is too short." The person may have to insist they are serious about the compliment before the other person will accept it.

When teenagers are struggling for a positive view of themselves and they make a mistake, they sometimes feel like they can't do anything right. While you are falling off the ladder the last thing you need is a lecture on safety tips. A person cannot learn very well in a highly emotional state. After calming down and thinking about a situation a person can begin to learn about their mistakes.

Praise the Task

Sensitive teenagers seem reluctant to believe positive things about themselves. You do well to focus your praise on their tasks or efforts rather than on them directly. As you praise their achievement, you will notice that your young person begins to believe more positively about him or herself. The notion is to praise the art rather than the artist. Indirectly, the sensitive teenager praises him or herself.

If you tell your teenager that he or she is always wonderful or perfect, your teenager is not likely to find these comments believable. If you say she is a great poet, she may compare herself to the great poets of all time. In comparison, she wants a more realistic appraisal. If you tell her that her poem moved you and made you think of what it would be like to be a snowflake, your teenager will find this comment believable. The next thing that happens is the teenager praises himself or herself. She says to herself, "I made my dad feel good with what I wrote. I did a good job."

What we can give our teenagers is descriptive recognition. That is, recognize the task and describe what the teenager did, "The yard looks like a garden." Then we add our feelings and thanks. "It is a treat to look at. Thank you." The teenager then registers that they did something important, it created a positive feeling in their parent and they were thanked. Then the teenager praises him or herself. And he says to himself, "I pleased my dad. I did a good job. I can do it again."

Respect the Individual

Many parents have said, "How can I be respectful to my teenager when he is so disrespectful to me?" This is a valid question, especially for the tired and tested parent. It is hard to maintain your cool in the face of such obnoxious behavior and defiance.

Because you are more mature than your teenager the weight of maintaining a respectful attitude rests on your shoulders. When you are antagonized by your teenager's response, you may, out of desperation, dish out the same kind of remarks with which your teenager taunts you. When you are fighting with your teenager on his or her immature level you are in a no win situation.

Your teenager needs you to respectfully comment on their behavior even when they annoy you (or infuriate you). He or she needs you to maintain calm in the face of their adolescent calamities, to respect their ability to choose and to present consequences in a courteous manner. It is parent's attitude of respect and capacity to believe in their dignity, that teaches them that, even in the heat of their rebellion, they too have the capacity to show concern and respect for others. When you respect the individual, the individual becomes more respectable in return.

What is Your Dream?

No one may have ever asked you, "What is your dream?" For many adults this question is posed too late in life. Your young person has a dream. If you can help him or her discover it, many wonderful and exciting things can happen.

There are always hurdles to one's dream, that is why so many people never achieve theirs. With each hurdle one must find a way over it, under it or around it so it does not block the way to success.

Help your young person by asking, "What is your dream? If you can dream it, in time, with persistence, you can do it."

Don't Let Them Settle for Anything Less

Most parents hope their teenager will have a secure sense of themselves, possess high self-esteem and believe they are capable of being successful. The key to this success is for your teenager to believe that he or she is liked by family, friends and those who care for him or her. Teenagers need to feel appreciated for their own person and have the things they do be recognized as important. To be respected as a person who is allowed to make choices for themselves and to live their own lives. To be trusted to be a good citizen and to do what is best and right for themselves. To be thought of as capable to be successful and encouraged to strive for their personal best. Most importantly young people need to be loved for being just the way they are.

Love them for who they are
Respect them for what they have the potential
to become
And don't ever let them settle for less
than their personal best

2

PUTTING SOLUTIONS INTO PRACTICE

CHAPTER SIX

Who is in Charge of my Decisions?

The Future is a path through the forest.
At every fork in the road you must make a decision
      that could alter your trek through life
Should you stray off the path your journey changes
      and you must find your way back on
You cannot turn back, for you have not a map
      and every tree looks the same as the last
Some paths may be bathed in sunlight,
      while others are dark and somber
You can see the path ahead of you
      but not enough to know what is there
Your path may end in a dark forest
      or a field of wildflowers and butterflies
The future is a path through the forest...

Courtney Drake

Teenagers make Decisions, Parents Guide

As the world grows more complex, so do your teenager's choices. What your young person chooses can have a big impact on his or her life. If he decides to do poorly in high school, it can effect his chance for college. If she chooses the wrong friends, she can end up with a reputation that takes years to shake. If he decides to drink and drive the consequences could be disastrous.

In the past, when you were a teenager, the world you had to deal with was not quite like the world your young person faces today. In the 1960's spit wads were a big concern in high school. Today, our young people deal with issues like violence, AIDS, drugs and alcohol. We don't live in small, close knit communities where we know our neighbors and it is safe for our kids to be in the park or to ride their bikes across town.

Our sons or daughters are pressured to grow up quickly. Some of our youngsters don't get to be kids for very long. The world around them bombards them with messages to drink, get high and be sexual. Amidst the advertising and hype, we lack models for moral excellence.

Your job is to help guide your teenager with the choices and decisions that lie before them. Your influence can make a significant difference in how your teenager chooses what he or she decides to do. Even though you may not feel ready for the kind of challenges your young person presents, dealing with them is a major part of your parenting task.

Our youth are influenced by the changes that occur in our society. Their peer group is far more sophisticated than those of your generation. Technological growth is replacing people skills with advanced electronics and computers. Crowded classrooms are commonplace. Television, music and movies influence our impressionable young people with powerful messages and expose them to the adult world at a much earlier age than you might have experienced as a youth. Crime and violence have significantly increased in our communities and sometimes we witness these in our own homes. Alcohol and drugs are more available to younger children. The drugs that are available to teenagers today are far more potent than the drugs of a generation ago. Gangs are alive and well in our society.

The American family has gone through profound changes, with a high percentage of divorced, single parent and remarried families. With transient children and complex family groups, fewer adults are consistently home to interact with our teenagers and children. With two parent working families or single parent families, our young people spend a great deal of time without adult supervision. Often they are alone.

The work ethic is different for many young people. In an age of modern conveniences, some children may never have to learn how to do household tasks or help with work that in the past was a big part of being a family member. Fast food and a fast pace leaves families with less dependence on each other.

In the past, many teenagers had a very short adolescence because they were required to take on adult responsibilities at a young age to help the family survive. They may have been responsible for raising young children or carrying a work load of a sick or deceased parent. A few generations past, many would marry at fifteen or sixteen and start a family of their own.

The teenagers of today have different choices than you probably did. They too have to face many more complex decisions at a much younger age than you did.

Only you can slow down your teenager's world. What balances the choices for our young people is the influence and loving attention from their parents. You can be a powerful balance because of your connection to your son or daughter. No one is a more capable of slowing down the fast pace of the world for your teenager than you.

Facing Choices is Hard for Parents Too

Parents have a hard time facing the choices of adolescence because *you care*. The last thing you want as a parent is to see your child hurt, through physical pain, emotional grief or social loss. Watching your child become a teenager sometimes brings suffering and struggling that can break your heart.

Sometimes parents of teenagers, especially young teenagers, initially wish to avoid looking at the issues of our young person's world unless forced to do so. With your attention to potential difficulties, your teenager has a more mature caring person to help guide him or her. The success your teenager experiences dealing with choices and decisions has much to do with a relationship *between you and your teenager*.

The Basics of Decision Making

How do we make wise choices? There is a process each of us goes through whether or not we are aware of all the steps to reach a final conclusion about what we will decide to do. Good decision making is honed by maturity and experience. Your decisions are guided by your values, morals, maturity and beliefs. It may be helpful for you to look at this process so you become more aware of the steps your teenager needs to learn.

The first step is to recognize that you have a decision to make. There may be one or two choices or many possibilities. Here is a common process many adults go through:

* **STEP ONE:**
     Define the problem or issue requiring a decision.
* **STEP TWO:**
     Recognize your possible choices.
         * Two choices available (like yes/no)

        * more than two choices or options
        * create your own choices

* STEP THREE:
    Gather information (pros and cons).
        * from past experiences
        * from asking others
        * from resources like books, movies, etc.

* STEP FOUR:
    Narrow choice options to your best ones.

* STEP FIVE:
    Evaluate.
        * what consequences with each choice? (pros/cons)

* STEP SIX:
    Take your time.

* STEP SEVEN:
    Make a decision (yes, no, etc.).

* STEP EIGHT:
    Evaluate your decision after it has been made.

The sixth step, taking your time, is usually the weakest in the decision making process for many adolescents. Not taking enough time to think through a decision can mean making a hurried or rushed decision, which teenagers do often.

This whole eight step process takes time. Time is necessary to weigh out the choices to think and do some research. Teenagers tend to be very impatient with this process. To help your teenager get comfortable with using this process, you must be patient and persistent. Initially you need to be able to communicate with your teenager. Then you have to spend a good deal of time asking questions and listening.

This decision making process also takes energy and effort. By encouraging your teenager to answer questions with each of these steps you will have a chance to teach them to think logically. They will need encouragement along the way to stay motivated. As your young person learns to take their time with decision-making it tends to reduce their impulsiveness.

A young teenager, driven by her impulsive nature, dealing with the pressure from peers, can easily develop a decision making process where she takes step one and then immediately jumps to step seven, making a decision, where she comes to a decision. The teenager thinks, "Should I skip school?" and then moves quickly to "Yeah, it would be fun." Your naïve young person may think that this is all it takes to make a good decision. Teenagers rely on a lot of luck, intuition and of course, the 'good sense' of their friends.

Feeling hurried, your teenager may think there is no time for the steps in between. Green about real life consequences, they just wait to see what happens. The adolescent learns *after* their choice rather than thinking about things *before* the decision. Learning, primarily through experience, can put your teenager at risk.

You will need to walk your teenager through the process until they get into a habit of using it. A good way to start teaching a good decision-making process is to review the decisions your teenager may face by writing them down. Write the pros and cons for something as simple as do they want a part time job or a more complex problem like what are the best classes to take during high school.

This process is not needed for common decisions like, "What do I want for dinner?" Or "Should I do my homework now?" These are daily decisions, usually reached quickly because your teenager makes them often. The pros and cons are familiar. The different ways to choose have been tested. For example, if they eat too much candy after school they might feel sick. Or if they don't do their homework the only thing dad or mom will do is sigh and nag them until they do. They quickly evaluate if those consequences are worth what their choice may bring.

With a new social world comes new choices. Other first time new choices intriguing to your teenager might be about breaking the rules, like "should I skip school today with my new friend?" Or choices that have more serious consequences like, "Should I smoke marijuana or take an opened bottle of beer?" These kind of first time situations can take your teenager by surprise. The choices may entice your young person who yearns to be included as part of his or her peer culture. The teenage environment is filled with energy and excitement and sometimes decisions are based on being there. Young teenagers are inclined to choose to be accepted by others rather than what may be the best for them.

A More Simple Way to Decide

This eight step decision process seems pretty complex especially for the young, impulsive young person. To make decision making more *user friendly* for your teenager, you can pare this process down into a more simplified version. First, pose a question about your teenager's decision; " *How will this decision make you feel...tomorrow?*" Note the word *tomorrow*. It is the critical word in the question. Typically, a teenager may want to make a decision that is right for the moment. For example he or she may think: "If I smoke marijuana with my friends, I will be cool. I will fit in. I will be part of the group. I will find out what it is like and I will have some fun."

Like other teenagers, her decision making *responds to the moment*. Most teenagers do not ask if their decisions will effect them *tomorrow*. This is an entirely different question than most adolescents will consider on their own.

Your teenager, unless taught differently, is likely to adopt experiential learning to teach them about their world. If your daughter or son decides "I will skip school now and see what happens" Or, "I will have sex with my girlfriend now and see what happens." You know your teenager may be putting him or herself at risk.

The *here and now* is what drives the experiential learner. *Now* is all that seems to matter to the impulsive adolescent. The important things to this learner are impulses, desires and drives. There is little need to think about tomorrow. The primary concern is the here and now for impulsive people.

The problem with *now* is that, in most cases, what happens today has a lot to do with *tomorrow*. Today's decision, based on one's impulsive desire, feels good for the moment. With the wrong decision we know that *tomorrow* may bring worry, sorrow, hopelessness and sometimes a lot of pain. The experience may not be worth what follows.

I think of a young man, sixteen, who was saying how sorry he was he had sex with his fifteen year-old girlfriend, who had just given birth to their son. He felt pushed out of her life, afraid of the consequences and was feeling the gravity of his situation. His important message to other teenagers is for them to *think* carefully before making a choice about sex while you are young. He said he thought he was too young to be sexually involved. Experience was his teacher. He said *now he knew* what the adults had been talking about, that teenagers are too young to have sex.

Your Head Versus Your Heart

Another way to simplify decision-making is to present your teenager's choice as a balance between one's *head* and one's *heart*.

 VS

When you listen only to your heart, you may make blind, emotional decisions. The heart is impulsive and careless. Many times relationship decisions can be followed with regrets that sometimes even turn out to be disasters. The old saying 'Love is blind' warns of this fact. Making a decision based solely on one's heart is using one's emotions as a guide.

One part of this decision process has to do with what their *heart* tells them to do. Their hearts are their impulsive thoughts (like the *child* part of their thinking). The teenager's heart doesn't want to look at the realistic side of choices. This heart seeks love, romance, excitement and the thrill of life. The heart yearns to feel passion and always seeks pleasure. It migrates to experiences that please for the moment, seeking immediate gratification. The adolescent heart wants life to be like those 'happy ever after' movies, filled with passionate bliss, every need or impulse met for the sole purpose of their happiness and satisfaction.

The other part of their thinking has to do with a teenager's *head*, or rational thinking. With their minds or head, teenager's logic leads them to contemplate what they ought to do. What they *should* do (like the *parent* part of their thinking) is what is really best. Rational thinking is a composite of what others teach and caution them about as well as what they believe to be true, right and wise for themselves. Their knowledge, apart from their impulsive heart, is rationally and realistically based. Though this is an adolescent mind, your son or daughter will be able to tell you about the 'should' part of most decisions. In your inquiry about what their *head* says, your teenager becomes more aware of his or her options.

Though the message from the teenager's *head* may not be popular with your young person, it is important for your teenager to pay attention to what their head is saying. This rational or moral advice is not what your teenager may want to act on.

Instead, he or she may choose what their romantic heart tells them to do.

The problem for the adolescent is that what their hearts say to do is many times in great opposition with what their heads say to do. So you can ask your teenager, "*What does you head tell you to do?*" And they usually can readily tell you. Your teenager may say, "I want may old boyfriend back even though he lied and cheated on me. I still love him and I miss him."

Then you can ask, "*What does your head tell you to do?*" Now the teenager may say, "I know he is not good for me. I know that if I go back to him, I will get hurt again. This relationship probably won't work for me." Now the fight is on, a struggle between the teenager's head and heart. The rational and the emotional begin the battle over what the teenager ought to do. By asking questions like this, you will help make your teenager more aware of the struggle between their head and heart.

As the battle progresses, your teenager will be more aware of where his or her decision comes from. If they make a decision based on what their heart says to do they can evaluate it and see what happens. In some cases it may work out just fine. In others, disaster can occur. As long as they are learning and have an opportunity for discussion and respectful evaluation with a parent, they are well on their way to successful decision-making.

The young adolescent usually has a strong, impulsive heart and is likely to be immature in his or her *head*. As your teenager matures and experiments with choices and values they become more aligned with the ideas of their *head*, and less occupied and swayed by the yearnings and impulsiveness of their *heart*.

The resource you can best invest in has less to do with you acting as a wise counsel. Instead you *tap your teenager's wisdom*. Contrary to popular beliefs, most adolescents have great capacity to make wise decisions about their lives. The more your teenager tells you about the differences between their heart and head the better you will understand the maturity level of your teenager. Greater knowledge and wisdom comes with both time and experience.

This respectful interchange between your teenager's head and heart can do so much for helping your young person look at the dilemmas of their choices. It can simplify some of the complexity too. The internal conversation in a teenager's mind may go like this:

* **Her heart**:
>   "I love this guy. He was my first love. If I go back to him I think he can change. I want to give him another chance."
* **Her head**:
>   "This will not work. He is not mature enough for you. He is not your guy. Look at the other girls he let down."
* **Her heart**:
>   "But I think I love him. He was so sweet sometimes. I know there could be a great guy inside."
* **Her head**:
>   "This guy may never change. He thinks he is a tough guy. He knew how to say the right things. But he isn't honest, he isn't true."
* **Her heart**:
>   "But I think I love him. I know I miss him. And he is so cute."
* **Her head**:
>   "Don't go back. You can do better than this guy. Just give someone else a chance."

In most emotional decisions, especially for teenagers, there is a battle between one's head and one's heart.

Choose to be Happy

A question to ask your teenager; "*Will this decision make you happy...tomorrow?*" Again, you bring the future into a question, your young person can look past the moment and get the bigger picture of their choices.

If your teenager can honestly answer that their decision makes them happy today and also make them happy in the future they are likely to be making a good decision for themselves. No one else can do a better job of insuring their own personal success.

As you know some of your teenager's decisions will change and mature over time. So your teenager may be quite sure today he or she will never go to college and want to play in a band. If your teenager can honestly admit that this choice will make them happy both today and in the future then for today it will have to be OK. These 'definite' decisions are likely to change over time in a week or a month or so. So don't decide too quickly to give away his or her college fund to some other needy young person. Accept for today your teenager is contemplating and making some decisions regarding his or her happiness.

Before and After

You will not always be there to guide your teenager about the best thing to do. Whether or not you can control what experiences your teenagers have, they still do need to know *how* to make important decisions *before* they are presented with situations. Your teenager is then prepared when and if certain situations ever occur.

Dealing with choices and situations after the fact means that you need to discuss the situation with your teenager. Once you have assessed what has occurred then parents need to create a *learning consequence* that is *the experience* that occurs because of their decisions and choices.

Sometimes it is too late to do anything about a situation. This may mean you and your teenager have a talk about what they subsequently learned.

It Won't Happen to Me

If a teenager thinks no matter what he does (drink, use drugs, drive recklessly, fail classes), his charm and youth will get him through, he may be in for a big surprise. So when he is expelled from school or sits in youth detention center it dawns on him that he must have been mistaken. Tough stuff does happen to teenagers.

Youth is not a protective shield. When you come across newpaper articles about teenager's mishaps in car accidents, drive by shooting or deadly accidents, show these stories to your young person. If your teenager ever knows another teenager who is critically ill or who dies, take your son or daughter to the hospital or the funeral. This real life experience will help teach your teenager he or she is not omnipotent.

Why are teenagers so blinded to the consequences of their actions? What encourages this pervasive nonchalance about the future? This kind of thinking is based on a youthful and naive notion many teenagers have about themselves. If you could hear the 'mind talk' of a teenager this is how it usually goes: "I will not get pregnant if I have sex and don't use birth control. That happens to "other" people."

Here are some examples of the kind of thinking that keeps our young people so naive:

"Bad things won't happen to me...
- Because I am really only a kid, even though I may look like an adult.
- Because I believe I am a nice person. Tragic things don't happen to nice people.
- Because this rough stuff only happens in the movies.
- Because I am too young to experience serious consequences.

Thus many teenagers are convinced: they won't get burned by the fire, they won't get hooked on smoking marijuana, they won't get addicted to alcohol, they are too young to get AIDS, and their relationships will not be like the others in high school. Theirs will not end in heartbreak. Why? Because they are... *Young. Omnipotent. Unique. Special. Untouchable.*

Sometimes presenting the reality that bad things do happen to teenagers just like them can be a big wake up call about the real consequences for poor decisions. What happens to a close friend can be a good learning experience for your teenager. A peer who is pregnant can have a big influence on her friends by helping them to think seriously about the consequences of choosing to have a sexual relationship when they are young. A friend's experience can help your teenager decide not to have sex. If a friend gets hooked on smoking marijuana and starts to change it can be a kind of second-hand learning about poor choices.

Seventeen year-old girl Erin told me she thought she was pregnant. She was filled with panic and shaking with anxiety. Her period was four weeks overdue. She had had one sexual experience. She and her partner were not using any birth control, which is typical for the majority of sexually active teenagers. This 'just happened', her sexual encounter was not planned.

After this experience, Erin said, "I learned I am too young to have sex. Now I know that." Did she listen to others who told her the same thing? Did she consider what her parents and other friends had warned her about? No, she did not want to believe that their advice would ever apply to her... until now. Now, with all her heart, Erin believed their warning. Now, with many regrets she wants to start all over. Erin knows things will never really be the same for her again.

The decisions that some teenagers make are far more serious than lighting a match. Some of those decisions can and will change the course of their lives. When something bad does happen, it is typical for a teenager to say, "It is not fair this happened to me!" The issue is not what is or is not fair, the issue is that it happened as part of real life. Teenagers need to realize that tough things that happen in life are real. Like the bumper sticker that reads, "Life is not a dress rehearsal." If a teenager chooses adult behaviors, he or she will have to face adult consequences. The choices your teenager faces today may bring grave consequences like contracting AIDS, being seriously injured, emotionally scarred or harmed in some tragic way that can last one's lifetime.

Real Life

Part of real life acceptance for teenagers that have made poor choices is to share their experiences and advise other teens. Especially if you have more mature teenagers, like seniors, talk with younger more impressionable teenagers (like seventh and eighth graders) in school. Here you can have a successful match of more mature young people teaching younger teenagers about real-life decisions.

Peers are very influential with each other. They really feel like they live in a time and world set apart from other people, especially parents. Listening to another teenager's tragic story of poor choices and pain can break this illusion that many teenagers have that traumatic events will not happen if they make similar choices. Peers are people they can relate to, where there is no generation or communication gap.

Situations Before They Occur

Talking with your teenager about issues they may face as they grow older can help prepare your young person when faced with difficult decisions. For instance, if your teenager is a ninth grader you can present possible situations he or she may face in tenth, eleventh or twelfth grade.

You can do all this by treating your teenager as the *expert*. He or she can also help you pose possible situational decisions by telling you what some of the older teenagers are doing. Your teenager will be more comfortable telling you what other teenagers should do, rather than you asking questions that put the focus on them directly. Situations you present could be those that could occur with any high school student. Like issues relating dating, school, drugs, violence, cheating or dealing with a relationship issues.

Below are some examples of how you can present a hypothetical situation to your young person who can lecture you on what the teenager in this situation could do.

Situation #1: There is a sophomore and she really likes this senior. He is going to take her to lunch. On the way he lights a joint while he is driving. What should she do?

Situation #2: Three seniors are driving together after school. There are two guys and one girl. They stop in a store. One of the fellows decides to steal a pack of cigarettes. What should the other two do as they watch their friend pick up the pack?

Situation #3 Two juniors are in a chemistry class. One is getting a "B" in the class. His friend is getting a "D". His friend motions to ask him to show him an answer on the exam they are taking. What should the guy do?

Situation #4 Two 16 year-old girls are best friends. One of the girls is dating a guy two years older than she is. She has been seeing him for two weeks. He says he really wants to have sex with her. How should her friend advise her?

Situation #5 A bunch of people are at a junior/senior party. There are no parents home (they are on vacation). Most of those attending are using either alcohol, marijuana and cocaine is being used by several. Two fellows at the party do not drink. Someone hands them each a beer. What should they do?

Situation #6 A sophomore is at a party. Several seniors ask him if he would like to come with them for a ride. He really wants to fit in. As he is heading for the car, he sees the driver stagger, with a beer in his hand. What should this fellow do?

Situation #7 Two girls sit in a tenth grade English class. They notice a boy near them puts a small amount of cocaine in his book and snorts it. A few minutes later they notice he has a revolver in his hands. What should they do?

Situation #8 A sophomore got asked out to the prom by a fellow she has liked for a long time. He recently broke up with his longtime girlfriend. His former girlfriend threatens to beat up this girl if she goes out with him. What should she do?

Situation #9 A freshman skipped school for a day. When she comes home she erases the message on her parent's answering machine, informing them she was not in school. She runs into her school counselor who says she has a meeting with this girl's mom tomorrow. Should she tell her parents she skipped before they find out from the counselor?

Situation #10 In a freshman English class, the seats are assigned. A boy sits next to this girl and says very vulgar things to her. He touches her and she wants him to stop but she is afraid of telling him 'no'. He keeps getting more aggressive. What should she do?

Situation #11 A junior has met a freshman girl and they are seeing each other. She is really rough with him, putting him down, hitting him and laughing at him when he tells her to stop. She seems to take pleasure in his pain. On Monday, he comes to school with a cast on his arm. He says he fell down and broke his arm. What should his friends do if they are suspicious about his story?

Situation #12 A senior, who gets good grades, does everything right and is always on time, seems really depressed. He has been talking about how there is really no future and school is just a waste of time. He seems out of it, stares off in space. He has stopped seeing his usual friends, his girlfriend broke up with him and he spends most of his time in his room. What should his one remaining friend do?

These are just a few situations to present to your teenager. In doing so, parents have the opportunity to explore decision making based on their family values. Knowing what values your teenager chooses to use in specific situations can help you know what to expect he or she might do.

You do not need to be an expert to develop hypothetical situations for your teenager. If you present an incorrect scenario, your expert, your teenager, will correct you. Remember you are talking to an authority about junior high or high school. Just listening to stories about what happens to others at your son or daughter's school can instruct you on how to present ideas.

These situations work best if they do not directly refer to your teenager in the situations. You may present situations you hope your teenager will never have to deal with. Preparation can help just in case they have to make tough decisions.

Most teenagers, because of their expertise about junior high and high school, will gladly share their knowledge about what they think other teenagers should do in these situations. They will be encouraged to tell you more if you are respectful of their expertise and their interpretation of what is happening around them. Here you are not the expert and you must not lecture them on what they should do. Your adolescent needs to be able to lecture you.

If your teenager is prepared to make decisions before he is faced with difficult or complex situations he has a much better chance to make good choices for himself. Thinking ahead will help prepare them. Some teenagers learn these lessons by watching an older brother or sister go through some tough adolescent times. By observing their friends facing hardships, your teenager can use these situations to practice how they would use their values and decision-making skills. Sometimes they can also give valuable advice to their friends in need.

Reinforcing your teenagers with praise and positive feedback about their good decision-making skills helps them make wise choices. With insightful answers you can respond to your teenager by saying, "You are so mature for your age." Or, "You have some great ideas." Or, "Your friends are so lucky to have such a good friend like you." Your teenager does like to know when his or her knowledge has impressed you.

Who Gets Hurt ?

When exploring possible situations you can ask your teenager, "Who will get hurt by poor decisions?" That is the potential problem that accompanies all poor decisions. Someone will get hurt emotionally or physically. Emotional traumas come from feeling used, belittled, degraded or being left out or let down. Not feeling loved or cared about causes great emotional pain (having a broken heart). All of these negative responses drain a young person of positive feelings of self-esteem and feelings of worth.

Avoiding pain, either emotional or physical, is the goal of many decisions people make. To avoid pain you must first be aware that the potential exists with the decisions you make.

By making wise decisions, your teenager has a good chance of escaping or avoiding some painful experiences such as a broken heart, a broken promise, a damaged car, a negative reputation at school, a black eye, a poor report card or the loss of a good friend. Wise decisions can save them from being traumatized, in contrast to a teenager who is reckless and haphazard in his or her decision-making. Without experimenting with too much pain, your teenager has a good shot at success in adulthood. The teenager that is a good decision-maker can learn a great deal from watching others around them, rather than needing to have all those experiences for themselves. They also develop a sense of high self-esteem and confidence about their capabilities by making good choices for themselves.

Being Perfect

It is unrealistic to expect or anticipate perfection from your teenager. A more realistic expectation for parenting is for you to hope your teenager does his or her personal best and strives to be capable, happy and successful. Working at being perfect can create a great deal of pressure for an adolescent who is maturing because perfection does not allow room for any error. It is certainly not human to be perfect. We all make mistakes; do the wrong things, think the worst. A young person experiences great guilt and rejection when perfection is what is expected when making attempts at the trial of life. Sometimes the best lessons are a result of your mistakes.

Unlike perfection, doing one's personal best is more realistic and it makes it easier to take a risk to try something new. Striving for one's personal best is different than what perfectionistic children and teenagers aim for. Young people who seek only perfection tend to go through life with a lot of anxiety and pressure of expectation they put on themselves to do things perfectly. Sometimes they crack.

It is also helpful to tell your children that you have made mistakes and poor choices for yourself. Some kids are amazed when their parents make a mistake. They are surprised that you are not perfect. It is a tough model to follow, if you believe your parent is perfect and they never make or have made a poor decision.

One day I put my grandmother's antique glass butter dish into my microwave to heat some butter. It cracked and shattered into tiny pieces. It was something I could never replace. My young daughter looked at me with surprise and said, "Mom, you make mistakes too!" I realized I needed to tell her that I have made a lot of mistakes in my life and that I was in no way even remotely close to her 'perfect' notion about me. She seemed relieved to know her mom made mistakes. And that it is OK to make errors, they were part of life. I told her I have learned a lot from the mistakes I have made and I make lots of them, everyday. It is best is to try every day to do your best. And if you do make a mistake, own up to them, ask for forgiveness, learn valuable lessons from them and try to not repeat the same mistake again.

Testing Out Teenager's Theories

Your teenager may sound like the typical teenager that has everything all figured out. She claims to know both herself and the world around her. You can help her test out this theory. You can allow her safe experimentation to see if she is on track. This can be difficult for the parent that knows what their teenager will learn in the test rather than tell the young person to just listen to his or her wisdom.

The teenager that does not want anyone to tell her what to do or what to think will learn well through safe experimentation. When she gets in deep and has to face consequences, it can be helpful to allow her to experience what comes of her decision, if there is no safety risk. That means asking yourself whether the situation involving your teenager can be a valuable learning experience.

Not excusing your young person from school or having him redo his work, without your help, can be great learning opportunities. It may be one of the *experiences of their life.* Your teenager can learn about their own notions and learn to take on their own responsibility.

Don't Do What I Did

The last thing we want for our teenagers is to have them repeat the mistakes we have made in our lives. We want to protect them from emotional and physical harm. Your teenager may need to learn some of life's lessons through their own experiences, in spite of what you have learned in your life.

Your young person will tune you out when they hear; "When I was a teenager." They may think you grew up in the dark ages and cannot fathom you were actually once young. You will need to incorporate your experiences in the questions you ask and with someone else's story.

Thinking it Through

Your teenagers will need help to learn to assess their choices and decisions they need to make today. *Thinking through* a decision requires the help of another person, preferably an adult.

Who needs to explore the possible answers to situations presented to your teenager? Your teenager. Asking questions allows your adolescent to become the expert. Your expert needs to be thinking through situations for her or himself. When your expert is heading out the door to that party, with car keys in hand, your communication with him can help you boost your confidence in his maturity. *Thinking through* situations with a teenager consists of having them *talk through* the possibilities. With this kind of rehearsal, if they say it, they can remember it and then they can do it.

Circle of Relationships

Imagine there is a circle of people that surrounds your teenager. Imagine the faces of those people that are in your young person's life. Who is the closest to him or her, the circle of influence around your teenager? That would be the person they rely on heavily to help and guide them. Who significantly influences them right now? A boyfriend or girlfriend? Is you teenager obsessed with someone?

Get ready for lectures from your teenager. These lectures to you about life will unfold by using the following chapters.You will find ways to guide your teenager with both daily and life choices by looking at the circle of people who influence them. Be sure to include parents in this circle. When you examine the circle, you will note peer group and friends will change, it is you who remains a constant influence in the life of your young person.

CHAPTER SEVEN

I Can Pick My Own Friends

Oh, I get by with a little help from my friends.

the Beatles

Choice About Friendships

What must you do to be a good friend to someone else? What makes friendship last over time? If you only have one really good true friend, is that enough? How do you know when a friend has failed you? These are just some of the questions your teenager should think about. You can begin to have interesting dialogues about this very important subject after you have first heard from your young expert.

As you watch your teenager, you will observe how your youngster learns what it takes to make a good friend as well as to be a good friend. Sometimes there is great pain in the learning.

Imagine a circle of individuals around your teenager who are his or her friends. Most will be peers. There are also adults whom your teenager has a friendly relationship with, a teacher, a coach, an aunt, an uncle, a grandparent, a group leader, a pastor, etc.

Who does your teenager choose for a friend? Is it someone who is a lot like them? Someone who is honest and sincere? Someone who is funny and nice? What attracts your teenager to some people and not to others?

The twelve to fourteen year-olds begin to experience their new independence and autonomy by choosing new kinds of friends. Their social worlds become significantly larger. For the first time they may have friends their parents do not know. Now, with more peers, they have a bigger selection of people to befriend. The peer group continues to enlarge as they progress through school.

A teenager finds in his or her new world that now they are able to choose friends apart from their parents' influence. They begin to meet other teenagers who may have very different backgrounds than their own. The social groups forming around them can be very intriguing and perplexing.

Your teenager's friends are likely to change throughout their adolescent years. With a few exceptions, close ties of friendship they had as a young teenager are not likely to last through high school. Their choice of friends is likely to change just as they do.

Motivation For Choosing Friends

The young teenager wishes to fit in and gain approval from those around them. Teenagers seek friends to share similar experiences. When dealing with the insecurity of adolescence, it is comforting to know you are not alone. When others have the same problems and dilemmas, your teenager does not feel so unusual. Getting positive feedback from a peer helps validate your young person. The comfort for your teenager is that he or she is not considered weird. The message: you are OK!

Within friendships and peer groups, a teenager finds comfort in not being alone. Here they can explore their new 'social self' in an expanding social world. These friends are important because they help them feel important. Without them this period of their lives could be lonely and depressing.

Comparing oneself to one's peers helps the teenager in his search for self. The crisis of youth brings togetherness. If two teenagers together experience going through a growth spurt, they can relate to each other, discussing for example, how many pairs of tennis shoes they have gone through this year. If someone is having trouble with parents, plenty of other teenagers share this experience too.

Establishing roles within the social structure of peers is an important development too. Who will become the class clown? Who will be in the tough group of kids? Who will be in the popular group? Who will be in the honors group? Who will become recognized athletes? Will they be seen as someone with a lot of friends or just a few good friends? Each teenager is vying for a position in their new social structure.

Getting to know the role your teenager has with friends can help you understand his or her friendships. Some teenagers help others. Some are motivators to their friends. Some are role models. Some leaders. Some thinkers. Some are team mates. Some are good listeners. Some are entertainers. Others are loyal followers.

Curiosity sometimes is the motivator in choosing certain kinds of friends. Your son or daughter may be open-minded and curious about different kinds of people. She may be inquisitive about how people are different. As budding social workers, some teenagers like to be helpful to other teenagers who are not as fortunate as they are.

A teenager with low self-esteem may choose the group who will readily accept him. Using alcohol or drugs is sometimes the way to get acceptance in. Often this group is made up of discouraged teenagers, sometimes failing in school and breaking the rules.

Do you sometimes worry about the qualities and characteristics of the friend your teenager may choose? Parents, with years of wisdom and experience, may be concerned that a teenager's choice of friends could prove harmful to him. Maybe the friendship could lead your young person to feel used or to be influenced to do things that are against his or her better judgement. Parents will quickly learn that their 'recommendations' to drop a friend can turn into a battle royal.

The parents of fifteen year-old Nicki share their concerns about a new girl their daughter had befriended. They think their daughter is a really nice girl and are proud of how well she is doing in school. They are perplexed by Nikki's new friend, Tanya, who comes from a rocky, single parent family and is having a lot of problems. Tanya's mother is not around and she is left alone a great deal. In contrast to Nikki, she is doing poorly in school and they describe her as really 'rough' compared to their daughter. Her hair is an odd style and her clothes are strange.They are concerned Nikki's new friend will influence her in negative ways.

Taking a closer look, this new friend spends a lot of time at their house. She seems to enjoy eating dinner with the family and the girls share some classes and do homework together. It seems Nikki is a significant influence on Tanya. And Tanya is benefiting from being near her family. Over a short period of time, Tanya's life starts to improve. Helping someone else makes Nikki feel important and valued. She has discovered a *meaningful role* in helping others. Over time, she may bring other young people into her family with the hope to provide support and encouragement to them as well.

What Does Not Work

Most teenagers are invested in choosing their friends for themselves. They do not like when parents tell them who to choose. If parents do not like a friend, especially one that they do not know, a teenager may decide it is his mission to prove his parents wrong. Just to spite you, your teenager may do *exactly the opposite* of what you want and will plan to keep their friend for life.

Giving advice to your teenager on what he or she 'should do' about a friend is not helpful either. Your teenager may be present during your dissertation but he or she is likely to tune you out. Most teenagers will choose their own friends.

Threatening your teenager to give up a certain friendship can make a situation worse. Threatening is not a positive motivator to any young person. It is an attempt to change a person through fear and intimidation.

Becoming angry with your teenager, taunting him by predicting he will become like his friend, may actually encourage your young person to prove you correct. A negative approach does not motivate your teenager to change.

Working with your teenager, rather than against your teenager, is more successful.

Who Decides?

You can encourage your teenager to think about the choices when they select their friends. You can say things like, "I think this person is really lucky to have a friend like you." Or, "You are such a nice person, I hope the friend you have is as nice to you as you are to them."

Teenagers need to feel you trust them to make wise choices. Making the right choices gives them confidence.

Friendships can change often during adolescence. A friend whom you may not like may no longer be in your teenager's circle in a month or two. Friendships often do not last when teenagers tend to be fickle. As your son or daughter's friendships come and go, so too will your concerns.

Knowledge is Powerful

Before you can influence your adolescent it is critical to understand your teenager's view of their friendships. You can only find out how they feel and think if they tell you. You can only really get to know your teenager's friends by actually meeting them. From a distance you may have a different impression than when you get to know your young person's friend.

Five young men are standing on a street corner. Their heads are shaved and they are huddled in a discussion. Most who pass give this intimidating group a wide berth. Are they skinhead Neo Nazis? Have they been thrown out of their homes for delinquent behavior? As I am driving by, the group is starting to cross the street. I stop and wave them on. Two of the young men smile and wave at me. You cannot fairly judge a person by their costume.

Inviting Friends Over

Having your teenager's friends over to your house is a great way to get to know them. Fear and worry come from not knowing. You may be pleasantly surprised to find you may really like your teenager's friends. Once you know these young people you have a better idea what is happening in your teenager's life.

The best way to reach your teenager's friends is to feed them. Food and teenagers seem to go hand in hand. They may even have fun decorating cookies, frosting a cake or putting on pizza toppings.

Another way is to plan fun activities for them to participate in. One family bought a trampoline so the teenagers could play outside. Another family set up a ping pong table in their garage. One family put in a swimming pool so their teenager's friends would gather at their house. Your house may become the place to hang out because of the pool table or because the group can practice their music in your garage.

Letting your teenager spend overnights with another family that you do not know is usually not a good idea. It is better to have your son or daughter's friend come to your house so you can get to know the friend and their family situation better. The desire to spend every weekend at a certain friend's house and refusing to bring that person to your home should make you suspicious.

You may feel pressure from other parents to have your teenager be with a family you do not know or you don't think will serve as an appropriate influence. You must take a stand using your values. If it doesn't seem right, say "No, not now." After you have had more time to get to know the family you may want to reconsider. Perhaps, there will be another time or situation when you feel more comfortable and will allow your young person to stay with his friend and his family.

If your teenager will not bring a friend over, find out the reason. If he feels uncomfortable in your home, try to learn why. If the friend refuses to come over, you can say to your teenager that if their friend won't come over to the house there must be something wrong with the friend.

The Chauffeur

Whenever Carly wanted to go somewhere with her friends her mom always volunteered to drive. She never said more than just 'hi' to the kids. She sat quietly behind the wheel and gained a wealth of information. Her daughter's friends became so accustomed to her driving, they sort of forgot she was there. They would talk about who liked whom and what the kids were up to. Carly's mom never talked to the kids while they were in the car, though she occasionally brought up information that really concerned her when she was alone with her daughter. She was a very well informed mother.

Become the chauffeur if your son or daughter is not able to drive. You too can be 'in the know' about friends.

'One Minute Lectures' on Friends

It is difficult for parents to shorten their lectures. Before discussing the issues of friends and peer group first condense your knowledge and personal values into three to four sentences. This can be real work for a parent who is accustomed to having good listeners to longer lectures.

After three or four sentences, *pause*, then exit. This creates several opportunities. It creates an opportunity for you to ask for your teenager's opinion and start a conversation. It is very difficult to fight if you state your opinion and then leave the room.

Here are some examples of *ONE MINUTE LECTURES* about friends:

- "Dad and I think that if someone is truly your friend they won't pressure you. They will respect you for your own choices."
- "Mom and I think that you may want to try using drugs if you spend so much time with this particular group of kids."
- "We think that if your friend tells someone else what you told her in confidence then she is not a true friend."
- " We don't think that you have to do everything that your friend does to be his friend. You should be able to have your own individual style and still be that person's friend."
- " Mom and I think that if your friend only calls you when she can't reach anyone else that she really doesn't value you and your friendship. She may be a 'convenient friend' rather than a true friend."
- "If you have something constructive to do with your friend, then mom and I will consider what you want to do. Just hanging out in the mall or at someone's house is not an option."

In your parenting statements, it is very helpful to speak as a team. You may have to discuss your ideas if they differ on issues or values so you can compromise. The 'We' comes from what you can both agree.

Setting Limits with Time

Though you may not be able to change your teenagers wish to associate with a particular group, you do have some say in how much time they can spend with others. Teenagers who have little to do often want to spend time with other bored teenagers.

It is important to know where your teenagers are and what they are doing. If they are not busy and active with something interesting, they are likely to be bored and bored teenagers, alone, with little to do are a combination for trouble.

Situations Beforehand

Presenting possible situations before they occur is a great way to teach your values and help your teenager look at the issues of friendship and peer pressure before something just 'happens'. These hypothetical situations and scenarios work best if they relate to other teenagers and do not focus directly on your young person.

Issues can be chosen from a variety of areas:
1. Actual situations involving teenagers you know about.
2. Hypothetical situations that could occur in the next year or two.
3. An experience you think is common for teenagers.
4. Something that happened when you were a teenager, put into a modern context.

When you present issues to your 'expert' (*your teenager*), your teenager will correct you if your example is not accurate. How your son or daughter discusses these situations allows you to be better informed about the issues facing your teenager. Ask questions. Do not give a lecture. Here are some examples:

Situation #1: Jenny, Beth and Dawn are three high school girls who are friends. Two of the girls start doing things together while ignoring Jenny. When confronted, Beth makes excuses, explaining they forgot to call her. How do you think that makes Jenny feel? What could Jenny do in this situation? Do you think that Beth and Dawn are being good friends to Jenny? Is it OK to let someone treat a friend this way?

Situation #2: Jessica and Sally, both sophomores, have been good friends for a year. Sally has a boyfriend, Jeff, whom she really likes. Things are not going well. Jeff tells Sally he wants to break-up with her and see someone else. He then asks Jessica out. What should Jessica do? Should she tell Sally? What is more important, a date or a friendship? Is Jeff being fair to ask out Sally's friend?

Situation #3: Tim and Eric have been friends since grade school. Tim is getting tired of Eric lying to others in order to get out of tight spots with teachers or his parents. He jokes about lying to his girlfriend. Tim wonders whether Eric is lying to him. How do you think Tim feels? What do you think makes Eric want to lie instead of telling the truth? How much trust do you think Tim has in Eric? Can Tim do anything about helping Eric not lie?

Situation #4: During their last year in high school, four young men became friends. One of them wants the other three to skip school for the afternoon. Ben says, "No, thanks, I can't" (parental death threat). His friends give him a hard time and try to talk him out of his reasons to stay at school. How does Ben feel? What would help Ben stick to his decision? Are these good friends to Ben? How do you think the other guys might feel if Ben is not with them?

Situation #5 A group of girls have been friends since grade school. In the first year of high school one of the girls, Kaylee, falls madly in love with Phil, who is a sophomore. She really changes. She ignores the girls, stops eating lunch with them. Sometimes in the middle of a conversation she will leave to join Phil and his friends in the hall. What do you think it feels like to be Kaylee's friends? Is it fair for a friend to drop girlfriends for a guy? What should Kaylee do so she doesn't hurt her friends? What could her friends do about this situation?

Situation #6   Donovan and Steve have played on the same baseball team for the past two years. Recently, Steve made the junior varsity team. Donovan didn't make the team. Steve seems to have changed; he is hanging around his new team mates and doesn't pay much attention to Donovan. He hasn't come over to his house after school like he usually does. When Donovan is around Steve and his new group of friends, he feels ignored and uncomfortable. What do you think is happening in this friendship? How do you think Donovan feels? What should Donovan do? What should Steve do to remain a good friend?

Situation #7   It is February and Michelle is new in school. She has moved from another state and is sorry she can't finish the eighth grade at her old school. Her brother is older and in high school, so she feels alone. How should she decide who she would like to be friends with? Could she tell anything about other kids by how they dress or act? What clues might indicate someone would *not* be a potential friend? How would you choose people to meet if you were in her situation?

Current Situations

Once you have discussed these hypothetical situations with your teenager, you may know more about how your young person has chosen his or her friends. This kind of dialogue helps your teenager begin to *think* about how they choose. It creates an opportunity to think about the balance between what your teenager feels in his or her *heart* and a logical approach in his or her *head*.

Once you understand your teenager better you can address issues with a current friend or peer group that your son or daughter has chosen. Gathering facts and meeting the friend are necessary before discussing the things you do not like. When you meet a new friend, you can talk about what the friend does or says that validates your opinion.

It is important to respect your teenager's choice of his or her friend by focusing on behavior rather than the character or personality of the friend. You will need to think about what behavior bothers you, such as crude language or aloof behavior rather than saying the person is rude or strange.

I am not as concerned about how a teenager dresses or wears his or her hair (unless it is inappropriate). The important thing is how the friend interacts and behaves. For instance if a friend comes over and is rude to you or someone else in the family, you will want to discuss the friend's behavior with your teenager.

Go slow before you draw conclusions about your teenager's friends. It is better to present issues that concern you and let your young person have time to think about them. It is your teenager's decision as to whether he or she should ultimately end a friendship. But you can guide him or her by presenting real concerns based on what you saw and heard.

Your young person will respect your willingness to both get to know his or her friend and not jump to conclusions. This allows time for your teenager to think about how a particular friendship or association effects them. You may be pleasantly surprised at times to find your initial impression was wrong.

Telling your teenager that you are willing to give their friends a chance is important. This encourages your son or daughter to share his or her friends with you. It reassures them that you have confidence in their ability to choose nice friends. It also gives your teenager the benefit of any of your doubts.

Parents Predict

There is no doubt you have had much more experience with friendships than your teenager. You want to protect your teenager and help them have successful friendships but sometimes your daughter (son) needs to learn lessons on her own. Evaluate the friendship, then predict what you think *might* happen. You might believe this person will eventually let your teenager down. Or that your teenager may feel pressured to do things that are not good for him or her. For instance, you might predict a new friend might not be a good choice because he only calls when his other friends are busy. Or that a friend isn't really true because when she starts dating a new guy she drops your daughter.

Once you have made your prediction, let your teenager make

his or her choices and see what happens. If you are right, your teenager will be wiser and give more serious consideration to the next time you make a prediction. To your teenager's delight, you may not always be right about friends. You can encourage your son or daughter to predict what will happen with other people as well as their friends.

Ask Questions

Here are some questions related to values that pertain to friendship that your teenager can answer for you:

Q. How do you know if a friend is a true friend?

Q. What do you think you need to do to be a good friend to someone?

Q. Do you think young men and women can just be friends?

Q. How do you know if a friend is the kind of person you can trust with your thoughts and feelings?

Q. What is the difference between being a friend and being an acquaintance?

Q. Will a friend respect you if you say "no"?

Q.What do you look for when you find a new friend?

Prepare A Leader

Brenda's son is in the ninth grade, in an overcrowded high school. "I don't think it matters where my son goes to school," she said. "He is a great kid and I trust him to make good decisions where ever he is."

When your adolescent is confident that his or her own individual style is what matters, not what everyone is wearing or doing, you know he or she shows leadership ability. One young teenager did not want to dress like all her other friends. She made a point in shopping out of town, buying things that no one else had. When she wore her new clothes, most of her friends wanted to copy her style. One day she started wearing blue mascara. A few weeks later when her friends started to wear blue mascara, she found something else that set her apart. Her leadership showed in her ability to be confident in her own taste and become a trend setter.

Be Respectful

Teenagers like it when parents respectfully listen to their ideas and choices before they react. When you have open communication with your teenager, both of you get a chance to be heard and your opinions valued.

Just slowing down before reaching a conclusion can create a trusting relationship you want with your teenager. Many times when we are alarmed about something, we feel pressured to resolve the problem immediately. With teenagers and their friends, unless they are in a dangerous or serious situation, you should take your time. If you would like your teenager to drop a friendship, it is best to back off and give them some time to think about all the issues.

Here are some ways of presenting feedback to your teenager in a respectful way:

- "I have never met anyone that had a Mohawk before. Do you like his hair?"
- "I didn't like your friends language. We don't think it is OK to talk like that in front of others. What do you think about what he said to dad?"
- "Your friends were really funny. I liked Mike's jokes. He seems like a nice guy."
- "I hope your friends liked the snacks. They were all pretty quiet. Are they all kind of shy?
- "Your friend sounded mean to you when you asked him if you could join him tomorrow. Do you think he was being mean to you?"

Everyone is Doing It, So It Must Be OK

First and foremost, peer pressure does not make a teenager do something. Your teenager has free will and ultimately will decide for himself or herself. Your teenager may wish to blame the peer group that 'made' them do something but they chose to let others influence him or her. The peer group can certainly make a big impression and influence a teenager into choices that are not good. Sometimes parents want to blame the peer group. Your teenager is not forced by the peer group; he or she alone makes the decision.

You Gotta Go!

Six young teenagers are at the beginning of the line to the biggest roller coaster in the theme park. It was well known for its thrilling ride, especially the big drop that feels like a free fall. Some of the people exiting the ride look like they are in shock. Two of the boys have gone on the ride before and try to convince the others to join them. They talk about how awesome the ride is and how it will be great fun. The others say they don't want to go. After several minutes of intense pressuring three of the four teenagers say, reluctantly, they will try it. The last girl, Beth, says "No way." The group then tries to persuade her to go with them. Someone offers her the choice of who she could sit with on the ride. One of the boys tells her he will buy her any stuffed animal in the park if she'll be brave and go with them. In spite of their efforts to convince her, she refuses to go. The group finally heads off toward the ride, looking sad. When they get to the line, they all wave, getting her attention. Then together they yell at the top of their lungs. "Beth, pleeeease come!" Beth smiles, shakes her head no and waits.

This is a great example of peer pressure. If you are not brave about roller coasters and you have experienced this kind of pressure, you know what it feels like. The difference from the 'coaster convincing' and the real world of peers is that the choices the group is making are not as safe as a roller coaster ride. What some young people want to do may seem to offer the same kind of thrill and excitement.

Future Neighbors

Some of the fascination with a peer group is that these young people will be important in your teenager's future. The collective group represents a small society. The questions teenagers pose are about who will become what, who will do what and who will be their friends or enemies? Curiosity about how others are different can be the reason your teenager migrates to a certain group.

The peer group begins to know itself as 'the next generation' and there is a recognition that each will move beyond the bounds of the family to be on their own and together. These young people are your son or daughter's future neighbors.

Parents Face Their Own Peer Pressure

Your teenager may tell you '*everybody elses parents*' have given permission for them to attend a particular party. And your teenager will say you are *so* outdated and over-protective. "You treat me like I am a baby!" your young person will complain. "I wish I had anyone else for parents!" Then, the door is slammed.

You begin to ask yourself are you really being overprotective? Are the other parents doing a better job than you? Do you need to re-evaluate your decisions?

You too may feel the pressure of your own peers. What does society think? How are parents portrayed on the TV? You may wonder how are other parents down the street deciding? You become like your teenager, feeling alone, wondering how you are doing compared to others. To hear such comparisons can leave you feeling vulnerable, maybe a little insecure and sometimes confused and worried.

Your son or daughter cannot learn about avoiding peer pressure if you have trouble with peer pressure yourself. The peer pressure you experience may come from social pressure as well. Your teenager will pay much more attention to what you *do* than what you *say*. If they watch you take a stand and then give in, not because it is right but because it is popular, that is a lesson your teenager will not forget.

It is normal to look at what other parents seem to be doing. I encourage you to check these things out and then take a stand. Believe in your beliefs and stand by your values.

One Thursday morning Dave, a junior, decided to skip school with two of his friends, Jason and Todd. The next day, the admissions office called the parents of the three boys inquiring about their sons' absences. All three parents told the office their sons should have been in school. If the absence was without permission, they would be suspended for the next three days. Dave's parents were very unhappy; he had a big chemistry test on Monday and his grade would automatically be lowered with a three day suspension. Both Jason's and Todd's parents were unhappy and also worried about the boys' chemistry grades and decided to make up a false excuse to avoid the boys' suspension. Dave begged his parents to write a false excuse like his buddies but they told him they would not lie. On Monday, Jason and Todd handed in their 'excuses' and Dave stayed out of school for the next three days.

That semester, Jason and Todd did better on their chemistry grades than Dave, who got a low C because he had missed his test. Dave did not blame his parents. He lost respect for his friends and their parents, who lied so they could take the easy way out.

Fake Cool VS Real Cool

A lot of things your young person's friends do can look really neat, like smoking, drinking or having sex. Parents know that there are pitfalls when immature young people make these kind of choices. Balancing what looks so harmless to a teenager and seems like fun can be a real challenge.

Teenagers typically do not make decisions based on their futures; rather they tend to make choices about what feels good for today. Parents need to help teenagers realize that doing the right thing rather than the popular thing is really cool. It takes a strong teenager to stay true to their values with some of their peers.

The Peer Family

When a teenager feels alienated, he will join his peers. In an extreme example, these unmet needs by the family can lead young people to a gang. It is not uncommon for a young gang to form a kind of family structure in which they care for members and where loyalty is expected from each member. The younger gang members are the most active while the older leaders direct and guide. To belong to something negative is better than being alone without anyone caring.

Being a Leader/ Being a Follower

How do you teach your teenager to be a leader is a delicate balance between allowing your teenager to make his or her own decisions but choosing what those decisions are about. A good leader is someone who can guide himself, herself or others in a decisive and direct manner, based on what is right. A leader leads by example. Followers are devoted and like having someone else make decisions for them.

The first person your teenager needs to lead is him or herself. A teenager then needs to learn to do this with friends, in spite of peer pressure and in difficult situations. Once your young people can say 'no' to what is wrong and 'yes' to what they feel is the right thing to do, they can then lead themselves.

Reinforce Positive Choices

Your teenager still has a lot of kid in him or her and needs parents' support and encouragement. With this kind of support, a teenager develops the courage and perseverance to face difficult challenges and make good choices. If your teenager tells a group he or she will not join in even though 'everybody' is doing it, your teenager needs to hear from you that you are proud of their maturity and independence.

Adopting Other Teenagers

When you develop a good relationship with your teenager and your home becomes a gathering place, some wonderful things can happen. Other young people may decide to adopt your family for a while. Being around your family may be better than being in their own family. In the course of your son's or daughter's adolescence you may be a significant influence on several other young people. Those are some of the rewards of doing a good job parenting.

One Minute Values

Here are some examples of condensing your valuable lectures:

- "Dad and I think that if someone is your friend they want you to do what is right, not what is wrong for you."
- "Your friends are always welcome in our home."
- "We will give any group of your friends a chance with our family."
- "Peer pressure is doing what is popular, not always doing what is right."
- "If you have a friend, we know your friend is very lucky to have you."
- "If your peer group drops you because you won't do what they say, they were not true friends."
- "Peer pressure doesn't make you do anything. What you do is your choice."
- "Some of your peers may not always have your best interest at heart."

Take a Walk in Someone Else's Shoes

Learning from other's mistakes helps teenagers understand what can happen as a result of making poor choices.

Mark and Patrick have known each other since fourth grade. Now in ninth grade they share several classes. This year several of Patrick and Mark's friends have started smoking. Both think they can hang around their friends and not smoke. Mark's biggest reason for not smoking has to do with playing baseball. Patrick really doesn't have a reason except that his parents don't want him to smoke. The two boys spend more and more time with their friends, who keep asking them to try smoking. Do you think if they keep staying around these friends they will eventually begin to smoke? How hard is it to resist trying what your friends are doing? Who do you think has the best reason to not smoke, Patrick or Mark? By deciding not to smoke together, will these fellows have a better chance of being true to their values? What should they do if it is getting harder to say 'no' to smoking?

Saying 'No' Rehearsal

Here are some ways to say 'no' to friends and peers:

- "I am going to pass this time."
- "My parents will kill me if I go."
- "No, thanks."
- "I don't smoke."
- "I don't smoke because of sports."
- "I don't want to use drugs."
- "I don't drink."
- "I'll see you later."
- "I don't think I should go right now."
- "It isn't my thing."
- "I can't, I have to go home."
- "Thanks for asking but I can't."
- "No way."
- Leave

Preparing your teenagers to lead themselves, instead of following others, encourages them to make good choices. If your teenager knows that you care, that your love and support will not fail, he or she is more likely to act as a leader. It is common for the independent teenager to have loving, supportive and respectful parents. A teenager does not feel alone if he has family support when he is left out by peers.

What Is Love?

love, luv, n. (O.E. *lufu* = O. H..G.) *luba,* love: **1** A feeling of intense personal connection and affection for someone or something **2** a passionate affection of, as for one of the opposite sex **3** difficult to wait for **4** rare and treasured, difficult to find. **5** those without it, suffer and pine for it **6** those who find the object of such affection; a sweetheart or lover, experience great joy **7** to flourish in, to grow and thrive like an animal or plant in a climate conducive to its needs **8** Momma says you can't rush it, you must wait; finding it will bring you joy you have never known; not finding it will break your heart **7** *Tennis* a score of zero – **vt. vi.** to feel love (for) – **in love** feeling love – **lov'a/ble** or **love'a/ble** *adj.* – **love'less** *adj.*

Love is basic to human survival. Once you have satisfied the basics needs, food, water and shelter, your need is for love. Research shows babies do not thrive without love and attention.[3] Everyone needs love, first love from parents and family. In adolescence one begins a search for a young adult love relationship. With the search comes the hope that this love will last a lifetime.

Let's go back in time to when you first fell in love. Do you remember what those feelings were like? Were you thrilled, scared, curious, delighted? How old were you? What intrigued you about the person you fell in love with? Did you feel social pressure played a role in your search for love? How long did it take until you fell in love? Falling in love is an experience one never forgets.

Our teenagers are curious and fascinated by love relationships. They may wonder what does it mean to be 'in love'? How do you know if you are 'in love'? Is there a difference between 'love' and 'lust'? What makes love last? Will anyone ever fall in love with me? Is there anyone out there for me to love? There is more than one answer to each of these questions.

Teenagers explore their ideas about love relationships with their friends, through their music, daydreams and discussions. Interest starts with an intense study of what is happening with their peers. The young teenager becomes an expert about seventh and eighth grade relationships, which usually last about one to three weeks. In high school 'love' relationships can last for years.

Finding someone to love complements the search for self. As teenagers mature they become more concerned about their love destiny. They wonder who will love them? Where and how will they find this special person? Some become desperate, as they wait for the answer.

The peer group and friends help support a young person seeking independence from parents and family. Finding a love relationship fills the wish to be loved, valued and cared about. In a sense, it replaces primary parental love. When a young adult moves beyond his or her family a love relationship makes this venture less risky and lonely. Together, boyfriend and girlfriend can become independent from family as they strive to create their own interdependence.

Can't Hurry Love

Many divorcees contend they were too young, too immature, to decide on a true life mate. They were eager to 'get' married and could not find the right person so they settled for someone who wasn't quite right for them.

With the age-old myth that true love can change a frog into a prince, many young women marry a man they think will make them happy *once I have changed him*. Or a man marries a young woman thinking he can mold her so that she becomes the ideal wife *Once I have changed her*. Then they learn a hard lesson. When it comes to the people you love, what you see is usually what you get.

When people divorce, many knew *before* they married, the match was not right. Some were afraid to back out, others felt too much social or family pressure. With such an important decision, they were impulsive and stubborn. Family and friends may have warned them they needed to look farther. They may even have been aware of an alcohol or drug problem, seen violent tendencies or disliked parts of the person's personality or felt uncomfortable with this person. Neveless, they married, hoping to change the person they married. Choices like these do not make marriages last.

Motivation for Love Relationships

Attraction in a love relationship is a powerful motivator. Sexual urges are some of the most potent feelings a person can have. Teenage boys feel hormonally driven. Teenage girls may be more intrigued with the emotions of love. Discovering the feelings of love can be exciting, joyful and gratifying. This is a whole new world with powerful new emotions.

When a teenager finds a new love, he or she may fear it won't last. This can make your young person desperate, vulnerable and possessive. Teenagers want to find someone they can love and who will love and admire them in return. Some young teenagers find a boyfriend or girlfriend experience scary. They feel pressured and wish it will last only a short time. As the teenager changes and discovers a new self, he or she may move from one relationship to another.

Older teenagers in high school tend to be more serious. They wish for a particular love to last forever. Forever is not a realistic goal for many teenagers. As they watch their friends, they observe relationships start and end in a period of weeks. Really falling in love can mean that a teenager will do anything to beat the odds so that his or her love relationship will endure.

A teenager who loses a love relationship may feel he has lost a big part of himself. If your teenager's love relationship collapses, his or her self-worth and self-esteem can seem to crumble too. During this time of grief and loss, a teenager usually looks to his parents to help him feel loved and validated.

Other reasons teenagers seek relationships is because these relationships give them status in their peer group. Some strive to achieve such a relationship as a mark of adulthood. They are looked upon as desirable and popular. Attention from another young person makes the teenager feel special and included. If she doesn't accept any relationship that comes along, she may think she will be left out of finding any love.

Both the social validation and feelings of being loved gives a teenager both hope and courage about the future. With this kind of validation, your young person has avoided the trap of thinking she is obscure, lost, a nobody. With someone to love, the teenager will not feel so lonely.

Once a teenager discovers she is attractive and desirable, the relationship may not be as important. With a new identity the adolescent may seek more independence from their love relationship. With a renewed confidence that young person can seek other relationships, instead of remaining loyal to the first love.

To find two teenagers who are mature enough to know how to maintain a lasting love relationship is rare. What is common in adolescent relationships are teenagers changing boyfriends and girlfriends like they do hats. Mature love requires two mature people.

Love and Lust

Imagine the young fellow, filled with energy. He sees a beautiful girl and instantly he is in awe. Or the young teenage girl sees a guy she thinks is gorgeous and suddenly she feels like she is floating. These feelings of attraction are indescribable for the young teenager. The feelings are so new and powerful a young person can feel lost in them. Some of those feelings are hormonally driven. The teenager must somehow decipher if this exciting feeling is love or lust.

The feeling of lust is intense and excessive. It can cloud a teenager's thinking, the feelings are so overwhelming, it is hard to think straight. The world seems to stop and the adolescent now lives in his own little world, obsessed and excited, lost in his new thoughts and feelings of exhilaration. When you talk to him, he just stares.

When a teenager or young adult feel mature love, their reaction is different. They are kind, loving and more aware of others. They have a pleasantness about them that is contagious. Happy, content, fulfilled and yet still excited, the young person has a sense of security rather than precariousness.

Many things can motivate your teenager in their choices about whom to like and love. At one time they may be motivated by curiosity or the pressure of needing to have a boyfriend or girlfriend. Other times your teenager may be inspired by the person with whom he or she falls in love because this person truly is the love of his or her life.

What is in a Relationship?

What is the basis of a great relationship? What are the things that are important? How do you know you can trust someone? Can loving someone make you miserable? These are the kind of things your teenager needs to know in order to have successful relationships. At a distance, teenagers begin to develop opinions and notions about love relationships in the adult world.

To achieve a great love, young people need to be instilled with strong values and high standards for both themselves and others. The world presents many choices and options. Each teenager seeks the path for his or her personal success. Successful teenagers believe they are worthwhile and find a partner who is a wonderful match. Success boils down to the best choices.

Rotten Relationships

Rotten relationships are obviously doomed for a short life. You may hear about the nice girl who dates the guy who just likes to be stoned and thinks the couch fabric is interesting. Even though he is cute, he is a dud. The relationship is likely to fail. Or the fellow who cheats on his girlfriend; she really doesn't want to know because she has invested her heart. Or the couple with nothing in common and who don't talk to each other. Some teenagers are so concerned about their status they do not really care about the person. They just want to boast about having a boyfriend or girlfriend. Other examples include the girlfriend who is really mean to her boyfriend. For some reason he just accepts it. Another disastrous relationship is the couple that fight all the time and yet stay together.

When teenagers talk about what makes a mismatch in relationships they are teaching themselves what does *not* work. In the explanation, teenagers begin to *think* about relationships rather than decide about them based solely on their feelings.

What Girls Want, What Guys Want

There are teenagers who find the love of their life when they are young. You hear about couples who met in grade school and only loved each other. Or couples at the high school reunion who are still together. These couples are rare.

Generally, adolescent girls are curious about love and lasting relationships and teenage boys tend to be more curious about sexual experiences. It is common that what boys and girls want in high school is pretty different; girls may say 'yes' to sex experimentation in order to keep a relationship and boys may say 'yes' to love seeking sexual experiences. Those differences still exist, though there are plenty of exceptions. Even in adult relationships, what men and women want can be radically different. Sexual response and emotional needs are different for males and females. Young women tend to value security and crave attention. Young men wish to be admired and attention is coupled with strong sexual interests.

Building Blocks of Relationships

Since your teenager learns through experience, here is a helpful way to help them explore how to build a relationship. This *relationship exercise* will help your teenager to assess and question the important aspects that build a healthy and happy relationship.

Below are a series of blocks that represent the components of an adult relationship. You can make blocks or just use pieces of paper. This can be a beneficial exercise to do with your teenager, with his or her friends or with your entire family.

- ❑ BLOCK A   acquaintance
- ❑ BLOCK F   friendship
- ❑ BLOCK IL   in love
- ❑ BLOCK L   love
- ❑ BLOCK H   honesty
- ❑ BLOCK C   commitment
- ❑ BLOCK S   sex
- ❑ BLOCK T   trust
- ❑ BLOCK R   respect
- ❑ BLOCK M   maturity
- ❑ BLOCK Ma   marriage

TIME LINE

Present these blocks to your teenager. Next ask your teenager begin to stack the blocks representing the building of a love relationship. Your teenager may leave out some blocks or use them all. He or she may change how the blocks are arranged, especially after you talk about them.

Once the blocks are compiled, you can put a *time line* next to the blocks and ask how much time each of the blocks takes to develop and maintain a healthy relationship. You can then discuss your teenager's arrangement of the blocks.

Here is an example of putting the blocks together:

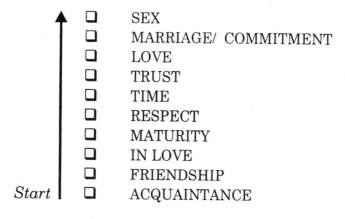

❏	SEX
❏	MARRIAGE/ COMMITMENT
❏	LOVE
❏	TRUST
❏	TIME
❏	RESPECT
❏	MATURITY
❏	IN LOVE
❏	FRIENDSHIP
Start ❏	ACQUAINTANCE

Acquaintance   Acquaintance is defined as meeting a person to whom you are attracted. Part of acquaintance is to have some initial idea or impression of what a person is like. This can be based largely on physical attraction. Most people are drawn by their physical attraction to each other at the beginning of a relationship. This is especially true for teenagers. You hear them say, "He is so gorgeous." Or, "She is so fine." Teenagers have to contend with having physically mature bodies often before they reach emotional maturity. Good questions to ask are: "What can you tell about a person when you first meet them?" "Have you ever met someone who you thought was a really nice person and later you found out you were wrong?" "How long does it take to know someone before you can be sure what he or she is like?"

Friendship   What does it take to form a friendship? Friendship takes time, energy, self-control and patience. To be friends means spending time together, caring for one another and getting to know each other, being knowledgeable about another's hopes, dreams and fears is part of the foundation of knowledge of one another. Think about your best friend. How long did it take you to really get to know that person? How did you meet your friend? How long did it take to develop the friendship? Did you like them right away or did it take time for you to grow to like each other? What do you have in common with your friend? What situations have tested the friendship? Is friendship important in a love relationship? It is important for you to talk about the meaning of your friendships with others and to give examples. Your teenager also needs to recognize signs that the friendship may not be true or that friendship is based on immature needs.

If more people based their decision of marriage on the quality of friendship maybe we would see a drop in the divorce rate. If you wait to find someone who will be your partner and friend it may take you as long as a year to even know if you can trust the person to be your friend. Your best friend will always be there for you...to love and respect you. Friends grow with you and understand you. A true friend will never fail you, even in the toughest of times.

In Love   Teenagers are so curious about falling *in love*. They dream of finding a wonderful person who will fall in love with them. Being *in love* is associated with romantic love, marked by infatuation, powerful sexual attraction, feelings of excitement and optimism that the relationship will last. Infatuation creates powerful emotions and can make a person feel intoxicated with their feelings of attraction. People *in love* are often impulsive and possess a narrow vision. *In love* is where a lot of teenagers lose sight of the importance of self-control. They are so intrigued and in awe of these new and powerful feelings that they do not always think clearly.

Some teenagers are so eager to meet someone who finds them attractive, they become desperate. This is a precarious stage of the love relationship. And most teenagers are not patient. Many want the security that their new relationship will last, so they will do anything they can to assure that the other person will not leave them. To the dismay of a number of teenagers this 'in love' can be fickle and changes over time. Sometimes it lasts only a short period of time, like an evening or week. One of the two people who are 'in love' changes his or her mind and moves on in search of another true love.

When being 'in love' fades and the relationship ends, it can make your teenager feel like his/her life is ending. A young person feels great despair. What helps heal their pain is the love and care from a parent and encouragement to keep going on. Losing a love is a great lesson about love relationships.

Here are some questions to ask your teenager: "How do you know if you are in love?" "How long can "in love" last?" "Have you ever had a friend fall in love and start to act differently toward you?" " Do you think people can know each other for a long time and then fall in love or does it happen right away when you meet someone?"

Maturity Maturity develops from knowing oneself. Maturity requires enough life experiences for a person to establish a consistent sense of self. Though the mature person can change he or she has a great deal of confidence in their identity. Mature people are able to give without relying on others to fill their own needs. It takes a lifetime to fully mature but the beginning of adult maturity starts in the middle twenties for most people. Teenagers may have a keen sense of themselves for the moment or day but their personalities and developing maturity is in considerable flux. Teenagers are in the process of becoming mature adults. And they are learning about becoming more mature. Maturity takes time.

Respect Respect is an essential ingredient in a mature loving relationship. It is the basis of most functioning healthy relationships between people. To genuinely respect others, as well as yourself, creates peace. If you respect another that person is free to have their own feelings and ideas. Respecting encourages that person to be him or herself without the need to change in some way. There is not only acceptance but celebration and admiration for who the person is. Self respect is to believe you are trying to be the best you can be for today... confident and accepting of yourself, as you are.

Love Love is the most profound feeling a person can have. Poets, writers, musicians and artists have attempted to capture this essential ingredient in life. Love takes maturity. You may think of love as kind, unselfish, patient, loyal and never failing. Love is tender, compassionate and passionate. It takes a lifetime for each of us to explore the question 'what is love?' This exploration is to somehow understand what we all seek and yet find so difficult to explain.

One of the most famous quotes graces many marriage ceremonies:

1 Corinthians 13: 4: "Love is patient, love is kind. It does not envy, it does not boast, it is not proud. It is not rude, it is not self-seeking, it is not easily angered, it keeps no record of wrongs. Love does not delight in evil but rejoices with the truth. It always protects, always trusts, always hopes, always preserves. Love never fails."

This is another saying about love; "Love is friendship caught on fire." -unknown

Love is to invest yourself, your feelings and interests truly in another person. To give up some of your own sense of possessing yourself and to share your heart and soul with another human being. Facing great odds, the risk is that by investing yourself, there is a chance you could lose your heart. Love endures, even if the other person changes. Real love is not based on the actions or responses from another person.

To love another, you treasure them and delight in who they are. You move beyond yourself, willingly give something of yourself to the person you love. Love takes maturity and discipline. Love is patient. Love is kind and considerate. Love is generous and accepting. Love takes time and heals great pains. Love knows no bounds.

Trust   Trusting another comes when you know a person well enough and long enough to believe they are reliable. When you trust you have confidence in a person and can rely on their actions without worry, concern or question. It takes great capacity to not only trust yourself but to risk trusting others. If you trust someone with your love and feelings, the risk is they may let you down. How easily one trusts another person may be based on their early experience growing up. Those children with secure love experiences with their primary caretakers usually find it easier to trust in others as adults.

Questions for your teenager about trust: "How long and how well do you need to know someone before you can trust them." "How well can someone trust you?" "What do you do if someone you trust lets you down?" "Whom do you trust?".

Commitment   Commitment is an act representing love, trust, respect and care for another. It is to invest yourself in a promise, either to yourself or another, that you will continue to care for that person over time. Commitment is a sign you are confident enough in your love, respect and trust that you can predict yourself in your future. Commitment that is true endures over time and remains intact when it is tested. Once truly committed, you don't change or give up on that commitment. Like becoming a parent, you commit yourself with the task of raising your child, no matter what hardships or heartaches you must face. Committed people do the best job they can with all their knowledge and strength. They may wear out but they do not give up.

Marriage Brown in <u>Life's Little Instruction Book</u> offers this wisdom: "Choose your life's mate carefully. From this one decision will come ninety percent of all your happiness."[4] A marriage that lasts today may mean a commitment that spans fifty to seventy years. This may be one of the most important decisions you will make in a lifetime. Who you marry can determine the quality of your life. Marrying the wrong person for you can bring you misery and pain.

If you choose your spouse carefully, you will know joy and pleasures in your life. Many people choose a person to marry based on what their heart tells them. More successful marriages are based on feelings of great love as well as finding the person who matches their dream of the ideal partner.

Sex This block is fascinating. Sex, coupled with love and commitment (marriage), may be one of the most exciting of all human experiences. It may be the most wonderful and passionate interpersonal physical experiences a person may ever have. It is a way two people, who love and are committed to each other, can express their love and affection. The intimacy of loving another through sex is a powerful experience.

Without first establishing trust, love and committment in a relationship, a couple may only experience sex as a physical pleasure without any emotional fulfillment, leaving the experience to be an empty one. It is important to explore your values about sex and share those values with your teenager.

To value chastity and fidelity and to share these values with your teenager may seem old-fashioned and out-dated. However, it is prudent we do so considering the emotional and spiritual risks of a young person. It does not matter what your experiences were as a youth because these are different times. We do live in the era of AIDS.

Ask yourself what do you really want for your son or daughter? Whatever you decide is what you should share with your child. If they ask you what your experience has been, you can share what you have learned. As you unfold your own maturity, you give your son or daughter a great gift and a great start, an opportunity to value themselves and what they have to offer another.

Here are some questions to ask: "Do you think teenagers are too young to have sex?" " What do you think it is like for a girl or guy when they have sex with someone and then the relationship ends?" "What is the difference between 'making love' and 'having sex'?" "Do teenagers get pregnant if they have sex?" "What are the reasons a girl or guy could give if they have decided not to have premarital sex?" "What should a person know about a partner before considering having sex with him/her?" " How would a person know for sure they were safe from sexually transmitted diseases like AIDS , herpes, gonorrhea?".

Putting the Blocks Together

Using these blocks may help you clarify what you want your young person to learn about the development of a love relationship. Talking about these aspects of being in love *before* they are in a serious relationship helps them respond to real life situations. They are prepared because they have clarified what is important in loving another rather than just letting the experience lead them. Sharing your *values* with your teenager answers important questions about developing a happy relationship.

Divorce

You can challenge your teenagers and ask them how they and their generation will change our current divorce rate. I like to ask teenagers this question when we talk about relationships. "What does it take to make a relationship last sixty years?" Sixty years of marriage may mean you will be in your eighties.

Divorce is alive and well in our teenagers' worlds. It is their generation that can make a dent in changing America's high rates of divorce. These are some of the things teenagers say they will do to make a difference. One is to marry later in life when they are more grown up. Others say they will choose their best friend to marry. Another answer is to marry someone with whom they have a great deal in common. Some think it is important to marry someone with whom they will not fight. A few teenagers, based on their family experiences, say they won't marry someone who uses drugs or abuses alcohol. Asking questions like this can really stimulate thinking about important relationship issues.

Other teenagers are less optimistic. They tell me they will probably get divorced at least once in their life. These young people do not have much confidence in their ability to choose well and lack faith in marriage. They need encouragement so that they do not anticipate failure as they approach long term relationships.

Tell Them Your Own Love Story

Teenagers, feeling so grown up, still like a few stories. So tell them your love story.

I always like to tease whenever I tell teenagers about my own love story that started back when the earth was cooling and dinosaurs roamed the earth. The teenagers usually just chuckle. They do seem to be pretty amazed by what it must have been like back 'in the olden days' when their parents were young.

Tell them how you two met. What you thought and felt. Did you know you would fall in love? Did you know what would happen in your relationship? What attracted you to mom or dad? What did you both look like back then? Tell them any funny or romantic stories about your courtship. How long were you together before you decided to marry. Who asked whom? What was it like to get married?

Teenagers love those happy ending too. So I hope you have one to tell them. If the marriage did not work for you, you can tell what you learned that may be important to their own decision-making. Our young people need the hope that their love relationship can last and endure the test of time.

The List

When I was about sixteen I learned a wonderful thing from my mother. As I was impatient for love, she told me to think of the qualities and characteristics of the perfect man I would like to meet and marry. So in my mind I made my mental list. Then as I dated, I compared my dates with my list. It was easy for me to figure out what qualities I did like about those fellows I dated. The list was my way of knowing I had not met the one I hoped to marry. There were many times I thought the guy on my list was too good to be true and I would never find him. My mom insisted if I waited and was patient I would eventually find him.

As time passed I found my list was a good guide. One amazing day I met the man that matched the list. I am still married to him today. He was definitely worth the wait.

For your teenagers and young adults, I recommend they write 'The List'. This list has all the qualities and characteristics of the perfect mate for your son or daughter. No two people will have the same list. Then when the teenager is dating he or she can compare the list with the person they are dating.

If the person your son or daughter is dating has several characteristics that contradict the characteristics on the list, then your teenager knows this *is not* the person for them. The person may be very nice and becomes a good friend, but should not be a seriously considered as a long-term partner. For example, a teenager has honesty on his list and he is dating a girl who has lied to him several times. He may not think of her as someone who has the potential for a long-term relationship with him.

The List helps teenagers rely more on their head than only on their hearts when it comes to the decision of who should be their partner in life. If your teenager chooses well, it can make a big difference in his or her personal happiness. A poor choice can make life hard and difficult.

Teenagers or young adults may have as many as fifty positive qualities and characteristics on their list. Some also write a list that has the qualities and characteristics that *will not* work for them. They should keep their lists with them. You may want to make copies and send the list to them later in life. As they grow and mature they can keep adding elements that are important to them.

You should encourage your son or daughter not to marry until they find the person that meets all the qualities and characteristics on their list. You may very well hear from your teenager that no such person exists. You need to encourage them to not give up, be patient and set high standards for themselves. If they keep looking, someday they will find someone worth waiting for. A comforting thought for the young person waiting, is that his or her future love is waiting for them too.

There is a flip side to this list too. As your teenager develops his or her list, these characteristics apply to them as well. It is a guide for the kind of person he or she wishes to become. So not only finding the right person is important but *becoming* the right person is part of the process of growing up and coupling.

Here is a list of the qualities and characteristics of a great person both to marry as well *as to be:*

- Honest
- Considerate
- Trustworthy
- Loyal
- Respectful
- Your best friend
- Kind
- Treats mother/ father/ brother/sister well
- Has courage and conviction
- Handsome/Beautiful
- Intelligent
- Creative
- Funny
- Fun
- Independent
- Integrity: strives to do what is right
- Handles his or her anger
- Athletic
- Good self-esteem
- Confident
- Dependable
- Hard worker
- Complimentary personality
- Value of money/spending similar
- Courageous
- Responsible
- Leadership skills
- Shares
- Doesn't fight, peaceful
- Doesn't try to change you, accepts you as you are
- Caring
- Helps and cares for others
- Respected by others
- No problems with alcohol
- Does not smoke or use drugs

- A good citizen

Not only does your young person need to find their ideal mate for life but they too must become this person's match by developing these qualities and characteristics for themselves.

Dating Starts with Dinner

Some parents are surprised when their teenagers are not very interested in dating. You may wonder why. When teenagers have a lot of unsupervised time, this creates the opportunity for teenagers getting together at someone's home after school. Some use this unsupervised free time to drink, have sex and socialize. Many teenagers, especially a boy, are not interested in dating if he can have a sexual relationship alone with a girlfriend during the day.

As a parent you certainly cannot set limits on when your teenager is allowed to have feelings for someone they like. Each family does need to decide about when it is OK for a son or daughter to have a boyfriend or girlfriend.

The first date can set the pace for your teenager. The foundation for the first date can be given to your son or daughter through an educational experience, rather than through lecture. Some parents will do this by the father taking his daughter out on outings like dates, where they spend time together. These outings show a young teenager how she should be treated respectfully and kindly. For the teenage boy, his mom takes him on his 'date'. She can talk with him about how he should be respectful of a girl he likes, the kind of behavior that girls like and admire. This is great preparation, in which you stress the importance of doing what is right. A 'date' can be a fun time to spend time with your teenager.

Working Together

No matter when your teenager develops interest in a love relationship, working together and keeping communication open is the key to guiding your teenager. Teenagers need adults to talk to when they are dealing with such complex issues as love relationships. They certainly do not have all the answers themselves.

Situations Ahead of Time

Offering situations for your teenager to think about helps prepare them for love and relationships. Remember, if the situation you present is not accurate, your expert will correct you.

Situation #1 Paula and Jerry have been dating about two months. Paula is outgoing and Jerry is usually quiet. She usually sets up the time they will see each which is often. Jerry just doesn't seem to pay enough attention to her, she complains to him. He doesn't like being told what to do but he doesn't know how to tell her. What do you think Jerry should do?

Situation #2 John and Kerri seem to be equally stubborn. Kerri is a junior and John is a senior and they have been dating for three months. They seem to fight about most things. They argue about what they are going to do, what each should do for the other. Their friends get pretty uncomfortable because they will fight when others are around. They have broken up three times for usually four or five days, then they make up and get back together. What is the prognosis for this relationship? What do you think they would be like if they got married?

Situation #3 Nikki is a really cute sophomore and she has been admiring the captain of the football team since the beginning of the school year. Troy is in one of her classes and she has helped him a couple of times with his history. One March day, he calls her and asks her out. She can't believe it. She tells him she would love to go out. In the back of her mind she remembers a friend warned her that Troy has got a reputation as a 'lady's man' and has used a number of girls. She forgets the warning when she thinks about how gorgeous he is. On Friday, he picks her up in his sports car and off they go. They get something to eat, meet up with several friends, go to a party and then he says he wants to leave. They start driving and Troy heads out of town and down a deserted dirt road. What should Nikki do? What if she tells him she doesn't want to go here and he tells her to relax and have a beer? What should she do if she tells him 'no' and he just laughs and keeps driving?

This a tough situation that I have asked many teenagers to discuss. I have had teenagers tell me Nikki should have double dated knowing the guy's reputation. Others have said she should have bailed out of the car, even at high speeds! One girl said Nikki should carry a cell phone so she could call for her parents for help, which I thought was a terrific suggestion.

Situation #4   The party is on and Cory is there with his buddies. Most of the seniors seem to be drinkers and Cory is no exception. Tonight he meets a gorgeous girl, Jennifer. She is a sophomore and she thinks Cory is a fun guy. When they start dating, Cory always seems to be drinking, at a party, out with friends or even when he is at home watching TV. Jennifer has not dated him when he has been sober. Should she be concerned? What should she do? How would you approach a friend like Cory about his problem?

Situation #5   Greg is a junior and hasn't dated much. The junior prom is coming up and Brittany asks him if he would like to go with her. He doesn't know her well, she runs with the 'popular' crowd and he thinks she is pretty. For the next three weeks, they see each other at school and she calls him. On the phone, she does most of the talking and he is a good listener. He asked her to go out one Friday night and she said she was busy. The prom night comes up and they are doubling with her best friend Angie and her steady boyfriend, Phil. They all meet at her house. Phil offers to drive. At the dance Brittany spends a good deal of time talking with her friends, Greg stands by quietly. They dance a few dances, stay late to help clean up. They go home, the other couple leaves and he says goodnight. The next school day she seems to be ignoring him. She stops calling and when he calls she is very short with him on the phone. What do you think Greg is feeling? Do you think Greg got used? What should he do?

Situation #6   This is the first date for Shelly and Craig. She is sixteen, a sophomore and he is a senior, almost eighteen. Off to the horse races they go. Shelly hasn't know him long but at school she thought he was a great looking guy. It is a fun date, he is very friendly and attentive. After the races they head to his house to get something to eat. This is the first time on a date a boy has asked Shelly to stop by his home to get something to eat. It seems kind of weird to her. Craig suggests they watch a movie. Shelly is getting uncomfortable. Then as they watch he has his hands all over her. She wants him to stop. She tries to get away from him and he grabs her and pulls her to him. What should Shelly do? What could she have done earlier to avoid this situation? Why did going to his house make her so uncomfortable? What could she have done before this date since she didn't know Craig very well? What could happen if she says 'no' and he doesn't take her seriously?

Grandma's Story of True Love

A woman told me about her wonderful grandmother. When she was sixteen she seemed to be in a daily struggle with her mother. After school each day, instead of walking home. she went to her grandmother's house. There she found her grandma, waiting for her, usually offering treats and milk. During her after school hours she told her grandmother her woes. She would complain about her mother and her grandmother would always listen. One spring day she arrived with great news. She was in love! After hearing her exciting story about this wonderful guy she couldn't live without, her grandmother gave her wise words of advice. She told how to find out if your love is true. She said love is like a bird in a cage. In order to find out if it is true, you must let it go. Not try to tame it or confine it, just let it go free. True love will always return to you. False love will fly away.

Over the next year she tested her first love and he flew off to college, never to return to her. She had other loves that flew off too. Later, she was relieved to have several of them take flight. Then a man, with eyes the color of the sea, stole her heart. Test after test, time apart, difficulties to handle, he always returned, only to love her more. This was the man of her dreams, his love was true.

How Your Teenager Starts Saying 'No'

Another basic guide is to help your teenager learn *how* to say 'no' to a poor choice whether the choice is a date or a boyfriend or girlfriend. Instead of telling your teenager to 'just say no', your teenager needs some basic information:

- Why do they say 'no'?
- What is the script to 'no' ?
- When do you say 'no'?
- What are the likely results from saying 'no'?
- What do people do after they say 'no'?
- Are you OK if you say 'no'?

The reasons for saying 'no' to a boyfriend or girlfriend must stem from your family values. If you don't tell your teenager why to say 'no', then they do not have a reason to say it. Teenagers need specifics of why, briefly in the *One Minute Lecture*. What is the reason based upon? It might be your religious beliefs or your personal beliefs. What is the moral reason? Why is saying 'yes' the wrong answer? In addition to moral and ethical reasons the other reason is because of your love and respect for your teenager. You must care enough about your young person to engage in a discussion and share your values.

Your teenager must be given the reason for saying 'no'. Your son or daughter must hear it and believe it so it becomes important to them and will influence how they choose to live their lives.

Love and Sex

Love and sex are closely tied in the minds of our young people. The world today does not care about the innocence of our children, especially our teenagers.

Being exposed to too much sexual material takes our young people's innocence. Parents have learned when they were young to trust TV, radio, magazines, even billboards. Things are not the same.

Many parents think of a movie as 'good' or TV as 'entertaining'. When they watch, much of it is how they remember it... *with a difference*. Even in "good" shows today, there may be material added that subtly corrupts our young people. Parents have a struggle of what to do. It is hard to accept that the entertainment that is so appealing has become morally irresponsible. Do you stop watching or do you just put up with it because it is too much of an inconvenience to walk out of a theater or turn off a TV?

Plastered on billboards, capitalized on our screens and appearing in most magazines a message is clearly sent: sex is cheap, fun, free and for everyone. By bombarding our young people, they lose the chance to dream and wonder, to grow up slowly, to think and become curious about the marvel of sexuality. Growing up too fast stunts our children and teenagers in many ways but most profoundly regarding relationships. Our young men are growing up not respecting girls (they have seen it all). And in turn, young women lose their respect and admiration for young men.

Parents in the Driver's Seat

If you are approaching a bad car accident and you want to protect your children from seeing the gore, what would you do? I would think if you could avoid it by driving another way you would do so or if that was not an option you might tell your children not to look. If they did look you would want to talk to them to help them understand in some meaningful way what they saw that was disturbing. You might say that is what a body looks like when it has been crushed and how sad it must be for that family today. Or that all of us will die someday and we are lucky it wasn't our car. You might also apologize for exposing them to something that was traumatic to them. The sad part about America is that when we drive by, we slow down to watch. We have forgotten who is in the car with us, our children.

Sex Sells Everything

Sex is everywhere you look. In America it sells, from sleek new automobiles to the whitest and brightest toothpaste. It is predominant in many types of music, movies, videos, T-shirts, news papers and magazines. Everywhere you look you can find something that uses sex to sell.

Violence also sells. For many viewers the more realistic the better. Combine sex with violence and the result is the worst kind of sensationalism.

Many times entertainment brings this conflict. What should parents do when they want to watch a movie or TV show that their children should not see? What your youngsters see and hear affects how they think, their beliefs, choices they will make and how they view others. And how they think can greatly affect how they eventually act, or at least believe they should act. Much media or entertainment is appropriate for adults but *not* for children and teenagers.

Much of the sex portrayed today in movies, television and advertising would be considered pornography when you were a teenager. What is the definition of pornography? Literature or art calculated solely to supply sexual excitement or other material that is sexually explicit and intended to arouse sexual passion; obscene literature or art. Selling with sex has become so common we really do not *think* about what we are watching. Using this definition you can find pornography in any magazine in the grocery line, in a package of pantyhose or in a TV beer commercial. Though it seems to be everywhere, you should ask yourself if you think it is good for your teenager. Advertisers would rather you *not think* about the impact on your young people because they make millions of dollars selling merchandise.

Parents should not ignore that sex arouses our young people. With so much saturation it is not hard to question the results... experimentation with little respect.

What is Parental Guidance?

Parental guidance is simple but not always very easy. Parental guidance begins by screening movies, TV, music, computer media, books and magazines *before* your teenager sees them (this means PG and PG13). Then, if you want your teenager *to look like, act like or talk like the people in the media they view... show it to them.* Using parental guidance you have to care about the things that have an effect on your son or daughter. It means you say no to all the media that is not appropriate (even top box office hits rated PG13 that *everybody and their children are watching*). You can edit video rental at home. TV control may mean a lock on your TV. Much of what your teenager may want to see will have to wait until your young person has matured and can discriminate what is real and what is Hollywood. You may find there is very little your teenager should see except G and PG movies, without editing.

If you really look at the content in the media, your young person should frequently hear this sound ... *CLICK*. It should become easier for you to *turn off the TV or say 'no' to a movie* than to turn it on. *CLICK* goes the TV, movie or radio. The station changes. Your teenagers and children will know you want what is best for them. When they are older and more mature they can see what they want. Ultimately, you are responsible for rating what your teenager sees as appropriate or not.

With *parental guidance* you will be doing a great job making mature and thoughtful decisions about what affects your children and teenager.

Like witnessing a car accident or traumatic event in your family you cannot take away that experience from your child. If they see it and hear it, it does affect them. It might be something they think about for years. Without knowing it, many children are allowed to watch media that is *traumatic or provocative* for them. Adults can *discriminate* media, so they may think their children can too.

In their formative years much of this media becomes part of their character development. Even though there are many great films and entertaining television, some great movies or shows may prove detrimental to our young people. Often only part of the film is inappropriate. Without previewing, you cannot know in advance when these scenes will occur, even if you are watching with them. And if you are not watching with them you will not know what they are viewing.

Parental Guidance means *you*, the parent, determines what your children should be watching. When you monitor the media, you allow your children to be kids longer. They have plenty of time ahead of them to learn about foul language, sex, violence and verbal aggression.

Molly's Story

Years ago I met a wonderful thirteen year-old. She was funny, cute and vivacious. Her grades were A's and she had a fun family. As I got to know Molly and her family better I saw 'Parental Guidance' in action. Her parents talked to her about what their family believed in and what they wanted for her in life. For example, she was not allowed to view an R rated movie (which are like most PG 13 movies today) until she was 17. During the next four years I knew her, when her friends decided to go to an R rated movie rather than the one Molly was allowed to view, Molly went to her own movie at the theater either by herself or sometimes with a friend who would join her. She would tell her parents about feeling left out and they always commended her for accepting the limits they set. On Molly's seventeenth birthday, her friends told her all the raciest movies they could think of. She watched several of them. When the shows were over, she said, "I didn't think it was that big of a deal". At 17 she was mature enough to make the right choices about the movies and media events she saw.

Media Impact

When we view the media we see very few examples of moral excellence. What sells is not moral excellence but glamorized sex. Real life relationship issues are not interesting to the majority of the viewing public. Watching people on the screen engage in sexual activity is interesting to viewers. But when the viewing public is under the age of sixteen they are not mature enough to discriminate what they view as real or make-believe.

What you typically see are *serial relationships*. One person having sex with a number of partners. This is glamorized *rule breaking*. The media portrays moral rule breaking as painless and rewarding. Breaking the rules becomes the norm.

For instance what does your teenager see on a soap opera? A man or woman may have three to five sexual partners over the course of a TV year. And these actor and actresses seem so real and familiar to a teenager who wants to be grown-up and cool too. Watching enough of these episodes, your young person begins to view such behaviors as normal. They incorporate what they have observed and learned as part if their belief system.

Our kids are like sponges. The soak up what they see and hear. Like the example in Chapter One, I needed to explain to Adam the portrayal of a pathological woman in a movie, using a a sledgehammer to break a man's legs, is *not commom or normal adult behavior*. Discussions between parent and teenager can make a movie less glamorous by bringing the real world into persepective. Young people need this kind of awareness because much of the media is packaged so well.

They Have Seen Too Much

First, tell your teenager or children you have rethought some things they have been allowed to watch. You are sorry they had seen things they were too young to understand. From now on you will screen what they see and stop or edit some of their viewing. If they throw a tantrum, they will know that you love them and are concerned for their welfare.

Here are some reasons to *edit* what your teenagers watch:

• Part of being a good parent is to monitor their shows because you care about them.

• You want them to learn good and positive things, not negative, violent things.

• They can see shows and movies when they are older and better able to understand it.

• You, as the parent, need to watch TV and movies first to decide if they are good for your child/teen.

- Some TV and movies do not portray real life.
- Too much violence can make teenagers and children think being violent is OK.
- Part of watching TV shows with your child is they cannot predict what is going to come next on the show. If part of a show is inappropriate it is not fair to let them watch and see something that is not good for them.
- Many TV shows and movies are made for adults and are not meant for kids because of bad words and adult actions.
- Many TV shows and movies show people doing morally wrong things and portray them in a glamorous way.
- Too much TV, video, computer and Nintendo is not good for your young people. It takes away your chance to do other fun things.
- TV and movies dull your imagination.
- *Parental Guidance* means you will watch new TV shows and PG and PG-13 movies first and then decide if it is good for your child/teen they can see it.
- You love them enough to say no to things that are not good.

Guiding Your Teenager

The media tells them to be sexually active, peers tell them to say 'yes', even toothpaste ads encourage early experimentation. They are told it is easy to have sex and it is satisfying both socially and physically. Do you wonder if being firm about your expectations and values will have an impact on your teenager's behavior or that maybe your ideals are not that important?

Ask yourself if you think any young person under the age of eighteen is mature enough to handle a sexual relationship? What do you think is right for your son or daughter? Should your son or daughter wait until he or she marries? What are the emotional costs when a sexual relationship ends? Are young people mature enough to maintain a long term relationship? Can any teenager handle the responsibilities that come with sexual activity...pregnancy, sexually transmitted diseases (Venereal Disease, Syphilis, and Herpes), or the risk of contracting AIDS?

If you do not think your teenager should be sexually active, how do you guide him or her? Does your teenager seem mature enough to decide about not being involved sexually? Are you confident your teenager could say 'no' and make a wiser decision to avoid feeling let down, hurt or used? When will your teenager be old enough to respect, love and care about the other person? Or be able to maintain a relationship that lasts years? Do you think your young person is capable of having a mature discussion with you and other family members? Parents need to decide *when* they think their young person is ready to make a decision about a sexual relationship. Though they may be reluctant to say it, many parents think sex belongs in marriage.

The best way to help your teenager is to openly discuss your values and explore the pressures that encourage young people to experiment with premarital sex . If parents are not open, teenagers turn to their peers and the media for information. Parents are the critical factor to balance all the things that influence a teenager.

Teenage Sexuality

Sexuality is different from sex. Sexuality is thinking of oneself as a sexual person.

Sexuality creates intense feelings, sexual urges, fears and wonder. These urges and feelings are powerful and passionate. Sexuality is not a choice, it is the amazing transformation from girl to woman or boy to man. Sometimes talking about your teenager's *sexuality* can be a good way to begin a discussion. Our teenagers are experiencing their identity with their new sexuality. Having sex is a choice. One's sexuality and sexual identity are part of the natural process of growing up to become a man or a woman.

When you discuss sexuality with a teenager, you can talk about their new and changing bodies. Do they feel enjoyment in the things that are happening to them as they become a young woman or young man. And what is it like to have to control one's feelings and impulses. What don't they like about growing up? Does your teenager value his or her virginity? Can your teenager be proud of their sexuality? Does your teenager believe in avoiding premarital sex? Also important is to discuss how they can be attractive to others around them as well as finding others attractive. And what do they do if they are obsessed? Your teenager will appreciate knowing this is a normal and natural experience.

How they respond to those new sexual urges profoundly

influences the decisions about having sex or waiting until they feel they are mature enough to decide which may not occur until marriage. A teenager can experience an interest in their sexuality and sexual attraction without needing to say 'yes' to sexual experience. A message to your teenager can be that a person with a positive feeling about one's sexuality can say 'no' to casual and experimental sexual experiences and look forward to waiting for one life long love.

Attitudes about sexuality are closely related to family values. Why is a sexual relationship worth waiting for? Is virginity important? How does your family value about self-respect, keeping something valuable and avoiding being hurt or having regrets? You already have the answers for your teenager. They come from your family values.

Teenagers Having Sex

It happens. Everyday. Young people are having sexual relations. In grade school, middle school and high school. With it comes broken hearts, degraded reputations, loss of innocence, positive HIV test, pregnancy and sometimes babies.

When Choices Match Values

Steps to Good Decision Making:

1. Learn the facts, get educated
2. Clarify your values (with parents and family help)
3. Understand the risks involved
4. Have a plan of action (how to say 'no', possible situations, rehearsed scripts)
5. Avoid risky situations (double date, group date, earlier curfew)

Decision Making in Risky Situations

1. Recognize how a situation puts the teenager 'at risk'. Cues about being uncomfortable or uneasy. The little voice says 'watch out'.
2. Make a good decision for self. Know why it is right to say 'no'.
3. Follow through with action to avoid making a mistake.

4. Talk to a parent. (Reinforce good decision-making)

Parenting Tips

1. Get educated about issues and situations.
2. Clarify values: yours and spouses and family.
3. Communicate values to teenager.   Why do they say 'no'.
4. Talk about situation BEFORE they occur and prepare your teenager with a plan and script.
5. Supervise, supervise, supervise (media, outings, dating).
6. REINFORCE good decision-making.
7. Role model your values.
8. Love your teenager. (Listen, respect, talk and touch)
9. Like your teenager.
10. Provide accurate information and communicate with teen ager on the issues.

How Do You Know You Really Are "In Love"

Infatuation	Love
Short lived	Maintained relationship
Intense preoccupation	Patient attention
Emphasis on physical attraction	Emphasis on personal attraction
Blind to faults of the self and of faults of other	Realistic acknowledgement of self and others
Ignore problems and differences	Able to work through problems and differences
Hide faults and weaknesses	Feel loved and accepted by their love
Fear of losing the relationship	Confidence in the relationship
Pressure to keep the relationship	Both people's values respected
Pressure to not change	Personal growth is encouraged
Change is discouraged	

Why Some Say "Yes"

In the 'olden days' young guys had to try hard to have sex with a girl. Most of the girls said no to the boys. There were a few girls who would 'give in'. What these willing girls got in return was not so good; bad reputations, damaged self-esteem, poor self images and in the end, feeling used and dumped. Guys would say they loved a girl so they could have sex with her and girls might say yes to sex so they could get loved. What has changed?

Today, here are fewer girls who say no to the guys. It is not as hard as it used to be for the guys to have sex with a girl. Now, there are even some girls who ask the guys if they want to have sex and some of the guys think they should not. It has almost gotten too easy for many young people. As one young man of eighteen said, "I don't think there are any nice girls left. The girls I know just come right out and ask to have sex and sometimes I don't want to. I'm going to college. Someday I would like to get married but I don't want to marry one of these girls. They're cheap. I don't think I will ever find a nice girl."

There are many reasons teenagers decide to have sex. The media has made premarital sex socially acceptable. Many teenagers feel they are old enough to handle sex. Their sex drive is strong. It looks like a great time on the screen or in the magazines, why not have sex? They believe having sex will bring them happiness. Why wait? It will makes them feel grown up. They are led to believe it is easy and uncomplicated. They find out quickly it is not at all like the movies.

Teenagers tend to be naïve. They feel confident their choices will not lead to pregnancy, HIV, AIDS, sexually transmitted diseases. They do not believe that AIDS is growing in epidemic proportions, especially among teenagers. Because of a belief that bad things won't happen to them, pregnancy will not be an issue. What is paramount is that they want to have sex and ignore the risks.

Teenagers who are sexually active *do not believe* in the consequent emotional risks. They think sex will enhance their emotional life and not become a problem. As relations progress they can certainly change their thinking about this. Like the girl who believes her boyfriend is true to her and then when he leaves she is devastated.

The peer group may look at a sexually active teenager and recognize them as mature and adult-like. Others look up to them because they are sexually active. Similar to peer recognition, a few teenagers say 'yes' because it is condoned by one or more parents. These teenagers are doing exactly what their parents want them to do. Some fathers and mothers actively encourage their sons and daughters to be sexually active. Their teenager behaves in a way that matches their parent's beliefs and values.

A rebellious teenager seeking love can quickly find himself in a sexual relationship. Many of these teenagers are seeking a replacement for the love they don't feel in their family. They don't want to be lonely and want to feel secure. Sex can seem like it bonds the relationship but that security may not last with immaturity. Other teenagers don't want to wait and do not want to control their impulses. What is paramount is sexual satisfaction.

Curiosity is a big reason teenagers become sexually active. The experience satisfies their need to know what it is like. It is not uncommon for some teenage girls to seek sex with the wish to have a child, looking for someone to love. A child represents someone to love them, not someone they will need to take care of and be responsible for.

Using drugs or alcohol can impair a teenager and decrease self-control and inhibitions. Many times girls who drink or use drugs become sexual targets. Under the influence, teenagers may get into situations they want to avoid, putting them at risk.

The most important reason is that these teenagers do not have a parent who tells them *why* they should say no and has a commitment to keep communicating about what is happening in their teenager's life.

Why Some Say 'No'

Some of the reasons teenagers postpone sexual activity during adolescence is because of religious convictions or belief in family values that agree to say 'no'. They typically have a close relationship to parents who guide them with values and encouragement. They are confident in their reasons to say 'no'. They can say 'no' because of their belief it is the right thing to do. These benefits outweigh any pressures about having premarital sex.

Teenagers who are confident and independent do not buckle to peer pressure. He or she is clear about what is best and tend to avoid others that may try to persuade them differently. These teenagers usually have a close relationship with their parents and feel loyal to their families.

Some teenagers feel they are not ready for a sexual relationship. They have seen what happens to others and know the risks and want to say 'no'. They have strong convictions about right and wrong. These young people enjoy dating, having a boyfriend or girlfriend and don't wish to change the relationship.

Fear of what could happen is another reason. Being aware of the emotional, physical and psychological risks helps teenagers say 'no'.

Future goals are another reason a teenager says 'no'. These teenagers have their sights on college, marriage and family. Their look to the future makes the present not seem so significant or important.

Teenagers also abstain because they wish to maintain a good relationship with their parents. They have confidence their parents have not misguided them and their support helps them with difficult situations. These teenagers can usually talk openly with parents about sexual issues.

Most teenagers are not only interested in sex and curious about their own budding sexuality but are intrigued with relationships as well. It is common that many teenager think that sex is supposed to be part of any teenage love relationship. There may be only a few moral models around them that do not include sex as part of teenage bonding.

Situations Ahead of Time

Situation # 1 Jackie is almost 16 and spends a lot of time with Kyle, now 17. She likes being with him and has a hard time thinking of anything else. She becomes jealous when other girls are near him. Though she can tell that Kyle likes her, she feels insecure and wonders what will happen with their relationship. Jackie tries to dress in a way to attract Kyle; she begins to ignore her friends and seeks out a new crowd who all know Kyle. Part of her new look is to smoke and dress more seductively. Kyle doesn't seem interested in dating her; he does not ask her out. He does invite her to spend time with him after school, usually at his house with friends. He talks openly with her about sex. She wonders if he will ask her to have sex with him. Is this situation risky for Jackie? Should she be more patient and wait to see if Kyle will ask her on a date? What do you think about the changes she has made? Do you think Kyle respects her?

Situation # 2 Steve is fourteen, loves to play baseball and is popular at school. One Friday he and some friends end up with some of the older guys who are heading up to the mountains for a gathering of friends. When they arrive there are about fifteen people there, all older than Steve and his friend. During their time in the hills, unknown to him, there are several sixteen year-old girls that make a bet that one of them can have sex with Steve. Nancy decides she will have sex with Steve. She asks him to take a walk with her to a nearby wooded area. There she seduces him and to his surprise, he doesn't think long about saying 'no'. He tells her this is his first sexual experience. She later rejoins her friends, 'reports' her success and 'wins' the bet.

The following Monday at school, Steve cannot believe his horror. Everyone seems to know what happened with him and Nancy. His buddies are congratulating him and laughing about how he is no longer a virgin. He cannot believe how awful he feels. Do you think Steve feels used? What do you think he should have done before he said yes so readily? Does Steve face any kind of risk?

Situation #3   Blair and Amy have been friends since 7th grade. Now they are in 9th grade and have been getting more serious about their relationship. It is Friday night and they have decided to go see a movie together. Their parents do not ask them what movie they are going to see. Together they watch a romantic R rated movie showing explicit sexual acts. Both are aroused by the film. Do you think this an appropriate dating situation for these young people? Why do you think the parents didn't ask what movie they were going to watch? Do you think Blair might be uncomfortable watching people have sex on the screen sitting with Amy? Do you think Amy is uncomfortable watching with Blair? Do you think this encourages this young couple to experiment like the actors in the movies?

Situation #4   Jerry has a eleven year-old daughter, Erica, and a nine year-old son, Ben. Erica has begged him to see a popular romantic film about a couple on the Titanic, rated PG13. Erica's mom is out for the evening so Jerry offers to take the kids out for dinner and a movie. Erica pleads and begs him to take them to this movie she says 'everybody' in her 5th grade class has seen. After dinner Jerry gives in to her request and they go to the movie. During a scene in the film the actress is bare breasted and then the actor and actress have sex in the back of a carriage. During the film, Jerry does not like what his kids are watching, he does not think it is good for them. Even though he is uncomfortable he sits through the film with them. On the way home Ben is upset. He said that girl should not have taken her shirt off. That night he has nightmares about his family drowning in the ocean. What do you think this dad should have done when he realized the content of this film was not appropriate for his children to watch? Do you think other families taking their young children to this film were bothered? Why do you think so many parents attend films like this? Do you think Jerry should have taken his children out of the movie instead of staying to watch? Should Jerry have paid attention to the film's rating?

Sex Education

Specific physiology and information is *best* taught by experts. This expertise should cover information about birth control, sexually transmitted diseases, sexual response and function. This is taught in school, seminars and found in books on the subject of sexuality. Teenagers do need to be informed *before* they make choices about sex. They are best informed by the experts in the field.

More informal information or *misinformation* is what they learn from their peers. Media can also provide informal and *partial education* usually leaving out many important aspects of the subject. Many teenagers have traumatic lives learning purely from direct experience about things like contracting herpes, venereal disease, becoming HIV positive or becoming pregnant. Once they have these experiences they cannot go back in time and erase the trauma.

Here is an example of an AIDS question for your teenager:

On a warm, sunny summer day Greg meets Sally at the park. They start talking. She is from out of town. Sally is eighteen and Greg is seventeen. Greg thinks Sally is great. Sally likes Greg too. After meeting each other over two days they find themselves sexually attracted to each other. Greg is a virgin. Sally is not. Should Greg have sex with Sally? Should Sally have sex with Greg? Is either one at risk of contracting any sexually transmitted disease like AIDS? Let's look at their sexual history charts:

Sexual Partners Chart

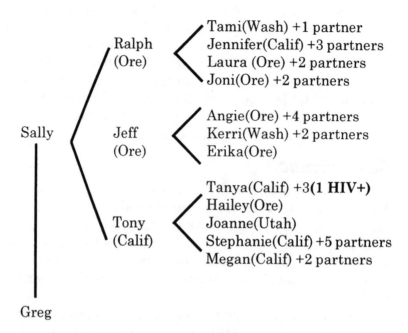

This chart shows the risks for Greg if he chooses Sally as a sexual partner. Sally has had three sexual partners, Jeff, Tony and Ralph. Jeff has had three sexual partners before his relationship with Sally. Tony has had five sexual partners before Sally, including Tanya who is HIV positive (undetected). Ralph has had four sexual partners before his relationship with Sally. So Greg will have a chance of being HIV positive from his one contact, just as Sally may have contracted AIDS from her relationship with Tony. By choosing to have sex with Sally, Greg has connection to at least 41 people on this sexual chart.

This is not an uncommon sexual history chart for some teenagers who are seventeen and eighteen. It really brings the issue of safety to the forefront. These young people are not just making a choice about sexual experience. They are making a choice that could profoundly affect their lives.

If you are a good listener, you will be able to guide your young person. They do need a more mature person to ask them questions and critically think through the issues they face when it comes to making choices about sex.

The Most Magnificent Christmas Present

Several years ago a young man of nineteen spoke to a group of teenagers about being proud of his virginity and would remain one until he was married. He said that waiting for him was like waiting for the most magnificent Christmas present imaginable. He said that if his future wife had had a sexual relationship with someone else it would be like someone else opening his most extraordinary present, then wrapping it up again and putting it under the tree. He treasured his virginity the same way, saying his future wife would feel cheated too if she was not the first opening his gift to her. This young man felt encouraged and courageous. He looked forward to the day he would marry.

The Pearl and Family Ring

One family had a special tradition for their teenage daughters. On each young girl's sixteenth birthday, they had a special celebration dinner and received a very special gift. The gift was a beautiful pearl ring. The ring represented their daughter's virginity, white and pure. The committment ring was given to remind each daughter about her promise of saving her virginity until marriage. It was worn most of the time, especially while dating. It was a reminder of her commitment to wait and say 'no' to premarital sex. Each daughter would eventually trade her ring in on their wedding day for a wedding band.

Though this family did not have sons, a committment ring could be given to a son with a family emblem on it so he would make the same promise of waiting.

Hot Pink Underwear

One father told me about a man from Philadelphia, who travels from school to school speaking to young people telling them to wait for marriage and to avoid premarital sex. He wears a hot pink jacket and is an inspiration to young people to value their virginity. After hearing this speaker, this father went out and bought his daughter hot pink underwear to wear on her senior prom night. The idea was that if for some reason she got undressed and saw her hot pink underwear, it was time to call home and say 'no'.

Starting Over Again

When teenagers realize they have make a mistake by saying yes to premarital sex, they may feel doomed to keep repeating their behavior. No longer a virgin, they will always say yes to sex. Parents may need to encourage a teenager once he or she realizes he or she should have said no. They can stop at any time and wait for marriage. Young people need to know their parents will recognize their mistakes, forgive them, let them learn and give them a chance to start over again. Then waiting for marriage can be resumed.

Ask Anything

Teenagers may be so curious or driven they feel they could not find a parent who would listen. When a teenager knows they can ask anything and their parent will answer, even if the questions are tough, teenager may find they can make better decisions by having this kind of open forum.

What is the Script?

Here are some choices for scripts to help your teenager rehearse how to say 'no' to pre-marital sex with boyfriend of girlfriend:

- "I am not ready for this."
- "I really like you but I have to say 'no' to this."
- "If this is what you need, you've got the wrong girlfriend."
- "I am waiting until I get married."
- "I need some time to think about this."
- "This is not working for me. I like you but I don't want to date you exclusively."
- "I would rather not do _____. It is fine to take me home if you want to go."

When Do You Say 'No'

Timing can be very critical for your teenager in dating situations. In exploring potential situations you and your teenager can work on the timing of how and when to say 'no'. For instance if a sixteen year-old girl is on a first date with a guy who wanted to drive down a deserted road, ask your teenager *when* should this girl say 'no'? If she waits too long and they have been driving for fifteen minutes she may be in a tough situation that may present some potential danger to her.

Part of timing has a lot to do with helping your teenager be sure of himself or herself. You may need to encourage and reinforce your belief about the strength and courage you see in your teenager. Rehearsal about situations are very helpful to develop a sense of what and when to say it.

What are the Results of Saying 'No'?

Your teenager may be afraid to say 'no'. She may feel she will be left out or will not be accepted into a certain group or she will lose a boyfriend. Others feel like an oddball because they feel they are the only one saying 'no'. Being able to say 'no' may seem like they are 'too good' and it is boring. You must find out what your teenager is most afraid of and provide balance. Most teenagers respect those who have the courage to do what is right rather than doing what is popular.

Teaching our children and teenagers our family values is like putting answers in their pockets. So if someone asks them if they want to buy crack cocaine they can reach into their pocket, pull out their family value and have a reason to say 'no'. A family value would sound like this: "No, that stuff will mess you up and ruin your life. No way do I want any." And when a boyfriend or girlfriend says, "Do you want to have sex with me?" a teenager might respond, "No, I am not going to. If you insist, you will need to find a new girlfriend."

Teenagers need to know *why* to say no. They need to know *when* to say no. And they know *how* to say no.

CHAPTER NINE

Saying "No" to Alcohol and Drugs

There is pain in their hearts

and confusion in their worlds.

The transition from childhood to adulthood is a process that can be fun, exciting, demanding, frustrating, confusing... and painful. When teenagers are ignored by friends or think parents are uncaring, it leaves them struggling with trauma. They are shocked to find that part of growing up is a painful and troublesome experience.

It is not easy to cast aside the security of childhood and take on the challenges of young adulthood. Becoming an adult requires self-reliance, responsibility and maturity.

Many teenagers find the new pressures of adolescence means they start to lose their innocence, their optimism or the ease of life as children. Many young people report they are surprised by the difficulties of adolescence, that no one warned them about the pains of growing up. Without knowing, a teenager may find himself or herself feeling disillusioned and unprepared when faced with painful issues.

The unprepared teenager, disappointed and bewildered, may have to confront a whole array of new and unexpected anxieties. There are a number of tough conflicts, on-going confusion about issues and relationships. Doubts and worries can consume them. Demanding or frustrating situations appear in their social worlds. Struggles with parents bring ambivalence, when teenagers seek distance while still needing to be close. In the midst of this kind of conflict and confusion, a teenager can feel alone.

No one likes tough challenges. It is easy to understand that your teenager wants to avoid these difficulties and frustrations. Teenagers are vulnerable and may be drawn to alcohol and drugs to alleviate discomfort and pain.

The American Message

In our society, we believe if you feel *pain*, you should find a *fast* and *instant relief*. When hungry, we drive up for fast food. With physical pain, we reach for products claiming the *fastest relief*. We do not want to tolerate pain or be inconvenienced by it. If something can take away the pain, use it.

What are the messages about *social and emotional pain*? What do some teenagers learn about dealing with discomfort, from not fitting into a particular group to a real crisis of losing a love relationship?

Some discouraged teenagers find relief in alcohol and drugs. The escape is a only short-lived relief. Using alcohol and drugs can create an imagined sense of security and pleasure.

Socializing can create a tremendous amount of anxiety for teenagers, especially young people who are socially clumsy. Some may find using alcohol or drugs soothes their anxiety and covers their lack of social skill. The alcohol and drugs can 'talk and interact' for a teenager. If things go poorly, they can always blame their social blunders on the alcohol or drugs.

Another message from the media about drugs and alcohol is that it is OK to use them recreationally but you should never get hooked. Addiction is socially unacceptable.

Millions of American drink. Thousand of people have dependencies. Teenagers having problems with alcohol or drugs may be harder to spot because many of our young people are just starting to experiment.

Escape the Pain

Drugs and alcohol make a person euphoric, happy, excited. Cares and worries dissipate. When they are high teenagers feel numb or safe, disengaged from their worries or concerns. Everything is wonderful when they are high.

Unfortunately some teenagers do not experience a 'natural high'. A 'natural high' comes from the excitement generated by your own accomplishments. This 'high' can be seen on the faces of the basketball team after their victorious win. Or the teenager who has just been asked out by someone she had fantasized would call her. Their life experience creates intense joy and satisfaction. These teenagers feel a great high on life.

Some teenagers, especially those without close adult relationships, are not as likely to have experiences that develop positive feelings about themselves. They lack enthusiasm, about themselves and their lives. They believe the good things sure don't outweigh the bad stuff. These young people are most at risk of never finding anything better than the drug or alcohol high. In their view drugs or alcohol is the best life has to offer.

Face the Pain

Our young people need to know that pain is part of life, especially during adolescence. Just because it may have looked like teenagers were enjoying a carefree life, that is not the way it really is for any young person. Let your teenagers know there will be tough times and growing up is not easy or pain-free.

Pain usually comes from losing people and things that are important to us. Grieving is a way of moving through the pain and finding a way to cope with the loss. To feel sad, lost, dejected or depressed make us feel real and those feelings are alright. Many times because of a loss, our lives become richer and sometimes better. There are important lessons to learn through our pain. We learn how close we are to feeling really human. For most of us, when we feel we are at our worst, we are really at our very best.

Drink and Be Merry

Alcohol can have a big affect on a teenager. Alcohol is a depressant that can affect a young person's mood, loosen control over what he or she says and does.

Drinking the first drink can make a teenager feel relaxed, calm and silly. The second drink can make even a shy teenager feel bold and energetic. She finds she cares less about what is right or appropriate and cares more about what feels good. He feels bolder and braver than ever before. By the third drink, a teenager may be out of control.

With continued drinking they may even black-out or pass out. No doubt the young person under the influence of alcohol is at risk of doing the wrong things when they are out of control. The adolescent can become an easy mark who can be taken advantage of by others.

Early experimentation with alcohol or drugs can be a novel experience done out of curiosity or just for fun.

If use continues, the young person succumbs to increased use, which can lead to *dependency*. With dependency the person is no longer self-reliant but now becomes dependent on their 'painkiller' of drugs or alcohol. What has become a *habit* can progress into an *addiction*. Then the drugs or alcohol are in charge. When addiction develops, the young person begins to feel *powerless* to the drug or alcohol.

Self-confidence and being an independent thinker helps a young person become more resilient to the lure of using alcohol and drugs. Any teenager having the skills to deal with tough issues of adolescence and the support of parents has a better chance of making positive decisions. Teenagers need to deal with pain and hardship by facing it rather than using something to avoid it. Caring parents available to talk about current issues and concerns offer a teenager the support and security your young person needs while growing up.

Get Informed

The drug scene will always change. Gathering information from both your teenager or from other experts about the types of drugs and kinds of alcohol that teenagers use today is critical to helping your son or daughter. The drugs that were available when you were a teenager are not the same drugs teenagers find now. They have changed in their potency and chemical make-up. Many drugs are cheaper, more accessible and stronger.

The information is twofold. It will be helpful for you and helpful to guide your teenager. When you have current and accurate information you can begin to comfortably talk to your teenager. You certainly do not have to be an expert. Being an informed opens a dialogue. You have a good chance to not only get educated about current issues but will be able to guide your teenager with values and choices.

Knowing the effects of drugs and alcohol on both mind and body assists you in asking relevant questions. Being knowledgeable can assist you identifying whether an alcohol or drug-related problem exists with your teenager. It is helpful to know the following 10 things:

1. Learn about the different types of drugs and alcohol most commonly used. Drugs like marijuana, cocaine, amphetamines, LSD, crack and sedatives. Alcohol includes beer, wine and hard liquor.

2. Know what the current drugs look like and the ways they are available.

3. Know the popular kinds of alcohol that are available to teenagers.

4. Understand the effects of alcohol on the immature brain of a teenager. How does one drink effect a teenager? How about two, three or four? How much alcohol does it take to have an illegal blood alcohol level?

5. Learn how alcohol can make a teenager lose consciousness. Know what an alcohol induced black-out is. A blackout occurs when a person becomes so intoxicated they do not know what they are saying or doing and what they said or did. To others they may look sober. The alcohol has 'blacked out' their conscious awareness and they will not remember anything they said or did.

6. Know the effects of each particular drug. What does the drug do? How do teenagers react to the drug? Why is the drug so attractive to teenagers? How addictive is the chemical?

7. How are the drugs typically used? Social use? During school? In combination with some particular activity? How often are they used?

8. Learn about the harmful effects. How does a particular drug affect their bodies? Their emotions? Their thinking process? Their concentration? Their motivation?

9. Be able to identify the paraphernalia associated with each drug.

10. Know the kinds of behaviors to watch for with each particular drug or alcohol. Both signs of *use* and *abuse*.

Parent Check

Your teenager not only learns from what you say but also from what you do, and that has a powerful influence on your teenager's behavior. What your teenager sees at home with you or any other family member with alcohol or drug use is likely to be his or her model.

The majority of teenagers who smoke have had a parent role model that either has been a smoker or is currently smoking. If teenagers have access to liquor or drugs at home, it is easier to begin using them.

Parent Values

Each parent develops their own feelings and notions about alcohol and drugs. Even if you have never used alcohol or drugs you have had some experience indirectly with them. Just watch some of the 40,000 beer commercials your teenager can view each year on TV. You may know others who drink or use drugs. Someone in your family may have had a serious problem with alcohol or drugs.

Each person has some relationship to alcohol or drugs. Abstaining from alcohol and drugs is one kind of relationship. Social drinking is another. Recovering from alcohol or drug addiction is still another.

Discussing alcohol and drug use can evoke passionate feelings. One parent may have grown up in an alcoholic family while another enjoys drinking socially with their family members. These differences are based on their different life experiences. Both may have very different views and concerns for their children and teenager. When parents have differing views, they tend to raise children who are better at critically thinking through issues.

It is important you share your personal values. This way you open up communication with your teenager on how he or she is developing an opinion about using alcohol and drugs. Your young person may reveal how he feels when he goes to school with teenagers who use alcohol and drugs. This is a common experience for many teenagers.

Let your teenager know where you stand on his or her use of drugs or alcohol when your young person is:

- Under age
- In school
- Alone
- While driving
- On dates
- As an escape from problems (school, personal)

* Out of curiosity
* Only on weekends
* To fit in

Parents must provide reasons *not to use* drugs and alcohol. You have to sincerely believe in what you say based on your personal values. You may believe teenagers are too young and immature to handle alcohol. You may not condone the use of any drugs or alcohol under any circumstance. You may enjoy having wine with some family meals. The range is vast and each family is different.

It is helpful to *listen* to what your teenager tells you about what he or she thinks other teenagers *should do* in a potential situation. If your son or daughter can tell you what someone else should do, recognizing the risks, they will probably give the same advice to themselves.

How Do You Drink?

As the years pass we become more knowledgeable about the physiology and psychology of drugs and alcohol. What we know today is important in helping your teenager make decisions.

Alcohol and drugs are a part of American life. Drinking is socially acceptable in most social situations. Having a drink in hand is not looked on as doing something that is out of the ordinary. Picturing a teenager with a beer in hand may not be unusual for your teenager either.

Social drinking and *problem drinking* are two very different things. Here is a guideline to teach your teenager about adult social drinking.

Social Use of Alcohol or Normal Drinking

1. One Drink per Hour

2. Only Drink Beer or Wine　　Only beer or wine is a *reliable measure* of an ounce of alcohol. With mixed drinks, depending on who is doing the mixing, one drink can be the equivalent of three or four beers.

3. Always Eat While Drinking　　Drinking on an empty

stomach produces a more immediate effect. Eating tends to allow the alcohol to be absorbed more slowly.

4. Never Drink Alone   Social drinking means not drinking in isolation or being the only person drinking alcohol in a group. This includes not drinking when you are alone with your children.

5. Never Drink When You Need a Drink   This is a key to being a social drinker. 'Needing a drink' is an indicator of a possible dependent or addicted relationship to alcohol. When a person 'needs' to have a drink they are not able to cope with the day or a situation without using alcohol.

6. Never Drink When You are Depressed   When you are depressed it is important to solve your problems before you would consider using alcohol. Using a depressant, like alcohol, while you are depressed is not considered part of social drinking. Once problems are solved, then you can drink socially.

When I offer this guideline to teenagers, they will tell me, "Nobody I know drinks like this." When most teenagers drink, they drink to get drunk. Drinking behavior for many adolescents is typically very different from this social use pattern.

Part of adolescent drinking behavior is their lack of knowledge and experience with alcohol. Teenagers usually get a crash course in 'How to Drink' from their peer group. And the rules are:

1. Usually drink until either ALL the alcohol is gone and or you are stumbling drunk (preferably both)

2. Anything goes when you are drunk and

3. Everyone can handle using alcohol or drugs. Nothing bad should happen.

Many of teenagers do not have frank conversations with their parents about drinking and their current social situations. They do not know their parents' reasoning or values other than 'My parents don't want me to drink' or 'I would get in *big trouble* if my parents ever found out about my drinking'. Drinking and using drugs should be an open topic of discussion between you and your teenager. Such dialogue can help can make wise choices.

As research continues we learn more about patterns of addiction. There is a clear genetic predisposition toward developing a problem with either alcohol or drugs. If any members of your family have had addictions over the past two or three generations, the more informed you can be about addiction the better the chances that the risk of addiction can be reduced.

Reasons To Use

Teenagers need to know *why* their peers chose to use alcohol and drugs. They may not explore the reasons until you discuss these ideas with them. They also may have a few more reasons they can add to the list.

Alcohol Means Maturity   Believing the media, a young person could easily be convinced that to be an adult you should smoke and drink. The peer group says being cool means you have to drink or use drugs to fit in. A young man who holds a beer at a party may feel he has achieved a new maturity, that he is considered more of a man by others. Or to be perceived as being a 'mature' young woman, a teenager thinks she has to drink to achieve this status.

The Maturity Balance Your teenager needs to understand that based on your *values* using drugs or alcohol does not make a person *better* or *mature*. If they have to use drugs or alcohol in order to fit into a group, that group isn't worth fitting into. Only a 'mature' person says 'no' to drinking.

Parents Use   If you do drink yourself, you may want to discuss at what age your teenager should begin experimenting. Your young person learns a great deal from your example. The drinking pattern your teenager observes is likely to serve as a model. Some parents attempt to try to convince their teenager to do as they say, not as they do. Teenagers don't find this believable.

The Parent Balance Be honest with your teenager about what is really happening in your family. You may want to share why you drink, what it does for you. Address any concerns or feelings your teenager has about it. Your teenager may have questions about what is happening with you or others in the family related to drugs or alcohol. Answering those questions honestly is the best approach.[5] Talk about what you have learned as an adult.

Having Fun A young man in therapy told me that all through high school he did not use drugs or alcohol. He had strong opinions and was confident that drugs and alcohol were really bad for young people. Now that he was twenty, he has been experimenting with drinking and tried smoking marijuana a few times. He said he was glad he waited until he was older and more mature before he started to experiment.

He also recognized the powerful nature of drugs and continuing to use could become a serious problem. He decided he would not smoke marijuana anymore. He was glad he waited to experiment until he was a young adult. He thought that young teenagers are too immature to handle this kind of experimentation.

He discovered something that really surprised him. He realized that he did not know how much *fun* the experience was going to be. No one ever told him that alcohol and drugs made you feel really good.

I think this is a mature experience from a young adult. He knew himself well enough to recognize he needed to limit his experimentation. He found that drinking and drugs provided some entertainment value. He was confident that he would not become a chronic user of either alcohol or drugs. Because of his age, maturity and experience of watching others use, he felt he could *now* handle his own experimentation. He felt he was mature enough.

The Fun Balance Parents need to discuss why consuming alcohol or drugs can begin as a fun thing to do but sometimes can turn into disaster. Your teenagers need real examples for this lesson to be meaningful. They may have a number of situations that their friends or peers.

Your teenager must learn how to have fun without using alcohol or drugs. They need to be reassured that their choice to be drug free has a *great benefit* for them.

Acceptance With Peers Just like your teenager has to face the pressure of fitting in with peers, parents face a similar pressure. Do you let your son or daughter do things that are not in their best interest so they can be accepted by their peers? If your young person wanted to play Russian Roulette, what would you do? This is a an obvious example of when parents need to take a stand. The risk is clearly *dangerous*. Playing this game with the group is not worth the risk.

If a peer offers cocaine the risk is certainly greater than drinking a beer. The invitation from a peer may not seem dangerous to your naïve teenager. A number of young teenagers will agree to using drugs or alcohol if there is *only a chance it might be dangerous*. It is not always an easy call for parents. On these more subtle issues it may be harder for parents to take a firm stand.

The Peer Balance To fit in is important. If your teenager is putting him or herself in a situation where they may be at risk, those friends may not be worth taking that chance. When your teenager has a good friend they form the 'buddy system' so together they can say 'no'.

Social Ease Many teenagers think that social ease is something that just happens to you when you become a teenager. When you don't know what to do or what to say it can make a teenager want to avoid this feeling of awkwardness. Using alcohol and drugs can become a crutch in these social situations. Your teenager may even notice this with you or other adults who consume alcohol for the same reasons. The tone of a party or social gathering can certainly be different when adults are drinking as compared to when they sober. The laughter is sometimes louder, the jokes funnier and the conversation has an easier flow. The drinkers may seem more jovial and animated. They are more at ease.

The Social Balance Teenagers need to learn *real life skills*. Your teenager will feel comforted to know it is normal to experience awkwardness and feel uneasy in certain social situations. Discussions with your teenage son about how to talk to girls can prove insightful for him. Some guys like to have a female friend so she can help them deal with a girlfriend. Talking with your teenage daughter about how to deal with social situations can help her out as well. Increasing their social skills and confidence helps reduce the need for alcohol and drugs. Your teenager needs to learn how to be the life of the party without a drink in his or her hand.

Boredom Teenagers are social creatures. They usually don't like doing things all alone. They prefer a friend or a groups of people. So this bored teenager is likely to seek out friends to spend time with to relieve their boredom together. Many bored teenagers experiment with alcohol and drugs.

Boredom Balance Busy teenagers don't have much time

to get bored because much of their energy is directed. They also develop a love of what they are doing which reduces boredom. Help your teenager find a healthy habit like basketball, karate, volleyball, drums or dirt bike racing.

False Self-confidence   For an adolescent who may have low self-esteem the effects of the 'high' from a chemical can create the illusion of a boost in their self-confidence. They may feel they are now socially adept and have developed a close kinship with their peers. Using alcohol or drugs can create a pseudo-friendship so they can drink or smoke together.

The Self-confidence Balance   Real self-confidence comes from the recognition that *who* they are is important and significant. And the reinforcement that *what they do* is positive and notable. Helping others is a great confidence booster.

Teenagers who don't have parents who can give them this kind of attention to develop their self-confidence need another adult to help them. That person may be a Big Brother or Sister, a neighbor, a grandparent, aunt or uncle, senior citizen or a mentor through the church.

Emotional Problems—Pain Killer   Our teenagers, vulnerable and unsteady in their own sense of themselves, can be overwhelmed by the losses life presents them. The resulting pain can linger. Without help, teenagers can feel like their life is unbearable. Using drugs and alcohol can lead to more losses: loss of time, losses in school achievement, loss in relationships, loss in ability to cope without the aid of a chemical, loss of self-confidence, loss of self-esteem.

Balance of the Pain Killer   Love can balance pain. Recognition and concern from parents is a better solution than any chemical could provide an ailing teenager. There is nothing better than your ability to listen and then offer a hug. Tell your son or daughter that no matter how difficult the problem may seem you will work together to help them to find a solution.

Rebellion   A teenager's use of alcohol or a drug certainly gets a parent's full attention. Part of rebellion has to do with breaking the rules; social rules, family rules and school rules. Drinking or using drugs is a way of breaking out and can be a grand way to get attention.

The Rebellion Balance   During the course of your teenager rebellion you may find that *when* you are able to listen to your teenager's complaints, you may find what you have said or done has been *misunderstood*. This is a common phenomenon during rebellion. A misunderstanding can throw a teenager into despair, feeling unloved and rejected by parents and family. And in their discouraged state they can easily act out in angry, rebellious ways. The balance is to be able to listen, even if you do not agree.

Curiosity   "What is it like to get drunk?" asks one teenager to another. Many teenagers are curious about the taste of alcohol and its effects. They want to know about what others are experiencing around them. Are they missing out by not joining their peers?

The Curiosity Balance   For some teenagers, a frank talk, answering questions honestly, is enough to satisfy their interest. This openness makes them more aware of the risks. Teenagers can talk with parents about what the others say, who is drinking, what drugs are they using and what your teenager sees happening with their use.

Other teenagers need more. Hands on experience may be the only way to satisfy their curiosity. Some parents with these kinds of learners have taken a different approach. Not only do they discuss the issues, they also allow their teenager to drink at home. Some parents offer alcohol as part of a family meal or a holiday celebration. There is an openness about alcohol and their teenagers have some direct experiences. They know what the alcohol tastes like and experience the effect. They are also well supervised in a family setting. Sometimes this backfires and the teenager really likes the experience so he or she decides to drink more.

Alcohol use is a harder decision for parents than decisions about drugs. Just because they might be curious about crack cocaine, it would never be a wise thing to let your teenager try.

Few teenagers benefit from using drugs or alcohol. I think it does put them in potentially dangerous situations. Their judgement has yet to reach maturity. Using alcohol or drugs weakens instead of strengthens their character. Alcohol or drug use may prevent them from learning and achieving for themselves.

Each teenager is different, as is each family. So your judgement is best when it comes to helping reduce the curiosity of your teenager.

Smoking

When discussing drugs and alcohol, nicotine falls into the category of drugs. Smoking, like alcohol, can be a mark of maturity to your teenager.

Teenagers most likely to smoke have either had or currently have a smoking parent. Developing a habit of smoking can easily turn into a nicotine addiction. Smoking is one of the toughest addictions to stop. Smoking is a difficult addiction to overcome because it becomes *paired* with breathing. To stop the habit a person has to learn how to breathe all over again. The majority of teenagers who are smokers eventually use other more powerful drugs. Smoking is a gateway to other drugs, such as marijuana, cocaine and speed.

The Smoking Balance

I know of a father who found his son smoking and became very upset. After a call to the doctor's office for medical advice, he handed his son a pack of cigarettes and told him if he was going to smoke them, he could eat them too. His son reluctantly tried to eat one. He did not have to eat the rest of the pack but did get very ill from the one he did eat. This is a tough but powerful way to learn about the dangers of smoking.

Parent need to know by condoning smoking it is the hardest addiction to stop. Harder than heroine, cocaine or marijuana. One experience for the teenager who has chosen to try smoking can be to visit a respiratory unit in the hospital and meet people with lung cancer and emphysema. Others have to do reports and show pictures of lungs of chronic smokers. I always have liked the poster of a woman who is smoking and 'wearing' her lungs outside her body. Her lungs are blackened and scared.

Inhalants

Many parents are not aware that children and teenagers inhale paint thinner, permanent markers or spray paint. Most of these first time users are in fourth to sixth grade. A common term is called 'huffing'. When the kids inhale these toxic substances, they get high and cut off the oxygen supply to their brain.

Which means they cause some **brain damage**. This damage may not show up until middle school when students are asked to think in more abstract ways. With enough damage to the brain, these students eventually become identified as learning disabled.

Offer Choices

Offer your teen *One Minute Lectures* about your ideas, ideals and values. Once you have shared your feelings and concerns then you can give your teenager the option of choices. Here are some examples of choices:

Basic Script: If you choose _____ then this happens....
You decide.

Situation A: If you choose to drink and drive, then you will lose your privilege to drive for the next month. You decide.

Situation B: If you choose to smoke marijuana, then you will lose your privilege to drive and to keep your job. You decide.

Situation C: You may go to the party. We are trusting that no matter what others are doing you will make good choices. If you do, there will be more parties to go to. If you make poor choices, you will not go out to any more parties until next semester. We expect no drinking or any drug use. You decide.

Situation D: We do not approve of you smoking. If you choose to continue, you will no longer have the privilege of having a drivers permit. You decide.

Situation E: We do not think your friend is a good influence on you. We are concerned since he is smoking pot that you will too. If you do use pot, you will lose your privilege of playing basketball this season. You decide.

If You're in Trouble, Phone Home

I think it is a good idea to *reward truthfulness, even after a poor choice* has been made. So you should go to rescue them from a bad situation. You get to know first from your teenager, rather than from some other source, like school, police or other parents.

If you pick up your teenager, it is critical to not get into a conversation while they are under the influence. Telling them you are glad they called and that they are safe. As the hours pass, they will sober up. If you give your teenager enough time to think, he will take a look at what he has done.

Time delay your reaction. Always reward the truth or some part of their decision-making that strikes you as mature. For instance you would want to reward your young person for calling you, even if the call came right before the police arrived. You can deal with the other poor choices later.

The next morning is a good time to *start* a discussion. By this time your teenager is sober. The best way to start is by letting your teenager explain what happened. It is helpful to tell your teenager that calling home and knowing it was time to leave the party or situation was a responsible thing to do. By listening you are likely to find out what your teenager has learned from his or her experience. When you have listened, shared your concerns, you can tell your young person what the consequences are for his or her choices.

Spotting a Potential Problem

How do you know if your teenager has a problem with alcohol? When does a person become 'hooked' or addicted to a drug? What is the difference between just using it because you are curious and having fun or having a problem with the use?

Not all who use alcohol or drugs end up having a problem or become addicted. Understanding the reasons your teenager may choose to use a substance can help you evaluate your son or daughter's relationship to either alcohol or drugs. Research has helped us recognize problem usage at a much younger age. There is a good deal of information that will help parents in assisting their teenagers.

A working definition of addiction is this: Addiction occurs when the drug or alcohol controls *you* rather than you control the use of the drug. This means an addicted person cannot just *stop* their use. If the drug or alcohol is available they will use it. Once they start using it you cannot control how much they use or when they will stop.

Alcohol or drugs may be used to reduce depression. When their life situation and depression do not change, they will continue to use more drug or alcohol while increasing their tolerance for the substances. Then the downward cycle starts. More use leads to more depression, which leads to more use.

DOWNWARD SPIRAL OF USE

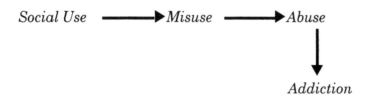

Social Use ⟶ *Misuse* ⟶ *Abuse*

Addiction

Here are behaviors outside *NORMAL DRINKING* which indicate a potential problem:[6]

- ☺ Paraphernalia
- ☺ Drinks alone
- ☺ Blackouts
- ☺ Gulps drinks
- ☺ Tolerance
- ☺ Preoccupation
- ☹ Lying, covering, denying
- ☹ Shame, guilt
- ☹ Break moral values under the influence
- ☹ Feeling out of control
- ☹ Protects supply

STAGES OF USE

STAGE 1: Experimentation (at home, away)
STAGE 2: Regular, repeated use
STAGE 3: Habituation and preoccupation
STAGE 4: Drug is the center of ones life

From Stage 2 to 4, Professional help is suggested.

Under the Influence

What can you do if you suspect a problem? First you need to have a *fact;* a urine test result, your teenager drinking, smoking or using, to begin a discussion about a problem.

If you find your son or daughter under the influence of either drugs or alcohol remember to *not discuss this issue while your teenager is under the influence.* Getting your teenager home safely to sober up is a good priority before having a dialog of any kind. Someone under the influence of alcohol or drugs is not likely to remember much of what you are saying.

Sometimes you may locate bottles of alcohol or some drug paraphernalia in your teenagers room, their pockets or in the car. This is a *fact* that you can ask your teenager about. If a teenager says it does not belong to him, then have them find the friend who owns it. It is best with any *fact* to rely on actual proof so you don't suspect your teenager if they are indeed innocent.

Another way information can be gathered is through a urinalysis(U.A.) at a local lab. I call this the *"But I DO believe you"* U.A. You can say that you want to believe your teenager. If he or she is not using anything, your young person won't mind giving you a urine sample. You need to be sure because of recent lying in the past. Your power in these situations are in your silence and composure. When you get a sample be sure to test it. If the results are negative, thank your teenager for being honest with you. Tell them this really helps you trust them.

The first step when confronting a problem is to have a loving discussion with your teenager. A non-confrontational style works the best when dealing with tough issues. Being angry or punitive may not allow you to obtain the truth. If you are angry your teenager will want to *avoid creating any more anger.* Harsh confrontation many times creates more distance, denial and secrecy when a person is having problems with control of either drugs or alcohol.

If your teenager is indeed in trouble they need an ally rather than an enemy. The direct and honest approach is respected by many young people. They appreciate that others can treat them with this kind of respect and maturity. To begin the conversation say you are concerned and why. Tell your teenager what you know that is *factual* such as finding a pack of cigarettes in her coat pocket or you see him drinking a beer.

The best way to start the questioning is to present the *fact* in a non-confrontational way. To say, "I would like you to tell me about these cigarettes." Then *wait*. Just launching into a lecture takes your teenager off the hook. Now it is your teenager's turn to respond.

If you do not reward your young person's truthfulness, it may become too risky to do anything but lie to parents. By offering amnesty, you reward the truth and *give consequences for the rule breaking behavior later.*

Here are some questions to ask your teenager. Be prepared to hear some difficult truths if your teenager honestly answers your questions. When asking your teenager *be direct, loving and honest:*

Q What is happening in your life?

Q Are you feeling badly about yourself?

Q Are you depressed?

Q How important is the drug or alcohol in your life?

Q What does using it do for you?

Q How does it (alcohol, marijuana, etc.) make you feel?

Q Do you feel pressured by others to use alcohol or drugs?

Q Do you feel you *need* this drug/alcohol?

Q Would it be hard to quit now?

Q Do you think the drug/alcohol is controlling you?

Q Are you gulping drinks? (or using the drug everyday?)

Q Do any of your friends worry about your use?

Q Have you ever blacked out?

Q Do you think this is problem for you?

Look for a Pattern

When your teenager's behavior changes drastically it can be without a significant reason. Behavior changes are part of a normal adolescence. When behavior changes become *chronic* and little seems to change over a long period of time then you may become more concerned. If you suspect that your teenager may be using either drugs or alcohol you may look at for a chronic pattern with some of these behavior changes:

*excessive sleeping   *change in their speech
*persistent avoidance or   *suspiciousness
    isolation
*drug paraphernalia   *a pattern of skipping school
*emotional outbursts   *lack of motivation and energy
*poor memory   *strange behavior
*increased secrecy   *increased seclusion

*irritability

*secrecy about friends

*drastic mood shifts,

*alcohol on breath

*giddiness

*inappropriate laughter

*stealing

*failing grades

*odd situations

*odd smell to their clothes

*unbalanced gait

*lying

*dilated or restricted pupils

Getting Help

If you have discovered that indeed your teenager is having a problem with either alcohol or drugs it is best to get professional help. Go to the experts. Usually this starts with an evaluation with a professional associated with an Alcohol and Drug Treatment Program.

After this step, you can evaluate their recommendations. In some cases treatment is not recommended. Sometimes the initial evaluation can be just the education your teenager needs to stop his or her use.

If treatment is recommended, it works best when your teenager agrees to it. If a young person is indeed having trouble with their use of either alcohol or drugs and they feel their parents are caring and supportive, they may be more willing to seek help. Some teenagers feel ashamed about their lack of control. Or think that admitting to having a problem will bring on more punishment.

If your teenager does need alcohol or drug treatment, I do recommend that the whole family be involved in the family component of their treatment. Then each of you can find out how to be supportive to your young person.

Our kids caught in the trap of drugs and alcohol are indeed lost. They need a supportive person to care for them and encourage them when things get hard. The love and support from parents and family members can make a big difference in the success of an adolescent recovering from addiction.

Reasons to Say 'No' to Alcohol and Drugs

When offered either alcohol or drugs your teenager needs to say either yes or no. Before they say 'no, thanks' they need to know *why*. This stems from their values, learned in their family.

Here are a variety of reasons *why* your teenager should say 'no':

- ☒ Alcohol and drugs can damage an immature brain, don't consume and save your brains.
- ☒ You are not missing anything worthwhile.
- ☒ There are genetic tendencies in family history and it is best to not take a chance you too will be at risk of becoming addicted.
- ☒ You have great capacity and potential to be a leader, not a follower.
- ☒ There is a lot more to life than getting high. Get highs out of doing life stuff, not a bottle or a joint.
- ☒ List the reasons saying 'no' is the best way to be smart. Don't take a chance.
- ☒ Using alcohol or drugs can put a young person in a situation that they may not be safe. It is not worth the chance of someone taking advantage of you or you being embarrassed by what you do.
- ☒ If your friends won't accept you because you refuse to be a user, then they are not true friends.
- ☒ Using drugs is stupid and you don't want to be stupid.
- ☒ There are lots of other ways to have fun instead of alcohol or drugs.
- ☒ You are the driver.
- ☒ You are an athlete and you should not use.
- ☒ Someone could take advantage of you if you use alcohol or drugs
- ☒ When you use you lose your morals and values.
- ☒ Marijuana turns you into a lazy, 'stupid' jerk.
- ☒ Inhalants cause permanent brain damage.
- ☒ Drugs and alcohol will not help you accomplish what you want in life.

Practical Solutions to Being Sober and Drug Free

Here are some things to *do instead* of using in social situations.

1. Be the 'Key person' at a party. You are the guy or gal who collects everyone's keys at the door. At the end of party, since you are sober, you decide who drives and who needs a ride.

2. Become the 'Designated driver'. This person drives their friends, some of whom *may* (or may not) be using alcohol, etc. You, the driver, do not drink or use. You stay sober and watch others. You have the role of a responsible person to take everyone else home.

3. Use the 'buddy system', when you are teamed up with a friend who choses not to drink or use drugs also. With the help of an adult, you both agree which choices are acceptable. You go together to be supportive of one another with these choices.

4. Become a chaperone who can be helpful to others who have impaired judgement.

5. When you are open and honest with others about your choice not to use alcohol or drugs you may find you recieve respect and recognition. This creates feelings of pride and strength.

6. Make your own 'drink' at a party or gathering. This gives you *control*. Others may think you are drinking alcohol and you are actually drinking soda.

7. Go to the parties and gatherings, have fun and be straight. You may be just as silly or funny as another teenagers under the influence. Others under the influence have impaired perceptions and are not aware of what is actually happening.

8. Be an observer. You can watch others make fools of themselves. This is a way to learn about why not to use.

9. Find support with friends who also do not use or drink or use drugs.

Ways to Say 'No'

It is helpful to rehearse *how* exactly to say 'no' rather than just tell your teenager to say no. It can be perplexing about exactly how to do so in certain situations. Some situations may seem to require more of an explanation than others. For example if a good friend asks, the answer may be more extensive than if someone the teenager does not know the person who asks. Here are some scripts:

"No thanks"

"This is not for me"

"No thanks. Not today"

"I don't use this stuff"

"I'll make my own drink, thanks"

"I'm doing fine. No thanks"

"Not today"

A Dozen Ways to Leave

Here are some ways for your teenager to get out of bad situations:

- Leave.
- Say you have to go soon.
- Say you need to go somewhere else , go home.
- Say you need to check in with your parents.
- Say you've got a new plan.
- Head outside. Then head home.
- Call and ask your folks to call you. Then leave.
- Leave with a friend.
- Leave with a whole group of friends.
- Head to the kitchen or bathroom and head home.
- Say 'excuse me' and then leave.
- Say your parents will kill you if they knew you were here and you must go. Then leave.

You can be a great help to your teenager by helping him or her make it through adolescence alcohol and drug free. Here is what one father did for his son, based on a lesson his grandfather taught him.

Jake's grandfather came to him when he was twelve. He made a deal with his young grandson. The agreement was that if Jake would not smoke or drink until he was nineteen his grandfather would give him two hundred dollars, in cash. Jake accepted the deal and party after party he declined to smoke or to drink. He was well known among his friends for having a coke in his hand. His close friends all knew his grandfather and Jake's deal and respected it. When Jake was seventeen, his grandfather died. Jake was even more adamant about not breaking his agreement in honor of his grandfather. He never got the two hundred dollars.

Now his son, Taylor, is thirteen and they have the same deal; only now, his son gets one thousand dollars on his nineteenth birthday. Jake feels confident his son knows how important this agreement is to him.

CHAPTER TEN

What grades do YOU want to get?

How your teenager performs in school will make a difference in your young person's future. Parents should become concerned when your student's grades take a drop. Many parents are not sure how to motivate their son or daughter. Lecturing them about what to do usually falls on deaf ears.

A critical question to ask your teenager is, "What grades do *you* want to get?" When I ask this question most teenagers think the question is, "What grades do *your parents* want you to get?" When your teenager answers the first questions, take a seat and listen. It is critical that you listen if your teenager tells you he wants to get A's and B's and currently he is barely passing his classes. The next step is once you have heard his desire to get much higher grades, ask what he needs to do to accomplish his goal. For instance: "What do you need to do to get an A in math... more homework, study for tests?" Then listen carefully when he tells you his plan. Remember you are not the expert, he is the expert and you need to listen to him.

Once you have listened to your teenager, tell him you are sure he can do well in school and you think his plan is a good one. Then stand back and let your young person get to work in his or her own way. Remember no lectures about what happened last week or last semester. Mentioning this can rob your teenager of his or her new hope for a change.

This is the way your young person builds a foundation so that he or she can begin to 'own' his or her grades. It is easy to sabotage grades if they belong to parents in order to get their goat. Particularly in high school, teenagers need to own their grades. They must learn to take responsibility for themselves.

Sometimes it is easy for parents to think the only 'good' grades are A's. Some students work very hard at school and when they give school work their best effort the result is C's. It is important to recognize that the teenager makes an 'A' effort. Another student may make a 'C' when he or she can easily get a 'B' or 'A'. Each teenager should be evaluated on effort, not merely outcome.

How Do You Learn?

People vary widely in how they learn. Some like to listen instead of read. Other teenagers do not want you to lecture or explain a subject, they just want to read about it. Some learn best by hands on experiences. There are three main orientations to learning; kinesthetic, visual and auditory. Each will be explained below. You may discover your main way of learning as well as your teenager's.

Visual Learners learn best by reading or looking at something. They pay attention to the detail of how something looks. When they speak they use 'visual' words like; "I see what you mean" or "I get the picture" and "look at this".

Auditory learners love the sound of things. They learn well if they hear someone speaking to them. They do well in lectures particularly if they like the person's voice. These people usually love music and will pay attention to how something sounds. The words they use are "I hear you", "That rings a bell" or "Listen...".

Kinesthetic learners do well when they can feel and touch the things they want to learn. They do not particularly do well with merely listening or reading. You know them when they say "I get it" or "If you show me, I'll get it" or "He can grasp it" or "I get the feeling...".

If you can discover your teenager's learning orientation you will better understand how he or she learns best. A movie can prove very helpful to visual learners struggling with history. For an auditory learner an auditory book may help with a boring novel. He or she may like listening to music while studying. Kinesthetic learners do well when they can manipulate objects to learn math concepts. Auditory learners would like you to explain a subject, visual learners would like you show them something they can read or study and kinesthetic learners want to watch how you do it.

Labels that Work

It is easy to view your teenager as still a child. When you are worried or discouraged about their past behavior it seems almost natural to label them: "You are so lazy" or "You never really apply yourself like you used to." Teenager do not respond to this reverse psychology. What you say is exactly what they will believe. So if you call them lazy they will show just how lazy they can be. Or if you say they are uncooperative, they will show you how contrary they can be.

Labels that work are not based on your young person's past struggles but on your hopes for the future. Labels that work are: "You have taken a very creative approach to your project" or " I know you can figure this out your own way." Other positive labels are: "You are really working hard at this" or "You are good at figuring out a way to get out of this" or "Now, that is a interesting excuse."

Handling Teachers

Teenagers having difficulties in class often are angry or unhappy with their teachers. Listen to why your teenager thinks a teacher is stupid or too hard. This way you can understand what your teenager is thinking about and how they are handling the class situation.

Here is how a conversation might go:

Teenager: "My math teacher is stupid!"

Parent: "What is stupid about her?"

Teenager: "Well, she wears a wig and it looks so dumb. She is really ugly".

Parent: "Anything else?"

Teenager: " Yeah. She has no idea how to teach math, she is so dumb".

Parent: "How do you think she ought to teach it?".

Teenager: "She should teach like Mrs. Smith did last year. I always understood her".

Parent: "Do you think you could talk to her about what isn't working?"

Teenager: "I don't want to. She wouldn't listen to me anyway".

Parent: "Do you want me to talk to her?".

Teenager: "No, it's OK".

All your teenager may need to do is explain or complain. Other teenagers need to come up with solutions to their problem such as talking to the teacher, writing a note to the teacher or doing their work despite how they feel about their teacher.

Doing Homework/ Creative Learning Experiments

Not getting homework done can be a big pitfall to getting good grades. If you are nagging your teenager, nagging about homework you should try to change your approach. The first thing to do is to ask your young person what he or she thinks is the best time to do their homework?

Do not be surprised if you don't like the answer. Your teenager may be a night owl and prime time may be between 9:00 p.m. and 11:00 p.m. If this is the case, you may demand they work much earlier. I suggest letting your teenager set up his or her own study schedule for these days (this is a college study schedule):

☽ Monday	study _____hours	time of day
☽ Tuesday	study _____hours	time of day
☽ Wednesday	study _____hours	time of day
☽ Thursday	study _____hours	time of day
☺ Friday	Have fun	
☺ Saturday	Have fun	
☽ Sunday	study _____hours	time of day

Initially, you may not think their schedule will work. Allowing your teenager to decide for him or herself can be a great experience. If the end result is good grades, it may not matter how or when your teenager studies.

Some teenagers will decide to experiment with starting homework at 9:00 p.m., Monday through Thursday. After the first week you may find that your young person falls asleep during the day or has trouble getting up in the morning. Suggest that your teenager might consider starting earlier so it is not so tiring.

I would also recommend that your teenager should not study in his or her room. Come to the kitchen or dining room (without TV on) and eat their favorite food during their study time. Most young people love chips, pizza, dessert or cereal. Save their favorite foods for study time (you may need to hide it until homework time).

I would recommend you encourage that your teenager listen to music when they study, especially with earphones. It can help your teenager focus by cutting down on distractions. I suggest classical music for math or any subject that requires a lot of concentration. Now if your teenager groans about the classical music have him (her) try it for one week and see what he thinks. Most kids will grow to like it.

Teenagers enjoy company. The best role for you as a parent is to drop in when your teenager is studying and have him or her share what he or she is learning. It is best if you are not the expert and let them explain to you what they are learning.

The experiment period can last for three to six weeks. Wait until the very end of the time period before asking your teenager to evaluate their homework experiment. Some teenagers have been successful studying with a friend, others with tutors, others by talking on the phone with friends.

If the end result is improved grades, let your young person continue with his/her new schedule.

How was School Today?

Do you keep getting the same answers to the same questions about school and homework? Do your conversations seems to go nowhere? Try to change the way you ask. For instance, the usual conversation goes like this:

Parent: "How was school today?"
Teenager: "Fine."
Parent: "Do you have homework?"
Teenager: "No."

Does this sound familiar? Your teenager has been answering the same questions over and over again for about eight or nine years.

These questions work better: "What are you learning in geometry?", "How is the basketball coming along?" or "I heard your theater arts group put on a skit for your class. Was it good?" or "Are things getting better with your English literature assignments?"

These questions imply you've been listening to your teenager and they encourage open discussion.

Taking Notes

Some teenagers have not learned how to take notes which can impede their work and learning. Here is a fun way to learn. Find a favorite science show on TV. One of our favorites is *Bill Nye the Science Guy*. Then you and your teenager watch the show together and both of you take notes. There is no specific way to take notes. Just see what your teenager comes up with. Show him or her your notes and then a few days later, repeat this experiment. Again, learning styles will show through. Some may draw diagrams with notes, others use key words and short descriptions and still others use examples or use different colors. When your teenager finds his or her own style to recall information, you have succeeded.

Math Stepping Stones

Solving math is like solving a puzzle. Learning math concepts requires learning one basic idea followed by the next. If your teenager fails to understand a concept learning math can be delayed. Your young person may need to return to the concept. It is like filling in the missing stepping stones. Sometimes if your teenager misses enough of the steps, he or she will need a tutor. There may be tutors available at school or you may want to hire a retired math teacher.

If your teenager says he or she doesn't want a tutor you may suggest, "How about we find some good looking high school senior to be your tutor?" When you have an older teenager as a tutor, like a neat senior guy for your daughter or senior girl to tutor your son, you may find your teenager become very interested in learning.

Effective tutoring can boost your teenager's confidence when it is discovered he or she can learn math and do well with it.

The Tutor

Ryan was struggling again in the beginning of his second semester of ninth grade. In middle school the same pattern seemed to occur. His parents had to get on his case so he could keep his grades up. They were hopeful with the start of high school this would no longer happen because his grades were now critical for college.

Though tutoring was offered before school in the mornings,

Ryan refused to go. So his parents told him they would provide a tutor at the house, to save him from any embarrassment, until he raised his grades.

Ryan said the tutor was a stupid idea and he would not participate. On Thursday at 4:00 p.m. there was a knock on the door. Mom let in the most gorgeous seventeen year-old girl he had ever seen. Mom introduced Ryan to Michelle, his new tutor! Ryan said, "This is not a stupid idea." He worked hard on his studies and when his grades improved he thought it was a good idea to keep his tutor so his grades would continue to improve.

Problems at School

Whose problem is it when your teenager fails a class? Some parents get over-involved. When they come to the rescue too soon the teenager does not become responsible for him or herself. When your son or daughter is called to a teacher-student-parent conference, who do you think should do the talking? When parents do not participate much in the discussion, their teenager has to assume responsibility. The next time this happens to you, ask yourself if this problem belongs to your teenage then try hard not to say anything.

Read for Success

With many subjects like math a young person may have certain times when they are most likely to be interested in learning or have developed an interest. If you teenager has not gotten interested in reading, especially by high school, you may wish to read a novel or story to your teenager to see if you can spark his or her interest. Some adolescents have an interest and they can read on their topic to see if they can develop an interest. If you have a disinterested reader make sure the book you do read is fascinating for your young person so they will want to read more. One mother started reading _The Incredible Journey_ to her seventh grade son who said he hated to read. Since reading that he now wants to have a book to read before going to bed at night.

Creating Consequences

When we create negative consequences, your teenager knows you are serious about changing his or her school behavior. For grades and school performance, it usually works best if after asking your teenager what he or she wants for grades, you can explain what will happen if your young person chooses to do poorly with their effort in school.

Some good consequences include losing a learner's permit, not using the phone or playing on the computer for a week. When the teenager brings a progress report from his or her teacher noting he or she has caught up, his or her privileges should be restored. The permit can be posted on the refrigerator while your teenager is restricted and the phone, CD player or computer games can be put in the trunk of your car.

Teenagers begin to realize when they work hard at school, privileges return. Hard work and it's rewards can create motivation to do their best.

Rewards

The best reward is the praise that comes from you. A weekly reward is a good incentive to work hard. In the end the motivation should come from your teenager. I do not recommend giving money for grades. Teenagers can lose interest in money and sometimes giving money as a reward can become very expensive.

Fifteen year-old Jessie came with his parents because of failing grades. He just did not feel like doing his work and his grades reflected his laziness. He needed to study to get good grades and do more than sit in class. Though he talked about college, it seemed too far in the future and thinking about it was not a motivation for him to work harder. So his parents agreed to do two things for him. Every week he brought home a progress report, signed by his teachers earned him a week of practice driving. He could also go to his favorite restaurant to eat his favorite food, lasagna. Jessie turned his grades around in two weeks. He was so delighted to have some short term incentive to help him keep motivated for his long range goal of attending college.

To create a reward for your son or daughter, talk to them about their grades and what might help them deal with the drudgery of everyday school. The rewards can cost very little, maybe a favorite food or a privilege like driving or using the family car. Some teenagers like the reward of staying up late or collecting music. Remember, unlike material rewards, your praise, attention and encouragement is priceless.

Find a Match

In some situations, school failure stems from a poor match between student and school. If you have unsuccessfully tried many things to get your teenager to raise his or her grades or your teenager is truly miserable at their school, you may need to make a change. First, try to help your teenager be successful in the school his or she is attending but after time passes you may realize your teenager is in the wrong school.

Some teenagers do not do well mingling with a sophisticated group of peers or they may feel they have very different interests than most of those students around them. Some teenagers find the whole situation of middle school or high school too high pressured for them. Think about your student needs and research other school options. Share your thoughts with your young person. Some options that have worked are a smaller private school, a school across town, a specialized school in science or liberal arts. For some home school has been an option. The kids sometimes only go to home school for a semester or a year and then return to a traditional institution. When your teenager is not stressed or anxious about attending school, it is usually a sign of a good match.

Motivating Your Teenager

The best motivator for your teenager is your time, caring and willingness to listen. When your young person has your support and encouragement, they cannot fail. So give your time, slow down to listen (with your eyes) and do not ever give up on the notion that your young person will become a great success!

$\overline{3}$

THE
PUZZLE
IS SOLVED

CHAPTER ELEVEN

The Puzzle is Solved....
Leaving the Nest

There are two lasting things
we can leave our children
One is roots
the other is wings
Unknown

This is a time of both monumental beginnings and sad endings. Our children need both the roots of security at the end of childhood and wings to soar in adulthood. At the onset of adolescence your young teenager looked a lot like a child, with an adult just beginning to emerge. By the end there seems to be very little child left. This turning point in your child's life marks the time your teenager has become your adult child. Along with this emerging maturity comes the inevitable departure from of home. Your young adult now seeks his or her place in the world, away from you and the family. He or she will create his or her own destiny.

A mixture of conflicting emotions abound. The future holds excitement, hopeful anticipations mixed with fears and worries. Young adults are sad when they say goodbye to old friends and their family and yet are eager to forge beyond what is familiar and secure. During this time they may still seek both reassurance and love from you as they move away and strive to become independent.

As the end of childhood approaches, you may realize you have learned as much from your children as you have ever taught them. These lessons of love and life are priceless.

We fear in letting go because we cannot predict what lies ahead. You cannot visit the house of tomorrow, discovering if your young adult's journey has been fruitful and fulfilling. Caring and not knowing, we become concerned and sometimes afraid for our children. Without knowledge, each of us is enveloped by the darkness of the unknown.

Where knowledge replaces fear, fears begin to diminish. Knowledge and understanding builds confidence and creates hope for a young person about their abilities and their future.

Things may be different now. Many parents view their teenagers as delightful young people by the time they graduate from high school. They are usually a pleasure to be around and parents have much more confidence in their young adults. Many are self-reliant, they know how to drive, work, laugh with parents, communicate, make a number of mature decisions and finish the things they start. Some of the pressures are off with the culmination of their twelve year accomplishment; graduation from high school.

Your relationship with them usually is much calmer, less intense. At the brink of adulthood our young adults are more curious about what parents have to offer. Your teenager, now becoming an adult, is still the same person you know but with maturity they are indeed different. The rough edges of growing up are smoothed. Now many parents are more assured their young person will do well in the adult world. By letting go, parents offer a gift of confidence to their maturing young person that speaks to hope for success in their future.

For most it is easier to leave someone or something than to be left behind. Your teenager may be very excited about the new opportunities that awaits him or her. It may be the anticipation of college, vocational training, a job, traveling or somewhere new to live and work. There is excitement and intrigue in what they have yet to discover. They are curious as to how they fit into the adult world, about everything they have yet to learn and things they have yet to become. For you, there is great loss. Your primary role as a parent is passing. It will never will be the same again.

Good Luck

We wish for our sons or daughters happiness, fulfillment, contentment, love, faith and joy. And we each hope our adult children will find good luck in all their endeavors.

Years ago I had the opportunity to hear an intriguing definition of 'good luck' from the late Dr. Harry Goreman, a well known veterinarian and researcher. Dr. Goreman was instrumental in the development of the artificial hip, pioneered in dogs, now used in humans. He was speaking at a baccalaureate ceremony I was attending.

Dr. Goreman wished the graduating class 'good luck' which he described as having two important parts. The first aspect is *opportunity*. The second is *preparation*. Both are required in order to bring a person good luck.

Opportunity is all around us. There are many possibilities, adventures and things you might enjoy and accomplish. All these opportunities are out there waiting for each of us.

The catch is, to take advantage of an opportunity, may require something from you... some kind of preparation. Without preparation, many of the opportunities in life will pass you by. Just wanting an opportunity is not enough for either you or for your teenager. If you want to be a physician, you can wish it with all your might but without the necessary education and training it will only be a dream. Each person must first prepare him or herself to successfully achieve what he or she wants.

You must take the time and do the work to become prepared. It may mean more education, a certain degree, vocational training, traveling, working, reading, an apprenticeship or some other kind of learning experience. Each person's dream requires a very different course of preparation.

Crossing the Bridge with Lessons Learned

The key to survival in the adult world (and doing it well) is for your young person to learn to care for themselves. Unlike early adolescence, your teenager does not need to learn everything on their own, in their own unique way. Learning basic tasks, from laundry to landlords, does not mean your young person needs to reinvent the wheel and figure everything out for themselves. Once they have new knowledge and skills they can use it in their own unique style.

How to instill the skills that are important to your young adult become more important and 'sinks in' the closer they get to leaving home. Avoiding learning adult living skills can be a way to slow down leaving. Their reluctance may be a way for you to know that facing adulthood can create fear. Fear of growing up, fear about being independent, fear of being alone and the *big* one...fear of failure.

How do you help to prepare your young adult so that he or she can prosper? Here is a list of the many things a young person needs to know in order to live successfully as an adult. As you read the list you may find there are other things you might want to add.

ADULT SURVIVAL SKILLS

Basic cooking: 3 breakfast, 3 lunch and 5 easy dinner menus
How to read a cookbook
How to use an oven
How to put out a stove/oven fire
Basic house cleaning:
    vacuum floors, dust
    bathroom
    windows
    kitchen
Basic laundry:
    wash/dry
    whites/color
    hand wash
    dry clean
    laundromat etiquette
Dishes
    with a dishwasher
    washing dishes by hand
Basic sewing
    buttons
    mending
    hand sewing/ machine
    tape instead of thread
Basic decision-making:
    1. gather information
    2. write pros and cons
    3. explore options
    4. take your time
    5. decide
Open a checking account
Balance a check book

What to do if a check bounces
How to create a budget
    managing money
How to live within a budget
Money from mom and dad (how and when to ask, etc.)
    loans from parents
    money as a gift from parents
    when to ask for more money
Basic bills
Basic commuter skills
Grocery shopping
Nutrition
First aid
    injury
    when should you see a doctor
    taking a temperature
    first aid kit
Basic health
Basic care of illness
Medical care/insurance
    insurance card and number
Car maintenance/ insurance
    gasoline type/ cost /filling
    how far can a car go on empty
    tire change
    oil change
    oil check
    winter tires
    winter preparations
    maintenance bills
Dental care/insurance
    what to do with it
    what to do without it
Sexually transmitted diseases
    What are they?
    How are they contracted?
    signs and symptoms
    treatment
Birth control
    options
Fatigue

how much sleep do you need?
Being discouraged/depressed
  How to detect?
  What to do about it
Self defense
  "The best defense"
Safety
    self-defense class
    set-up situations that are unsafe
        (alone at night, etc.)
Etiquette
Choosing friends
Living with a roommate
    how to share
    getting along
    how to pick a roommate
    solving differences
Preparing for college
    classes
    getting enough sleep
    dorm life
    study skills
    grades
    test taking
    roommate issues
    sorority/fraternity
    handling homesickness
    calling home
    writing home
Spiritual life
    choosing a church to attend
    important basics
Issues with alcohol/drugs
Job hunting
    filling out an application
    how to dress
    how often to go back
    first impressions, second and third
Job responsibility
    how to keep a job
    being on time

working in a team
being a hard worker
Appropriate dress
Social and professional roles
Being a good friend
    getting along
    how to solve disagreements
Being a good neighbor
    getting along
    how to solve disagreements
Dating
Basic safety
Driving
Choosing a life mate
Adjusting to being alone
Being independent
Missing home
Long-distance phone calls
Holidays away from home
Basic drains
Setting goals
Being in charge of your life
Career choices/ professions
Interest tests
Saying goodbye

This is a long list. To your delight you may discover that your teenager knows a number of these life skills. Others may feel panic, wondering if there is enough time to learn them. Once your young adult learns the basics for successful living he or she will be prepared for the opportunities that lie ahead.

The Bon Voyage Care Package

Sending a care package is helpful for your newly launched young adult. Here is a list of several things that may help you make up a first year away kit:

new socks
rolls of quarters
band aids
postcards with stamps
coupons to the frozen yogurt store

Swiss army knife or small tool set
ear plugs
sunscreen
pain reliever
portable alarm clock
candy bars/ energy bars
tooth brush
picture of the family
insect bite lotion
can opener
mace spray
an extra key chain
address book (with numbers and addresses)
city map
cookbook
extra gloves, hat (for cold climates)
T-shirt, hat and water bottle (for warm weather)
first aid kit
home baked cookies
candy, gum

In the box, here are some wishes:
♥   Believe in yourself
♥   Search for what you love to do
♥   No one but you can make you happy
♥   Let yourself dream of how you can make the world
     a better place
♥   Be persistent in your efforts and work hard
♥   The choices you make today will shape the rest of your
     life
♥   Never lose faith in God.
♥   Have faith in what you believe in and your dreams
     will come true
♥   Anything is possible in your life... and never
     settle for anything than less than your personal
     best.
♥   Out of struggle comes great strength

The Hundred Dollar Grocery List

Jodie hands her sixteen year-old daughter, Stacy, a hundred dollar bill and a grocery list. Stacy drives to the grocery store and carefully compares the prices of each item on the shelf. What was the motivation for this young woman to shop so conservatively? At the check out she will pay her bill with the money her mom gave her and what is left over is hers. Stacy will use her extra money for gasoline, clothes, food or anything else she wants. Careful shopping pays off.

Experience is a great teacher for a teenager. For many everyday skills, the best way to learn is hands on, direct, 'do it yourself' experiences. To learn about a check book encourage your teenager to open his or her own checking account. Your teenager will understand better the reason why it is important to balance a checkbook if he or she bounces a check and has to pay the NSF fee. Your young person will begin to understand what happens when you mix up a few numbers.

Learning skills is like the boot camp of adulthood. It takes patience on your part to allow your teenager to learn these lessons. Doing it themselves gives a whole new meaning to learning. Be ready for some pretty interesting meals, tinted laundry and creative cleaning.

You can certainly lend a hand at times with the lessons of adult life but only when asked. Remember to do not do for your teenagers what they can do for themselves.

The Steps of Success

During adolescence our young people insist on learning how to be successful by trial and error. And sometimes a good deal of 'error' in order to learn that life offers some hard knocks. Young people tend to have no real concept of what it takes to accomplish their dreams as an adult.

Closer to leaving home, completing the 'Do it yourself' course of growing up is much more interesting now that their futures hold college, technical schools, jobs, living independently and anticipating love and a new life.

Success in life means completion or accomplishing what is *attempted* or what is *intended or desired*. Simply, it means attaining one's goals in life. The most important accomplishments *influence or enhance the lives of others* in a *positive way.* Some examples are developing the Polio vaccine, a Nobel peace prize, a prosperous company that offers products or services to consumers. Or for many of us, the privilege of becoming a parent.

We achieve because we have a cause or others gives us inspiration. A young person can be inspired by a mentor, a teacher, their religion, an accomplished person, as well as our faith in them. Inspiration comes from one's belief about what makes life *good and meaningful.*

High school graduates know well the steps that lead to success. Without following each step, your young person will not graduate. Leaving one out would foil the game plan for success in life.

1. Success begins with an *idea, a dream, a vision.* What you could create or do, in your own unique style. The student in high school dreams of graduating and going somewhere, a certain college or a technical school or off to Europe for work, travel and adventure.

2. *Believing* in *your idea* is the next step. Like graduating from high school. Your young person believed in his or her idea and *saw a vision* that indeed the day would come he or she would wear that graduation gown and carry a diploma in hand. They developed *faith* they could finish what they started, mastering completion of twelve years of school.

3. Most importantly your young person's belief in their idea was followed by *action. Their persistent effort* toward completion was what got them here. Despite the times that seemed hard, your teenager persisted. Occasionally part of the journey may have seem impossible. The closer they get to the finish line, the more hopeful they become. With persistent effort, backed by their faith in their ability to complete their task, your young person found sweet success. You know it by that smile on graduation day.

Those who are successful in their adult lives many times feel very alone in their course toward what they believe can happen. It is not uncommon for others to try to talk a person out of their dream. It is truly the person's own determination not to quit that can make the difference between winning and losing. Giving up will never get you where you want to be.

Leaving Home

We all hope our children can move into adulthood as self-reliant, capable and successful. In order to accomplish this they must become independent from us.

Here is a question about the subject:

Q. Can a young adult emancipate from parents with the following choices?
   A. living at home
   B. living in the same home town
   C. living in the same state

Leaving home may be different for each of your adult children. Some remain at home and seem to resist becoming independent. Others are eager to leave home at a young age. In leaving so young they take on the responsibility for themselves long before their eighteenth birthday or before graduation from high school. Others leave in a planned fashion, whether to attend college or a move across town. These are on a continuum of choices.

For those who stay, some do not feel mature enough to be away from home or their parents do not believe they are ready for life beyond the family. Others feel financially ill equipped to be on their own. They may want to attend a local college and the most economical way to do so is to room at home. For others it is easier and cheaper to live at home. Some young adults have tried either college or living away and could not make it on their own, so they return home.

Some young adults may choose to live across town, in a local college dorm or down the street. They feel more independent than away from home. Often the young adult may drop in to see parents, usually at dinner time. They consult with parents frequently. They find comfort when parents are nearby.

Others take the courageous step of living far away. This demands the most independence and self-confidence. The young adult no longer has the easy access to parents for guidance, food or money. A young person must test of their abilities to care for themselves. College is probably one of the easiest stepping stones to move far away from family. Dorm life provides a family of peers for support and encouragement. Some are very self-assured and take on a job or venture to travel which is more risky because of a lack of financial security.

The Boxes of Life

Growing up our children move through a series of boxes. The first box is the family box. This box is small and familiar. It is secure and comfortable. At the age of five or six the child ventures beyond their box into the next bigger one, the elementary school box. Here they find new relationships, new neighbors. After this the child finds a bigger more complex box of junior high or middle school to explore. The last is the big box of high school, with a lot of windows and doors to peer into the adult world beyond.

Upon graduation, all the walls of the boxes collapse. There stands your teenager facing the world of adulthood. When the walls collapse some teenagers have plans in hand; entrance to college, further schooling, a job. Some have no plans at all. Some young people throw caution to the wind and jump into the world to explore their way. Others, also without plans, timidly step into the unknown and intimidating world of adulthood.

Your encouragement can influence the path for your young adult is likely to take.

7 WAYS TO LEAVE HOME

Here is a continuum about leaving home:

LEAVE EARLY (angry, abrupt)

LEAVE AS SOON AS POSSIBLE (and not return for years)

LEAVE (returning occasionally, 2-4 X year)

LEAVE in a planned manner

LEAVE GRADUALLY (returning often for short stays)

KEEP RETURNING HOME TO LIVE

REFUSE TO LEAVE HOME

Leaving home so important because it is the first big step into adulthood. You have to leave your family to get there. Each young person must find out for themselves that they can be independent.

As you see on the continuum there are many ways of leaving home. Some are rapid and can be abrupt. Other ways are slower and allow for more planning and preparation before saying goodbye.

When leaving is rapid and abrupt, everyone can be dismayed. Early leaving usually means no one is really prepared for the departure. Many times people are angry with one another. If your young person has not had enough time to get prepared then it makes their road ahead difficult and sometimes even dangerous.

The opposite end of the continuum poses another set of problems. The oldest adult child that I worked with was a thirty three year-old who had never left home. He was capable of going to work but was not able to break the ties with his parents. His parents were sad that he could not make an independent life for himself but they were caught in the trap of overprotecting him.

Advice from Erma Bombeck suggests a way to encourage your adult children to leave home was to leave the refrigerator sparse with only the food the parents will eat. When there is only a small selection of non-fat milk (blue milk), prunes and bran on the shelves, the young adult is suppose to get the hint about leaving.

Potential problems exist for those young adults living at home or close by. Your sons and daughters may not be able to build confidence in their ability to succeed on their own. This failure to become independent is more likely to occur with those young people who cannot leave. The comforts of parents and home are just too enticing and life seems easy.

Parents also may find it difficult to live with an emancipating young person under their roof. It is hard for a parent to switch from being a parent and start acting like a landlord. Battles occur when their son or daughter wants to live by his or her own rules, no longer respecting the limits and expectation of parents. They like to come and go as they please, sometimes not coming home at night. This kind of independence can create a dilemma for parents, especially if there are younger children at home. It may not be the best example to the others. Parents become uncomfortable being so close to their autonomous, experimenting (by their) adult son or daughter.

What Do You Want?

How and when do you want your teenager to leave home? Right now might be your answer if your thirteen year-old is making you tear your hair out. You may say 'as early as humanly possible'. If you are getting the invitations for graduation together, you may say you are not ready at all for your young adult to leave you. Wherever you are in your parenting career, begin to think about this question. How about a year after he or she graduates? The fall after they graduate? Are things so good between the two of you that you would choose never?

You need to decide on the best timing for your young adult and for you. You and your young adults may have very different ideas.

Try talking about this with your son or daughter. Graduation from home can be a planned event. The goal is meeting your young adults needs and wishes and also including some of yours.

The Ritual of Leaving Home

There are markers in our society that signify both beginnings and endings. Rituals help people establish new relationships. In our cultures and in our society we have a variety of rituals for such transitions, special things we do for births, graduation, marriage, for death and grieving, for baptisms and for birthdays.

When you think about leaving home do any rituals come to mind? If you say none, you are certainly not in the minority. The ritual of graduation signifies the right of passage from high school into adulthood. This celebration may or may not coincide with when a young person actually leaves home.

When you develop a ritual for your son or daughter leaving home it can help all of you with this difficult transition. The act of a ritual or tradition in our society helps us to move forward in life even if that move is painful like the death of someone you love. Gathering together in a formal way helps us make a transition. It marks an end of one way to be and signifies a transformation into another state.

Here are some stories of rituals for the launching of children into adulthood.

The Butterfly

Sarah, Mark and Jenny's oldest daughter, went to an out of state college, struggled and failed her freshman year. When Sarah returned and she challenged all her parent's rules. She stayed out all night, came home drunk, was drinking and driving and was very demanding her 'rights' as an adult. As her younger brother and sisters looked on, her parents were disturbed and perplexed, not knowing what to do with their daughter. This was not what they expected would happen.

Her parents finally told Sarah they were retiring from parenthood and announced their new roles as landlords. The bottom line was that if she chose to continue disrespecting their rules she had to leave home.

So Sarah left. They worried. She floundered. Sarah struggled trying to make it in an efficiency apartment. She had difficulty keeping a job. Struggling both financially as well in her relationships, Sarah became more depressed. During this time she faced a major crisis. She became pregnant and returned home in desperation. Sarah had to face her responsibility as an adult. Her parents supported her through this very difficult period of time. She courageously decided to carry her baby and to give it up for adoption.

After the birth, with the support of her parents, she remained at home, recovering from this trauma. Months after the birth, she was having difficulty keeping a job. Unsure about their ability to help her, her parents brought Sarah to therapy.

We discussed a way to help her regain her confidence in herself. Her parents decided to help her emancipate herself by creating a deadline for her to move out. Sarah agreed to a date. She had enrolled in a local college and got an evening job. And with this goal, she started to save. A week before she was due to leave she told her parents she had found an apartment in a nearby town.

On the eve of her departure date arrived. Her parents invited her to have dinner with them at home. They prepared her favorite foods. She was greeted with flowers on the table, a linen table cloth, the good china and candle light. Her parents were dressed up, emphasizing the importance of this occasion. During dinner they talked about all the fun times they remembered with Sarah, growing up.

After dinner her parents presented her with several small packages. With the opening of each package they each read something that they had written to her.

In the first package was a small butterfly necklace. Her mother began reading.

Dearest Sarah;

You have spent a number of years struggling in your cocoon. It has been hard for you. But in the struggle you have shown us how courageous and resourceful you are. You have faced great hardships and you have become much wiser and capable.

We know that today you are a butterfly. You are strong. We are confident you can take of yourself away from us. Wear this proudly.

We love you,

Mom and Dad

In the second package was a beautiful water color of a butterfly. Her father began to read.

Dear Sarah;

You are a beautiful person. You have wonderful qualities. You are gentle and kind. You have a terrific laugh. You know how to be a great friend and a sister. You are sensitive to others. One of your best qualities is what a great listener you are to others. You are gentle like a butterfly. On your travels in life we wish you the best. Many safe journeys. We wish in your life you will find all the pleasures and joys you deserve.

This picture is to remind you that you don't have to go back to the cocoon. You are a butterfly now. We are very proud of you.

We love you very much,

Dad and mom

In the third package was a small diamond ring in the shape of a butterfly. With it came this note:

Sarah,

This ring is diamond. To remind you that you are precious to us. We would like to thank you for all the joy and happiness you have brought us. It has been a privilege to be your parents. You are a wonderful daughter. Though we will miss you, we are confident that you need to make your own life for yourself. Always remember our love and care for you.

Mom and Dad

The evening was filled with tears and laughter. Enough hugs to melt anyone's heart. Saying good bye to the old and hello to the new, in a ritual of launching.

Did Sarah launch? Yes, indeed. These gifts will always be with her. They symbolize the confidence her parents gave to her and the hope for her future as an adult.

The Sports Car

During Alex's high school years he talked about the kind of life he wanted. He wanted to be wealthy, living in a big house and own his favorite sports car, a Jaguar. Like his father, Alan, he had a real interest in sports cars. He was less interested in working hard and more interested in dreaming.

His father had many long talks with his son about how important it was for him to work hard, in school and his job, in order to obtain the kind of lifestyle he wanted so badly. To his dissatisfaction, his son was not so convinced, shirking his job and school work. Alan was not optimistic his son would attain what he wanted with his seemingly mediocre work ethic and nonchalance about saving money.

When it came to saying good-bye, they had a last dinner together and his parents gave Alex gifts for his college. Lots of new socks, money for the laundry, post cards (stamped, addressed to home). He got a leather backpack and a new walk-man. His parents talked about missing his company and their hopes for his future.

Alex was the kind of kid that loved money more than anything else. His father said it was hard for him to give his son money because he was concerned Alex would just think money comes too easily from his parents and he would not learn to work hard for it.

When saying their final good byes at the airport, his father handed him a small package. It contained a note in his father's handwriting. Alex read how much his parents loved him and they were sure he would get everything he wanted in his life. The package also contained a shinny, little replica of a Jaguar and in it was rolled five one hundred dollar bills, money Alex could use toward that sport car he dreamed about.

With tears in his eyes, Alex was shocked. He hugged his dad. Alan, who was always reluctant to give his son money, outdid himself. Off Alex went to college with a huge dose of confidence clutched in that little box.

Apron Strings

A mother of a teenager told me a story about her own launching from home. During her years growing up Christine had a close relationship with her mother. After high school graduation, reluctantly she ventured about 200 miles away to college. Terribly homesick and lonely, Christine called her mother everyday. Several times she seriously entertained the thought of quitting college to return to the comforts of home.

After visiting home during the holiday break her mother and father insisted she stay and finish her first year before deciding to quit. It took every ounce of courage Christine had to return to college.

In the spring of her freshman year, a small package arrived from home. In the box was an endearing letter from her mother. She wrote telling Christine what a wonderful daughter she was and how proud her parents were of her. Accompanying the letter was a set of freshly cut apron strings, symbolizing her mother's confidence in her daughter.

She was very moved by the power of the letter and the apron strings. She proudly hung the blue and white checkered cloth strips on her dorm wall. Christine continued on with college, completing her degree. Throughout college, those precious apron strings remained on her wall.

Symbols

There is meaning in having gifts that have symbolism attached to them. Our young people will hang on to those things that represent love and confidence. Things they can wear or carry are especially thoughtful. They know your wishes are always with them. Much like wedding bands these symbols are daily reminders of our confidence and care.

You will notice things that are common to all these rituals. The gathering together of family and sometimes friends, flowers, formal dress, gifts and special food represents an end to some way of being and celebrates or recognizes a transformation into another. A transformation from one state to another, saying goodbye to the past and hello to the future (like being single and through a ritual becoming married).

New Roles for Parents

There is difficulty giving up your parenting, though you still remain a parent. You now have a different role with your young adult leaving home. It reminds me of the mama blue bird who must bail her little birdies from the nest. On their first flights, the little birds precariously plummet toward the ground. Some hit the ground hard and bruise. Mama bird encourages them to try again. Their survival depends on learning how to soar on their own.

When parents are not prepared for their children leaving they may experience the 'empty nest' syndrome, where parents feel sad and lost with their children gone. The best thing to do to avoid this experience is to plan for the things you would like to do when you are busy chauffeuring and helping your teenager. Keep track of all the things you wish you had time for like gardening, a hobby, getting in shape, volunteering in your community or most importantly, spending time with your spouse. One of the biggest mistakes is to not spend enough time working on your marriage so it too feels empty when the children leave.

Saying Goodbye

This season of life will someday pass. Things will not be the same again.

Saying goodbye is a painful thing to do. It means dealing with all those feelings, facing all the love and sorrow. Feeling some regrets of having to let go as your parenting comes to an end. Also enjoying all the hope in your son's or daughter's chance at their bright futures. Though your days at parenting do seem endless, your day will come to have to say goodbye.

Prepare your young adult with your love and your kindness. With your firmness, offer your expectation for their excellence. Do not give up with a persistent effort to be involved as their parent. Offer your patience and faith in your young person's abilities. And give your commitment to your parenting efforts so your son or daughter has a great shot to succeed in life.

Last but not least, here is a 'thank you' for you (since you will probably have to wait for years to get a thank you from your teenager).

There are times we cannot
find words to express ourselves
to say
thank you

For standing by me through thick and thin
For never giving up on me even when I didn't win
For your patience when I kept pushing you away
For caring for me when I said I no longer needed you today

When I was weak, I always could count on your strength
When I asked for support, you always went the length
When I was sad, you readily brought a smile
When I was full of joy you laughed with me all the while
When I lost my way, you got me back on track
In my pain, your comfort and love brought me back

When I wanted to give up, you gave me faith and hope
When I was confused you taught me a way to cope
You gave me faith in love and
helped me believe in myself
Leaving you I know will break your heart

Thanks for all the happiness you brought my life
Sorry for all the times I brought you strife
You caught me when I was ready to fall
Taught me to always stand tall
When I needed you, you were never further than a call

You are my mom and dad
To you, I will be forever grateful
Even though there are times
We cannot find words
to express ourselves

This book is a tribute to you, for all your love, concern and diligence raising your teenager.

Endnotes

1. H. Stephen Glenn, *Raising Self-Reliant Children in a Self-Indulgent World* (New York, St. Martin's Press,1988), pp. 40, 99, 117.

2. A. H. Maslow: Calvin Hall, Gardner Lindzey, *Theories of Personality* (New York , John Wiley & Sons), 1978 pp. 269

3. Helen L Bee, Sandra K Mitchell, *The Developing Person, A Lifetime Approach, (*New York, Harper & Row Publisher), 1980 pp. 132

4. H. Jackson Brown, Jr. *Life's Little Instruction Book*, (Tennessee, Rutledge Hill Press), 1993, Instruction #93

5.Michael D. Resnick; Peter S. Bearman; Robert W. Blum; Karl E Bauman; Kathleen M. Harris; Jo Jones; Joyce Tabor; Trish Beuhring; Renee E. Sieving; Marcia Shew; Majorie Ireland; Linda H. Bearinger; J. Richard Udry. *Protecting adolescents from harm: finding from the National Longitudinal Study on Adolescent Health.* JAMA, The Journal of the American Medical Association, Sept. 10, 1998, p. 1007 v278n10

6.Dick Schaefer, *Choices and Consequences. What to Do When a Teenager Uses Alcohol/Drugs: A Step-by-Step System that Really Works.* (Minneapolis, Johnson Institute QVS, Inc.), 1996

Index

ORDER FORM

Help Me... I Have a Teenager!!

The Nitty Gritty Guide to Parental Sanity

Qty	Description	Unit Price	Total
	Help Me... I Have a Teenager!!	$16.95(US)	
		SUBTOTAL	
	Shipping /Handling ($4.00 first book; $2.50each additional book)		
	Texas residents add 8.25% sales tax		
		TOTAL	

✉ Postal Orders: Duckworks Publishing
541 Louis Henna Blvd.
Round Rock, TX 78664

✱ Phone :   (512) 345-7270

✱ Fax Orders   (512) 310-1675

   e-mail: Anniedrake@aol.com   www.teenager-help.com

SHIP TO:

_____

Name / Organization

_____

Street Address

_____

City/State   Zip   Phone #

Charge: ❑Visa ❑MC   Exp. Date _____   ❑Check Enclosed

Name on card:_____

Account # | | | | | | | | | | | | | | | | | | | | |

_____

Cardholder Signature

ORDER FORM

Help Me... I Have a Teenager!!

The Nitty Gritty Guide to Parental Sanity

Qty	Description	Unit Price	Total
	Help Me... I Have a Teenager!!	$16.95(US)	
		SUBTOTAL	
	Shipping /Handling ($4.00 first book; $2.50each additional book)		
	Texas residents add 8.25% sales tax		
		TOTAL	

⊠ Postal Orders: Duckworks Publishing
541 Louis Henna Blvd.
Round Rock, TX 78664

✶ Phone :   (512) 345-7270

✶ Fax Orders   (512) 310-1675

e-mail: Anniedrake@aol.com   www.teenager-help.com

SHIP TO:

_____

Name / Organization

_____

Street Address

_____

City/State   Zip   Phone #

Charge: ❑Visa ❑MC   Exp. Date _____   ❑Check Enclosed

Name on card:_____

Account # | | | | | | | | | | | | | | | | | | |

_____

Cardholder Signature

ORDER FORM

Help Me... I Have a Teenager!!

The Nitty Gritty Guide to Parental Sanity

Qty	Description	Unit Price	Total
	Help Me... I Have a Teenager!!	$16.95(US)	
		SUBTOTAL	
	Shipping /Handling ($4.00 first book; $2.50each additional book)		
	Texas residents add 8.25% sales tax		
		TOTAL	

✉ Postal Orders: Duckworks Publishing
541 Louis Henna Blvd.
Round Rock, TX 78664

✴ Phone : (512) 345-7270

✴ Fax Orders (512) 310-1675

e-mail: Anniedrake@aol.com www.teenager-help.com

SHIP TO:

_____

Name / Organization

_____

Street Address

_____

City/State Zip Phone #

Charge: ❑Visa ❑MC Exp. Date _____ ❑Check Enclosed

Name on card:_____

Account # | | | | | | | | | | | | | | | | |

_____

Cardholder Signature

ORDER FORM

Help Me... I Have a Teenager!!

The Nitty Gritty Guide to Parental Sanity

Qty	Description	Unit Price	Total
	Help Me... I Have a Teenager!!	$16.95(US)	
		SUBTOTAL	
	Shipping /Handling ($4.00 first book; $2.50each additional book)		
	Texas residents add 8.25% sales tax		
		TOTAL	

✉ Postal Orders: Duckworks Publishing
    541 Louis Henna Blvd.
    Round Rock, TX 78664

✴ Phone :   (512) 345-7270
✴ Fax Orders   (512) 310-1675
    e-mail: Anniedrake@aol.com   www.teenager-help.com

SHIP TO:

_____

Name / Organization

_____

Street Address

_____

City/State   Zip   Phone #

Charge: ❏Visa ❏MC   Exp. Date _____   ❏Check Enclosed

Name on card:_____

Account # | | | | | | | | | | | | | | | | | | |

_____

Cardholder Signature